Sex and Self-Ownership

Sex and Self-Ownership

Essays on Consent and the Criminal Law

JESSE WALL

Associate Professor, Faculty of Law, University of Auckland, New Zealand

OXFORD
UNIVERSITY PRESS

OXFORD
UNIVERSITY PRESS

Great Clarendon Street, Oxford, OX2 6DP,
United Kingdom

Oxford University Press is a department of the University of Oxford.
It furthers the University's objective of excellence in research, scholarship,
and education by publishing worldwide. Oxford is a registered trade mark of
Oxford University Press in the UK and in certain other countries.

Published in the United States of America by Oxford University Press
198 Madison Avenue, New York, NY 10016, United States of America.

British Library Cataloguing in Publication Data
Data available

Library of Congress Control Number: 2025934611

ISBN 9780198876267

DOI: 10.1093/9780191987809.001.0001

Printed and bound by
CPI Group (UK) Ltd., Croydon, CR0 4YY

MIX
Paper | Supporting
responsible forestry
FSC® C013604
FSC
www.fsc.org

The manufacturer's authorised representative in the EU for product safety is
Oxford University Press España S.A., Parque Empresarial San Fernando de Henares,
Avenida de Castilla, 2 – 28830 Madrid (www.oup.es/en or product.safety@oup.com).
OUP España S.A. also acts as importer into Spain of products made by the manufacturer.

To Caleb

Acknowledgements

I was inspired to start (what has become) *Sex and Self-Ownership* by the two great 'Oxford Jo(h)ns': Herring and Gardner. With their hearts and minds in the right place, their work continues to inspire. This work would also not have been possible without writing it under the supportive aegides of Mindy Chen-Wishart, Mark Henaghan, and Janet McLean.

Many brilliant friends and colleagues have shared their thoughts and insights on various parts of this work, and I would like to specifically acknowledge Marcelo Rodriguez Ferrere; Nicole Roughan, Arie Rosen, and the New Zealand Centre for Legal and Political Theory; Lulu Weis, Dale Smith, and the Melbourne University Legal Theory Workshop; Andrew Halpin, James Penner, Andrew Simester, Mark McBride, and the Centre for Legal Theory at the National University of Singapore; Anna High and the New Zealand Symposium on Sexual Violence; Tim Mulgan and the Department of Philosophy at the University of Auckland; and Grant Gillett, Andrew Moore, and the Department of Philosophy at the University of Otago.

To Laura, thank you for your endless belief in me. To Evelyn and Vivien, I am so very proud of you both (and let's talk about *Sex and Self-Ownership* when you are a bit older).

Contents

Introduction

'From women's point of view', Catherine MacKinnon famously claimed, 'rape is not prohibited; it is regulated' by the state.[1] If 'sexuality is central to women's definition, and forced sex is central to sexuality', then 'rape is indigenous, not exceptional, to women's social condition'.[2] From this feminist point of view, it is true that any intervention by the state into forced or unwanted sex is merely regulatory. The claim is also true from another—more detached—point of view: if rape is unwanted sex, but the criminal law accommodates the acquittal of a person who mistakenly believed that the other person consented to the sex that was forced upon them, then the state only regulates (and does not prohibit) rape. Now, there are reasons for this: the criminal law is configured towards culpable conduct that ought to attract state punishment and public censure, and therefore has as its focal point the wrongful behaviour and blameworthy state of mind of the defendant. The point nonetheless remains: by focusing on retribution, the state only regulates rather than prohibits unwanted sex.

This book is ultimately concerned with the legal category of the exculpatory mistaken belief in consent. It seeks to explain why this category ought to be narrowed, and how it can be narrowed without departing from criminal law's retributive morality and principles of criminalisation. Whilst each essay in this book will also develop a standalone claim about sex and consent, the essays combine to construct a central argument about the exculpatory mistaken belief. In this way, the essays should be read as being mutually supportive: the ideas in subsequent essays will build from ideas in earlier essays. Skeletally, 'the central argument' is as follows:

1. All instances of (penetrative) sex 'instrumentalise' and 'objectify' the person (B) through A's (forceful) use of B's body.
2. All sex therefore 'requires' (ie triggers a moral and legal obligation on) A to have (explanatory and guiding) reasons to believe that B agrees to A's treatment of B.

[1] Catharine A MacKinnon, *Toward a Feminist Theory of the State* (Harvard UP 1989) 179.
[2] MacKinnon (n 1) 172.

Sex and Self-Ownership. Jesse Wall, Oxford University Press. © Jesse Wall 2025.
DOI: 10.1093/9780191987809.001.0001

3. B's agreement at (2) is 'transcendent'; it represents 'a point of view that A cannot have a point of view on'.
4. It follows from (2) and (3) that A's reasons to believe in B's agreement must be 'objective' and 'B-specific' reasons.
5. A's failure to act on the reasons at (4) is a culpable wrong since it represents an unwillingness to be guided by a value (the 'non-use value' of person B) that the state is responsible for promoting.
6. The finder of fact ought to identify A's failure to act on the reasons at (4) by having regard (only) to the steps A had taken to attend to, and ascertain, whether B expressed B's agreement by words or overt acts.

To introduce the book more thoroughly, I would like to take the time here to explain how these essays fit together, how the ideas connect, and how the separate claims develop in a mutually supportive way. This provides an overview of the separate claims in each essay and an indication of how each essay contributes to the central argument.

It is helpful to think of each essay as being occupied with both a foreground and a background problem to solve. In Essay 1 ('The Problem with Sex in General') is the characterisation that all instances of sex instrumentalise and objectify another person. In the foreground of the essay is an exploration of how the principle of consent-astuteness ameliorates the problem of instrumentalism. This grounds three foundational ideas. First, I argue for the primacy of consent-astuteness (over consent in fact) as the antidote to the instrumental use of the body of another person. Second, I explain how the principle of consent-astuteness is motivated by the 'non-use value' of each person. Third, I pull apart instrumentalism from objectification to consider the compounding effect of both together, in order to ground the claim that it is the instrumental use of the body (as an object) that explains the wrongfulness of all instances of rape.

There is, however, a methodological claim that sits behind the third foundational idea. The methodological claim is that these 'essential properties' of sex—instrumentalism and objectification—can explain the moral content of the (albeit contingent) features that we associate with 'real rape'. More broadly, I defend a detached and analytical account of sexual wrongdoing that starts by stripping away all of the 'contingent features' in order to isolate the 'necessary' or 'essential' properties of the wrong. Whilst we can be sceptical of an analytical account on the basis that '[a]bstract reasoning around competing moral values too often leads to the excision of concepts from their context',[3] I nonetheless

[3] Joanne Conaghan, 'The Essence of Rape' (2019) 39 OJLS 151, 180.

contend here that our context-specific concerns of harm, trauma, erasure, compulsion, misogyny, subordination (and so on) all stem from the essential properties of sex: namely, the instrumental use of the body.

Essay 2 ('A Prop in Someone Else's Fantasy') is closely related to the first. In the foreground is the relationship between instrumentalism and objectification. I suggest that even when we address the instrumental use of a person through being consent-astute, we may nonetheless be objectifying the person in one of two ways: by 'using a person in their capacity as a thing' (weak objectification) or 'using a person as if they were a thing' (strong objectification). In an analysis that is informed as much as it is haunted by Immanuel Kant's writing on sex and marriage, I attempt to explain how both forms of objectification are morally problematic and how they are general features of sex. I then provide an account of the possible solutions to the problems that both forms of objectification identify. One solution that emerges suggests that, to ameliorate the problem of objectifying another person, we need to be motivationally astute; that we ought to respond to, or share in, the reasons for the person's agreement to the treatment of them.

There is a further reason that we need to concern ourselves with objectification. In the background of Essay 2 is an account of how our view of even consensual sex may be a morally mismanaged view. If sex is, fundamentally or essentially, only objectifying in the weak sense, 'sexual practice' may nonetheless 'express objectifying social structures' in the strong sense.[4] Sex-as-we-know-it, then, is sex with a person that is 'conceptually unrelated to any and all person-related characteristics or abilities' that the person might have.[5] In the background of Essay 2 is the question of whether it is possible to escape from the web of objectifying social structures and possess a moral outlook that is consistent with the principles of consent-astuteness and motivational astuteness.

Essay 3 ('Choice Under Pressure') concerns the application of pressure (the presentation of unappealing options that fall short of threats of violence) to obtain consent from a putative victim. The foreground question is whether coercion is a form of wrongdoing that ought to concern the criminal law. The essay isolates two different functions of coercion. First, a finding of coercion can 'determine whether A's conduct is at least prima facially wrongful or . . . blameworthy'.[6] Second, a finding of coercion can defeat 'the typical normative results

[4] Barbara Herman, 'Could It Be Worth Thinking About Kant on Sex and Marriage?' in Louise Antony and Charlotte Witt (eds), *A Mind of One's Own: Feminist Essays on Reason and Objectivity* (2nd edn, Westview Press 2002) 63.

[5] Melinda Vadas, 'The Manufacture-for-use of Pornography and Women's Inequality' (2005) 13 J Political Philos 174, 190.

[6] Mitchell N Berman, 'The Normative Functions of Coercion Claims' (2002) 8 Leg Theory 45, 49.

of [B's] choice' that was coerced.[7] With regards to the first function, I develop in this essay the notion that coercive conduct, itself, can be a standalone wrong, where the pressure transgresses normative phenomena. Specifically, where the application of pressure aims to remove options that a person would otherwise be entitled to pursue, the pressure rescinds the assumption that the person's consent represents their assessment of their interests. Moreover, I argue that the standalone wrong is a criminalisable wrong: knowingly requiring another person to forgo options that they would otherwise be entitled to pursue is conduct that represents an unwillingness to be guided by a value that the state is responsible for promoting.

The functional duality of coercion helps us to begin to consider the different functions of consent itself. When force is threated, and a choice is coerced, the willing or acquiescing attitude of the consenting person no longer has the moral quality to grant permission to another person. Here, the expression of consent by one person does not grant the permission to the other person. Moreover, when pressure is applied, the choice between unappealing options may still be an autonomous one, but the applier of pressure is nonetheless knowingly requiring the person to act contrary to their rights or interests. The application of pressure can be a standalone wrong committed by one person against another. From this, three dimensions of consent begin to emerge: consent is an attitude or choice (that can be valid or vitiated), consent is an expression of a person's interests (that can be reliable or unreliable), and consent is a normative power that can be exercised (to change the normative relationship between two people).

Essay 4 ('That Was Then, This Is Now') then relies upon these three dimensions of consent to evaluate the plausibility of a particular type of excuse. In adopting Michelle Madden Dempsey's concern with whether the claim 'but that used to be okay'[8] can excuse conduct that is now considered wrongful, Essay 4 considers the relationship between norms (which can change) and moral reasons (which a person may be unaware of). To understand the excuse ('but that used to be okay') is to appreciate the relationship between a change in a normative practice and a person's claim to ignorance. This requires us to isolate the view of consent as a normative power (and the practice-given reasons that it is predicated upon) from the view of consent as being concerned with a person's attitude or a person's interests. I explain in the essay how a worthwhile social practice can generate moral reasons, and to the extent that

[7] Kimberly K Ferzan, 'Consent and Coercion' (2018) 50 Ariz St LJ 951, 968.
[8] Michelle Madden Dempsey, 'Coercion, Consent, and Time' (2021) 131 Ethics 345.

social practices can change over time, so too can the moral reasons that the practice generates.

Behind the excuse ('but that used to be okay') is an assertion of ignorance or unawareness of a contemporary norm. Hence, to evaluate the excuse, the essay considers the general exculpatory principle: that a person is not blameworthy for 'failing to respond to a reason he is unaware applies to his conduct'.[9] Whilst the general exculpatory principle may be able to excuse past conduct in the context of past norms, it does not seem to excuse contemporary conduct relying on past norms. To affirm this intuition, Essay 4 considers inculpatory exceptions that can be carved out of the general exculpatory principle. Whilst a person can be blameworthy for being unaware of the moral reasons they acted contrary to (in the lesser sense, where they are culpable *for* their ignorance), I suggest here that there are also instances where a person can be blameworthy for acting against those reasons where the accompanying ignorance of the moral reasons works to sustain their culpability for their actions (in this greater sense, where they are culpable for their wrongdoing *through* their ignorance). I also suggest that a person is only culpable in the latter, greater, sense where they have mismanaged their moral outlook, and where that mismanagement resulted in the lack of awareness of the moral reasons they acted against.

Essay 5 ('General Reasons Not to Have Sex') focuses on the distinction within the criminal law between the inculpatory elements of a criminal offence and the exculpatory elements of a defence. One way to understand this distinction is that under the criminal law, there are general reasons against performing the act that constitute the criminal offence, whereas a defence represents specific reasons in favour of performing the act. In relying upon this distinction, I argue that there are general reasons against penetrative sex, thereby implying that penetrative sex ought to be a criminal wrong that requires a justification or excuse. The argument for this '*pro tanto* legal wrong thesis' emerges from engagement with Herring and Dempsey's seminal '*pro tanto* moral wrong thesis', which suggests that penetrative sex is a moral wrong that calls for an explanation.[10] The common thread is the observation that all penetrative sex involves the application of force to a person's body, which calls for an explanation (as a *pro tanto* moral wrong) or is contrary to an obligation (as a *pro tanto* legal wrong).

[9] Douglas Husak, *Ignorance of Law: A Philosophical Inquiry* (OUP 2016) 52.

[10] Michelle Madden Dempsey and Jonathan Herring, 'Why Sexual Penetration Requires Justification' (2007) 27 OJLS 467.

In the background of the formulation of the *pro tanto* legal wrong thesis is the convergence of two ideas through the conduit of 'the right to self-ownership'. The first idea (from Essay 1) is that each person has a 'non-use value'. Whatever choices or uses a person makes of their own body, it is valuable that they are able to make those choices. The second idea (from Essay 4) is that normative phenomena—such rights, wrongs, and obligations—are generated by worthwhile social practices. A person can exercise a normative power, and enact a change in normative phenomena, where it is 'all things considered, desirable that that person should be able to bring the change' by exercising the normative power.[11] The *pro tanto* legal wrong thesis represents a normative practice (a set of rights and obligations) where there is an obligation not to apply force to a person's body unless and until that person suspends the obligation through their consent (the 'yes means yes' convention). As opposed to the current legal practice, where the obligation not to apply force to a person's body (when it comes to sex) is generated by the person's non-consent (the 'no means no' convention). The *pro tanto* legal wrong thesis ultimately represents the claim that the 'yes means yes' convention better promotes the non-use value of every person.

The difference between the absence of consent being an inculpatory element and the provision of consent being an exculpatory defence might seem to represent 'no significant practical distinction'.[12] Essay 6 ('Justify and Excusing Sex') explains how, by reallocating consent to the defence side of the offence–defence distinction, the consent that is now required is consent that complies with the demands of justifications and excuses for wrongdoing (rather than a form of consent that merely negates the allegation of wrongdoing). Specifically, justifications and excuses are predicated upon 'explanatory' reasons (the reasons that the defendant did act on) and 'guiding' reasons (the reasons that the defendant ought to have acted on). Justifications require the defendant to have acted on both guiding and explanatory reasons, and excuses require the defendant to be justified in acting on their explanatory reasons. In comparison, if there is no norm against sexual penetration (if the prohibitory norm requires the further inculpatory element of the absence of consent), then sexual penetration is normatively inert, and there is no requirement for belief in consent to rely on reasons.

[11] Joseph Raz, 'Normative Powers (revised)' (2019) Oxf J Leg Stud Research Paper 36/2019, 2 <https://ssrn.com/abstract=3379368> accessed 1 December 2024.

[12] Michelle Madden Dempsey, 'The Normative Force of Consent in Moral, Political, and Legal Perspective' in Tatjana Hörnle (ed), *Sexual Assault: Law Reform in a Comparative Perspective* (OUP 2023) 24.

There is a further implication of requiring consent to align with practical reasoning of justifications and excuses that emerges in Essay 6: if consent is required to obey the logic of justifications and excuses, then only a particular definition of consent (the 'expressive consent standard') can satisfy that logic. In most jurisdictions, and for most commentators, consent is an internal or subjective phenomenon; it is an attitude of willingness, intention, acceptance, or acquiescence ('attitudinal consent standard'). For a few commentators, and a few jurisdictions, consent is defined as an external or objective phenomenon that expresses that attitude through overt words or actions ('expressive consent'). It follows from the *pro tanto* legal wrong thesis that consent ought to be defined in terms of the objective elements (the overt words and actions) that express the subjective elements (the attitudes of acceptance, willingness, or acquiescence). This is because only the objective elements of consent can furnish a defendant with the guiding and explanatory reasons that the practical reasoning of justifications and excuses requires of the defendant. The practical implication of reallocating consent to the defence side of the offence–defence distinction is to require the more demanding standard of expressive consent.

After endorsing the expressive consent standard in Essay 6, I then set out to undermine it in Essay 7 ('The Expressive Consent Dilemma'). I undermine it only with a view to later improving it. I suggest in Essay 7 that different formulations of the expressive consent standard confront the same dilemma. At one horn of the dilemma, the expressive consent standard directs the finder of fact to perform the same task as if the attitudinal consent standard were being applied (this is 'the collapse' of expressive consent into attitudinal consent). At the other horn of the dilemma, the expressive consent standard only identifies culpable conduct in the weak sense: that a person is culpable for their ignorance, but not culpable for their wrongdoing. There is a gap between the culpable conduct that ought to be criminalised and the culpable conduct that the expressive consent standard captures (this is 'the culpability gap'). Regardless of whether the 'words and overt actions' that the expressive consent standard requires are 'reasonable', 'public', or 'objective', the standard either collapses into the attitudinal standard or criminalises non-culpable conduct.

In the background of Essay 7 is a dichotomy. In order to connect the expressive elements of consent (words or overt actions) with the attitudinal elements (willingness or acceptance), we rely upon social and semantic rules (a 'sexual script') that link the intended meaning of the consenting person with the recognised meaning of the person relying upon their consent. The expressive consent dilemma is predicated on the dichotomy of the finder of fact either accommodating the social and semantic rules as they are practised ('describing the sexual script') or requiring that certain social and semantic rules be followed ('prescribing the sexual script'). By describing the script, the finder of fact makes the same accommodations for mistaken belief in consent that we encounter under the attitudinal standard (the collapse). By prescribing the script, the finder of fact conflates culpability for wrongdoing with culpability for being ignorant of the applicable social and semantic rules (the culpability gap).

A lot of unfinished business is left for Essay 8 ('I Don't Know About You'). It nonetheless foregrounds a new question: if being consent-astute means having reasons to believe that another person agrees to my treatment of them, how can I be justified in believing that they possess that mental state? I consider in Essay 8 the apparent tension between two intuitions about the mental states of other people. One intuition is that the mental state of another person remains beyond my full comprehension ('the alterity intuition'), and the other is that we are nonetheless capable of having an epistemically justified belief in the mental state of another person ('the knowledge intuition'). To resolve this tension, I consider the 'asymmetry' between our knowledge of our own mental states and our justified beliefs in the mental states of others. This then enables two claims about mental states. One is that 'self-knowledge' and 'justified beliefs' are both inferential (we infer from (p) promptings to a (P) proposition through (l) linking assumptions). The other is that the (l) linking assumptions required for a justified belief (in the mental state of another person (B)) must be grounded in B-specific reasons that B is expressing a mental state.

I consider the problems of other minds with a background agenda already in place: I need to provide a way out of the expressive consent dilemma by identifying a standard of inference (from behaviour to attitude) that is neither descriptive of sexual scripts nor prescriptive of them. The way out of the dilemma is to view the problem of other minds as an epistemic problem as well as an empirical one. When the expressive consent standard is either describing or prescribing sexual scripts, it is applying or requiring the use of certain social tools. The burden of the expressive consent standard ought to be, however, an epistemic burden: to have a justified belief in the mental state of another person. The above requirement—that the linking assumption required for a justified belief must be grounded in B-specific reasons that B is expressing a mental state—is an epistemic standard that the expressive consent standard ought to embody.

Moreover, when the expressive consent standard does embody the epistemic standard, it avoids the expressive consent dilemma. It can avoid the first horn of the dilemma (the collapse) by shifting away from an empirical-descriptive standard of inference (how, in the ordinary course of life, people assess others' consenting attitudes) to an epistemic standard of inference (how a person can have a justified belief in the consenting attitude of another person). Avoiding the second horn of the dilemma (the culpability gap) calls upon some earlier-developed ideas: if culpable ignorance that is the result of the mismanagement of a moral outlook sustains the culpability for the wrongdoing (Essay 4), and if a failure to provide B-specific reasons for the belief that B agreed to A's treatment of B is the result of the mismanagement of a moral outlook (Essay 2), then the failure to provide B-specific reasons sustains the culpability for the wrongdoing. It therefore follows that the legal standard of consent ought to require not only objective or observable 'words or overt actions' that express an internal attitude of 'willingness, acceptance or agreement' but also reasons that those words and overt actions were her (his/their) expression of her (his/their) attitude of willingness or acceptance. This requires that any reasons for a belief in the consent of another person be person-specific reasons.

I conclude by revisiting the three main reforms advocated for in these essays with specific reference to the Sexual Offences Act 2003 (United Kingdom) and the Tentative Draft No 6 of the Model Penal Code (American Law Institute). With an eye on practicalities, I consider these reforms in light of a general principle of criminal procedure, that 'the prosecution must prove every offense element (beyond reasonable doubt)' which 'means—procedurally speaking—it must also disprove—"negative"—justifications and excuses'.[13] The first reform is that the provision of consent and the mistaken belief in consent ought to be available to a defendant as a justification and excuse, rather than their negation being an element of the offence. However, even with this reform, the prosecution retains the formal/persuasive burden of disproving any justifications or excuses, and thereby retains the burden of proving non-consent beyond reasonable doubt. Whilst consent-as-a-defence does not change the formal burden, it nonetheless reshapes the exculpatory mistaken belief in consent that needs to be disproven by the prosecution. This reshaping can be seen in the further reforms. The second reform is that consent itself should be defined in terms of the objective elements (the words or overt actions) that express the subjective element (the attitude of willingness, acceptance, or acquiescence). And the third concerns how expressive consent is interpreted: it ought to be interpreted as requiring complainant-specific reasons for believing

[13] Markus D Dubber, *An Introduction to the Model Penal Code* (2nd edn, OUP 2015) 143, citing American Law Institute, 'Model Penal Code: Official Draft and Explanatory Notes (Complete Text of Model Penal Code as Adopted at the 1962 Annual Meeting of the American Law Institute at Washington, D.C., May 24, 1962)' (1985) ss 1.12(1) and 1.12(2)(a).

that they were expressing the attitude of willingness, acceptance, or acquiescence through the words or overt actions that were relied upon. As I explain, this takes the legal form of directing the finder of fact that 'whether a belief is exculpatory is to be determined (solely) by having regard to the steps (if any) A has taken to ascertain whether B consents'. This 'failure to ascertain standard' represents a significant shift, from (the open-ended) 'having regard to all the circumstances' directions to the (closed) 'having regard to the steps A has taken to ascertain whether B consents' factual inquiry. It is a shift that reshapes the legal standard (that determines considerations that go to an exculpatory mistaken belief) without shifting the burden on the prosecution (to disprove the exculpatory mistaken belief beyond reasonable doubt). It is also a shift that rebalances the inquiry and interrogation towards the behaviour of the defendant (in ascertaining consent) and away from the general behaviour of the complainant.

It will be clear by now that this is a book by a fox and not a hedgehog.[14] It chases ideas through methodological disputes and feminist reconstructions of Kant, across accounts of moral responsibility and criminal accountability, and through normative powers and moral reasons. It tracks the structure of the criminal law and criminal procedure, and explores ideas from linguistic theory, phenomenology, and the problem(s) of other minds. All the while trying to understand one interaction—sex—and all the while trying to merely narrow the legal category of the exculpatory mistaken belief in consent.

In formulating the central argument (about the exculpatory mistaken belief), I also make a range of collateral demands: we should be astute not only to another's consent but also to their reasons for their consent, we are under a duty to somehow escape the social forces that mould how we understand sex, we cannot rely on the consent of another where we know their choice is contrary to their own interests, we should excuse some instances of past wrongful behaviour, all of our sex calls for a moral explanation, we ought to adopt more expressive sexual scripts, and so on. I doubt that I am right about all of these collateral claims, but I am hopeful that I am sustaining the right discussion; that is, I am hopeful that I am foregrounding the concerns that should worry us, I am highlighting some of the many ideas that are worth discussing, and I am maintaining a worthwhile tradition of inquiry. Even if it is just sex for foxes.

Or, more accurately, it is heterosex for foxes. For a lot of the analysis that follows, it is assumed that the sex is heterosex, the complainant is a woman, and

[14] Isaiah Berlin, *The Hedgehog and the Fox* (Weidenfeld & Nicolson 1953).

the ostensible wrongdoer is a man. This narrows the scope of the analysis and limits the implications that can be drawn from it. The narrow scope follows from a methodological commitment. As I touched upon in the first paragraph, and as we are about to encounter more thoroughly in Essay 1, any theoretical account of sex needs to grapple with the level of abstraction and detachment (from particular experiences and social contexts) that is appropriate, considering the aim or purpose of the account. There is a level of abstraction that would strip away the sex and gender of those in the interaction. At times, the discussion here ascends to that level of detachment. For example, in Essay 5, I make the claim that 'a general feature of penetrative sex is the application of force to a person's body'. The claim itself does not embody any assumptions about the sex or gender identity of the applier of force or the person being penetrated (nor does it assume that the applier of force cannot be the person being penetrated). At other times, however, the discussion remains abstracted whilst being orientated towards the sex and gender of those in the interaction. For example, in Essay 2, I suggest that 'sex being about male dominance might be a contingent and yet universal feature of sex-as-we-know-it'. The commitment here is that whilst gender identity and sexual orientation may be contingent features of sex and physical intimacy, they are nonetheless necessary to understanding some of the concerns and observations that I develop in some of these essays. That is not to presume that all sexual contexts, interactions, and orientations are the same, and that is not to say that the concerns about sex—beyond heterosex—do not matter. Fortunately, there is no shortage of robust scholarship that takes up these concerns.[15] Whether any of the puzzles, preoccupations, observations, and arguments in these essays applies beyond heterosex is an inquiry that I have not taken up here. But I hope someone will.

[15] Matthew Ball, *Criminology and Queer Theory: Dangerous Bedfellows?* (Palgrave Macmillan 2016); Carrie L Buist and Emily Lenning, *Queer Criminology* (Routledge 2016); Angela Dwyer, Matthew Ball and Thomas Crofts (eds), *Queering Criminology* (Palgrave Macmillan 2016); Jeff Ferrell and Clinton Sanders (eds), *Cultural Criminology.* (Northeastern UP 1995); Charlotte Knight and Kath Wilson, *Lesbian, Gay, Bisexual, and Trans People (LGBT) and the Criminal Justice System* (Palgrave Macmillan 2016); Joey L Mogul, Andrea J Ritchie and Kay Whitlock, *Queer (In)Justice: The Criminalization of LGBT People in the United States* (Beacon Press 2011).

1

The Problem with Sex in General

1.1

It is 'difficult to reconcile', according to Joanna Conaghan, the 'embeddedness of rape and its normative investment in a particular conception of sexual relations' with 'any formal articulation of essential properties abstracted from the context and conditions in which they apply'.[1] This is because, Conaghan warns, a 'formalistic approach' to rape is 'likely to yield an impoverished account of the operational parameters of the concept'.[2] And yet, despite this warning, this is exactly what I will do here, and over subsequent essays. That is, articulate the essential properties of sex, consent, and sexual offences, abstracted away from the context and social conditions in which these concepts apply. And then, eventually, locate how the 'embeddedness of rape and its normative investment in a particular conception of sexual relations' is relevant to the formal elements of sexual offences.

In this particular essay, I attempt to isolate the morally relevant, and essential, properties of sex. In other words, I seek to locate the features and characteristics that sex has *in general*—the features that arise in all instances of sex—which are also features or characteristics that inform how we *ought* to treat one another. Such an analytical approach, which isolates 'essential properties', can be alienating. It can be alienating because our understanding of, and familiarity with, sex is based upon our experiences, and these experiences are varied and contextual. Sex may have been coupled with experiences of trust or the betrayal of trust, of choice or compulsion, of affirmation or denigration, of subordination or equality, and so on. Being 'analytical' about sex starts by stripping away all of these 'contingent features'—or what we might call 'distracting epiphenomena'[3]—in order to isolate its 'necessary' or 'essential' properties. This is a problematic method of inquiry. 'Let us not forget', Stephen Shute and

[1] Joanne Conaghan, 'The Essence of Rape' (2019) 39 OJLS 151, 163.
[2] Conaghan (n 1) 163.
[3] John Gardner and Stephen Shute, 'The Wrongness of Rape' in Jeremy Horder (ed), *Oxford Essays in Jurisprudence: Fourth Series* (OUP 2000) 197.

Sex and Self-Ownership. Jesse Wall, Oxford University Press. © Jesse Wall 2025.
DOI: 10.1093/9780191987809.003.0001

John Gardner remind us, 'that some victims of rape have had unspeakable experiences'.[4] Whilst Shute and Gardner themselves strip away 'the distracting epiphenomena' of experiences, they are mindful that 'a philosopher, for whom no aspect of a subject can ultimately be left unspoken if the subject is chosen for study' might be 'guilty of serious insensitivity in taking up the study of unspeakable experiences'.[5]

In addition to being alienating and insensitive, the approach taken here may even be impossible. In order to operate at a level of *generality*—in order to capture the features that arise in all instances of sex—the concepts developed here are abstracted and detached, not just from social context but from any given moral or normative property. The methodology employed here might be normatively inert. This is the methodological problem with thinking about sex in general: there may be no essential moral properties, nor moral pitfalls, of sex in general.

With all this doubt in mind, I nonetheless start to construct in this essay a general—ie an analytical and essentialist—account of sex. In this essay, I will defend three 'essentialist' propositions about the problem with sex in general:

1. All sex instrumentalises another person.
2. All sex (also) objectifies another person.
3. The instrumental use of the person as an object explains the wrongfulness of all instances of rape.

The first two essentialist propositions ((1) instrumentalism and (2) objectification) follow from a viewpoint that I will attempt to ground as the methodological starting point, namely that the analysis ought to adopt

4. a second-person perspective that considers how a person can act on the consent of another person (rather than the first-person perspective that considers the consenting attitude of a person).

The third essentialist proposition ((3) the wrongfulness) also embodies a contentious methodological claim, that

5. the essential properties of rape can explain the moral content of the (albeit contingent) features that we associate with 'real rape'.

[4] Gardner and Shute (n 3) 195.
[5] Gardner and Shute (n 3) 195.

The discussion at 1.2 introduces the essentialist propositions, along with some initial puzzles. I then explain (at 1.3) how the moral primacy of the duty of consent-astuteness (over consent in fact), as the antidote to the instrumental use of the body of another person, follows from the second-person perspective. At 1.4, I start to pull apart instrumentalism from objectification to consider the compounding effect of both together. I then consider (at 1.5) the relationship between the harmfulness and wrongfulness of rape (and sexual violation and other sexual offences), alongside the relationship between the essential properties of rape and its further contingent features.

1.2

The challenge here is to say something morally relevant (something that informs how we ought to act) about sex in general (that pertains to all instances of sex). To attempt to do so, let me start with two basic assumptions. The first being that sex is an embodied interaction, insofar as it involves another person and their body. It is an interaction mediated through the *bodies* of two people (in broad terms, it is the penetration of one person's orifice by another person's body part, it is the stimulation of one person's genitalia by another person's genitalia or body part). The second assumption is that sex is an *action* (or series or sequence of actions) that one or two agent(s) perform, either reciprocally or unilaterally. If sex is an action (rather than an accident or involuntary reflex), then any given sex act is accompanied by an intention, motivation, or purpose that can explain the action. For instance, sometimes towards a long-term goal or aspiration (reproduction), and sometimes towards the immediate aim of orgasm. At times, the goals or aims may not be shared between participants. In any case, it is an act done with some purpose in mind.

If these two basic assumptions hold, then sex is intentional engagement with the body of another person. Which seems benign enough. It is benign until we make three substitutions: replace 'engagement' with 'use', load the 'use' with the language of 'means', and replace 'intentional' with the language of 'ends'. With these substitutions, sex becomes the use of a person's body with a view to pursue some kind of purpose or end.

Sex—in all cases—then becomes:

Instrumental: the use of another person's body as a means to an end.

Which is now more provocative. The shift in vocabulary deliberately invokes the notion that sex—necessarily—*instrumentalises* the other person, along with all the Kantian baggage that comes with it.

However, instrumentalism, by itself, might not render a wrong. As Leslie Green explains:

> We *must* treat others as instruments, for we need their skills, their company, and their bodies—in fact, there is little that we social creatures can do on our own, and so little of that is fulfilling.[6]

Moreover, '[m]ost people desperately *want* to be of use to others' but they 'want to be of use and used subject to certain constraints'.[7] We might then want to say that describing sex as 'using another person' is analytically sound in its generality, but overwhelmingly uninteresting and normatively inert. By itself, the allegation of instrumentalism does not seem to inform us as to how we ought to relate to one another. This is because we can readily reach for the antidote at the first sight of the symptom. That is, upon encountering 'instrumentalism' we redirect the inquiry to a discussion about the consent of the other person (and any other conditions that license the use of the person).

I want to resist this movement from instrumentalism of the person (as the problem) to the person's consent (as the solution). The tendency is to ground the analysis in the first-person perspective of the consenting (or non-consenting) person, their attitude that permits (or does not permit) the use of them, and the harms to the person that can ensue when they do not consent. According to the first-person perspective, it is consent—a person's attitude of willingness, acceptance, or acquiescence—that performs the 'moral magic'[8] of changing 'the moral and legal relationship between persons who engage in consent and to whom the consent is directed'.[9] Consent can 'transform a wrong into a right when it constitutes an autonomous exercise of will that conveys a permission on another that he would not otherwise have'.[10] Moreover, according to moral magicians, it is because of this transformative power that '[t]he primary harm of rape is a function of a putative victim's mental state'.[11]

[6] Leslie Green, 'Pornographies' (2000) 8 J Polit Philos 27, 44.

[7] Green (n 6) 45.

[8] Heidi M Hurd, 'The Moral Magic of Consent' (1996) 2 Leg Theory 121, 124; Larry Alexander, 'The Moral Magic of Consent (II)' (1996) 2 Leg Theory 165, 166.

[9] Peter Westen, *The Logic of Consent: The Diversity and Deceptiveness of Consent as a Defense to Criminal Conduct* (Routledge 2016) 15.

[10] Heidi M Hurd, 'Was the Frog Prince Sexually Molested?: A Review of Peter Westen's "The Logic of Consent"' (2005) 103 Mich L Rev 1329, 1331; Hurd, 'The Moral Magic of Consent' (n 8) 124–25.

[11] Westen (n 9) 151.

It then follows that if a putative victim 'does not subjectively and voluntarily choose an act of sexual intercourse',[12] then the putative victim suffers the primary harm of rape.

In comparison, I will ground the analysis here in a second-person perspective, where the focus is on how one person can respond to, and rely on, the consent of the other person. There are three main reasons for this commitment. Let me mention the first two here (and the third reason at 1.3). First, the second-person perspective brings the analysis of sex closer aligned with the practice and experience of sex itself, in one important regard: when we encounter the embodied person, we do so without direct access to the moral magic that licenses our use of them: their consenting attitude. Whilst we can have a justified, and true, belief in another person's attitude, the second-person perspective isolates the moral duties that we need to discharge to be justified in that belief (and thereby resolve or ameliorate the problem of our instrumental use of the other person). Second, if we are ultimately interested in the retributive morality of the criminal law, then second-person perspective (of the defendant) is the lens through which we can assess the culpability of the defendant. To the extent that a defendant's belief in the consent of the complainant (even when the complainant did not consent) is exculpatory, we need to understand how a person can be justified in that belief.

To help us step back from the first-person perspective of consent, and maintain the second-person perspective, let us subtract the consenting attitude from our moral calculus. We can do so by considering the following three scenarios:

1(a) Martha's Pillow: Martha is 'lying around with [her] lover on the bed, and use[s] his stomach as pillow' while 'he's asleep, with a reasonable belief that he would not mind . . . without causing him pain' (and 'in the context of a relationship in which he is generally treated as more than a pillow').[13]

2(a) Shute and Gardner's 'pure case of rape': A victim is 'drugged or drunk to the point of unconsciousness when the rape was committed, and the rapist wore a condom', the victim 'has no feelings about the incident, since she knows nothing of it . . . except possibly a hangover in the morning; otherwise the victim's life goes on exactly as before'. The rapist is then 'run over by a bus as he leaves the house'.[14]

[12] Westen (n 9) 151.
[13] Martha C Nussbaum, 'Objectification' (1995) 24 Philos Public Aff 249, 265.
[14] Gardner and Shute (n 3) 196.

3(a) While You Were Sleeping: Lucy (a by-stander) rescues Peter from being hit by a train. At the hospital Lucy is mistaken for Peter's fiancée (after being overheard saying 'I was going to marry that man'), whilst Peter is comatose. Lucy sustains the misunderstanding, out of affection for Peter's family, ultimately so she can develop a romantic relationship with Peter's brother, Jack.[15]

Even placing these three scenarios alongside each other may seem insensitive to the fundamental differences between them. And they are fundamentally different: Martha has committed no wrong to her lover, the rapist in the 'pure case of rape' has committed a serious (and, arguably, paradigmatic) wrong to the victim, and Lucy has committed a trivial wrong to Peter.

All three scenarios nonetheless share three common elements. The first is that Martha, the rapist, and Lucy used (or instrumentalised) another person; Martha used her lover as a pillow for comfort, the rapist used the victim as an object for sexual ends, and Lucy used Peter's relationship status to gain access and trust. The second common element is that Martha's lover, the victim, and Peter did not (and could not) accept or agree to the treatment of them. It was all while they were sleeping. To understand why there was no wrong (pillow), a serious wrong (rape), and a trivial wrong (fiancée) we need to look elsewhere, beyond the used person's consent. The third common element is that Martha's lover, the victim, and Peter were not 'harmed' by the use of them. It follows that if we want to explain the wrongfulness of the second (and third) scenario(s), then we must also consider the relationship between the wrongs committed and the (ultimately 'contingent') harms that may follow from wrongdoing.

1.3

We can now unpack these fundamental differences by explaining why Martha's instrumentalism was 'benign', why Lucy's instrumentalism was trivial, and why the harmless instrumentalism in the 'pure case of rape' is not just a serious wrong but a paradigmatic one.

Let us start with our first substantive question: how was Martha able to use her lover as a pillow without using him *merely* as a pillow? Recall that the standard answer—her lover's consent—is unavailable to us. We can, nonetheless, consider the relationship between Martha's actions and her lover's

[15] Jon Turteltaub, *While You Were Sleeping* (Buena Vista Pictures 1995).

consent, and suggest that Martha's actions were consent-astute. Her use of him (as a pillow) was astute as to 'what he would have agreed to'. She directed her attention towards 'the range of expectations that the touched individual would have given the nature of his or her relationship'.[16] Here, we can say that Martha performed the duty of consent-astuteness where the duty requires that

> Person A must have reasons to believe that Person B would agree to A's treatment of B.

In being sufficiently consent-astute, Martha is treating her lover as a person, as someone whose expectations and attitudes determine the permissibility of the use or treatment of them. By discharging her duty to be consent-astute, we can say that Martha used her lover, without her lover's consent, without committing a wrong.

It is tempting, however, to consider this explanation to be only a fallback position, which only works as a second best to consent itself. Again, the tendency—which I am resisting—is to take consent-astuteness to be morally secondary and consent (the other person's willingness, acceptance, or agreement) itself to be primary. It would follow that for 1(a) Martha's Pillow, we needed to invoke consent-astuteness only because consent in fact is removed from consideration by the construction of the scenario. We might then feel a little uneasy, or less confident, about our initial assessment that 'Martha committed no wrong to her lover' than if her lover had in fact consented to the use of him, because we are relying upon a second-best explanation of the permissibility of her actions.

I am attempting here to develop an alternative account to the moral magic of the first-person perspective. I suggest that we ought to maintain the second-person perspective, and not relegate consent-astuteness to being morally secondary. To explain, let me ask a further question about 2(a) the 'pure case of rape': does the wrongfulness of the rapist's act differ depending on the victim's attitude? Consider a variation on the scenario:

> 2(b) the pure case (entrapment): The putative victim drugged herself to the point of unconsciousness at a party in order to entrap the rapist by recording the rape. The remainder of 2(a) then ensues.

[16] Michael Plaxton, 'Nussbaum on Sexual Instrumentalization' (2016) 10 Crim Law Philos 1, 11.

I doubt that the putative victim's so-called 'moral magic' (their attitude of willingness, acceptance, or acquiescence) transformed the moral relationship between the rapist and the putative victim. If the rapist found the victim unresponsive and then proceeded to use the victim as merely a means to a sexual end, with complete disregard for the victim as a person, then the rapist's wrongful instrumentalism of the victim seems to be independent of (2(a)) the victim's unawareness of the use of her, or (2(b)) the victim's aim or intention to be used. The rapist in 2(a) and 2(b) committed the same wrong by breaching their duty of astuteness in the same way.

Hence, what we take to be morally primary depends upon our viewpoint. If we start with the second-person perspective, and posit that sex, in all cases, is the use of a person, then what calls for an explanation is how a person can use another person without committing a wrong. In this way, since we are concerned with instrumentalism, consent-astuteness becomes morally primary. In comparison, if we start with the first-person perspective, and posit that sex, in all cases, should be the exercise of a choice, then consent is morally primary. There is no denying the appeal of the first-person perspective, in light of how 'having a system of sexual relations in which people control by consent the treatment of their own bodies secures optimally respect for the ultimate value of people'.[17] Moreover, if 'to be an autonomous moral agent is to have the ability to create and dispel rights and duties' and if '[t]o respect persons as autonomous is thus to recognize them as the givers and takers of permissions and obligations',[18] then it might seem that our entry point ought to be the permission-giving powers of the other person.

Still, despite the appeal of the other perspective, consent-astuteness is taken as the starting point here. This is for an important, third, reason. The third reason for favouring the second-person perspective (and, in doing so, focusing on the duty of consent-astuteness) is that it helps us frame the 'non-use value' of the other person.[19] Whilst the body of another person can be used 'like other tools and receptacles and artefacts' (and thereby has *use-value*),[20] and whilst '[m]ost people desperately *want* to be of use to others',[21] each person has a value beyond their use; each person has a value—'non-use value'—independent of their use or usefulness. It is this value that is denied when we instrumentalise

[17] Gardner and Shute (n 3) 208.
[18] Heidi M Hurd, 'The Normative Force of Consent' in Peter Schaber and Andreas Müller (eds), *Routledge Handbook on the Ethics of Consent* (Routledge 2018) 46.
[19] Gardner and Shute (n 3) 207.
[20] Gardner and Shute (n 3) 207.
[21] Green (n 6) 45.

them. Whilst the right to sexual autonomy enables a series of choices, and uses of the body, the value of sexual autonomy ought to be understood without reference to those choices or uses. It is instead understood, here, with reference to the fact that each person has those choices; the right is valuable independently of how it is exercised, and the person has a value independently of the use we might make of them.

Approaching sex through consenting attitudes focuses our attention on how a person may choose to use their body; it foregrounds their use of their body. Approaching sex through instrumentalism, in comparison, foregrounds the non-use value. An analogy with property rights might help: rather than detailing the ways in which a property rights-holder might use an item or object, we can carve out a sphere of 'indefinite and undefined'[22] use by focusing on the duties that duty-bearers must perform to respect the right. By focusing on the duties that correlate with the property right, we afford the rights-holder 'an *open-ended* set' of privileges in the property.[23] In the same way, rather than detailing the choices that a person may make with regard to their own body, we ought to afford the person an open-ended (but not limitless) set of privileges in their body. That is, to recognise that whatever choices or uses a person makes of their own body, they are entitled to make those choices, and the exercise of that choice has a value independent of what that choice may be (a non-use value). This sphere of undefined activity around the body is carved out by the duties we owe the person, such as the duty of consent-astuteness.

This explains why we are concerned with instrumentalism (making use of a person), and, hence, we take the duty of astuteness to be our primary concern. It therefore follows that the reason Martha is able to use her lover without using him merely as a means is because she discharged her duty of astuteness (we have otherwise bracketed her lover's right of self-ownership, for now). But we need something further.

To understand why Martha's instrumentalism of her lover was benign, we need to appreciate why, in context, Martha's duty of astuteness was easy to discharge. Martha was able to discharge her duty of astuteness only because of how the duty is calibrated by its non-sexualised context. Recall how she used her lover: her lover's stomach (a typically non-sexualised part of his body) as a pillow (a typically non-sexual feature of his body). Similar to using another person's knees as a footrest on a couch, or another person's shoulder as a headrest in an aeroplane, using someone in this way provides a functional or

[22] James E Penner, *The Idea of Property in Law* (OUP 1997) 72.
[23] JW Harris, *Property and Justice* (Clarendon Press 1996) 160.

practical benefit for you that is tolerated by the other person. Perhaps there is more to the scenario; perhaps Martha's use of her lover as a pillow was an affirming or emotionally comforting reminder of their relationship. Either way, it was a non-sexualised use of the person, where they were used only as a physical or emotional prop, for the benefit of the other person.

In comparison, consider a variation on Martha's Pillow, where

> 1(b) Martha used her lover's body for a sexual end while her lover was sleeping.

In 1(b), we would be unwilling to accept that Martha committed no wrong. This is because the sexualised use of another heightens the duty of astuteness. Unlike the functional use of the body of another (as a pillow, footrest, or headrest), the sexual use of the body *ought to be* more than functional. Part of what makes a sexual experience pleasurable, valuable, and affirming of personhood is that it is a shared experience, of 'pursuing a meaningful activity with another who will recognize its significance and welcome pursuing it with us'.[24] It is reciprocally 'intentional' in the sense that we intend for another person to intend the same thing.[25] It is, in shorthand, a 'subject–subject' relationship,[26] or (in the Kantian language of the next essay) 'a unity of will'.[27] The body-object does not drop out of the picture; rather, the intention is still directed towards the use of the body, but with the aim that the other person also intends the shared embodied experience. Now, what makes the sexual use of a person without performing the duty of astuteness *particularly* wrongful is that it inverts the subject–subject relationship (into a subject–object relationship). It is the one-sided, or self-regarding, pursuit of an experience without sufficient regard, or with disregard, for the experience of the other person; it undermines or inverts the value that the interaction is capable of having.

In the context of 1(b), the fact that Martha has reason to believe that her lover 'wouldn't mind' her sexual touching of him whilst he is asleep would now seem insufficient to discharge the duty of consent-astuteness. We can go further and suggest that it is not possible to discharge the duty of astuteness when the other person is asleep. This is because the duty of astuteness now requires us to believe that our lover has an attitude of willingness or acceptance of the

[24] Plaxton (n 16) 5.
[25] Roger Scruton, *Sexual Desire: A Moral Philosophy of the Erotic* (Free Press 1986) 18.
[26] Gardner and Shute (n 3) 207.
[27] Immanuel Kant, *Lectures on Ethics* (Louis Infield tr, Harper and Row 1963) 167.

sexual experience, and they simply cannot accept an experience that they are not experiencing.

When it comes to Martha's *functional* use of her lover's stomach as a pillow (1(a)), I have suggested that we can accept Nussbaum's claim that Martha used her lover without committing a wrong. This is because Martha discharged her duty of astuteness in the context of the non-sexual use of her lover's body. There are two ways in which we might describe 1(a): either Martha, by performing the duty of astuteness, *absolved* the wrongfulness of the instrumentalism ('benign instrumentalism') or Martha, by performing the duty of astuteness, pre-empted the instrumentalism from arising ('non-instrumentalism'). This might seem like a meaningless distinction, and for the purpose of the present inquiry, it is. In this inquiry—which is uninhibited by a structure of norms—the distinction between benign instrumentalism and non-instrumentalism is meaningless because the problem (instrumentalism) and solution (consent-astuteness) are concurrent. However, when we later confront normative phenomena (rights, wrongs, and obligations), it is a non-trivial question whether a *pro tanto* wrong was justified or whether no wrongdoing occurred.

In order to account for why Martha's instrumentalism was 'benign', we have relied on three observations. The first has been that, by orientating her behaviour around the choices and expectations of her lover, Martha discharged the duty of astuteness. I have contended further that, following the second-person perspective, the duty of astuteness is morally primary. The second is that the duty of astuteness is calibrated by how another person is used. The functional use of the body (as a pillow) differs from the sexual use on the basis that sexual experiences ought to be (and are expected to be) shared experiences. It follows, I suggest, that it is not possible to discharge the duty of astuteness for the sexual use of a sleeping or unresponsive person. The third is that our finding—that the instrumentalism was 'benign'—can (in the context of this inquiry) be equated with the finding that there was no instrumentalism.

1.4

Martha may not have instrumentalised her lover, but Lucy did use a comatose Peter as merely a means (to be with Jack). We can now turn to consider our second question and explain why Lucy's instrumentalism was 'trivial'. We have so far been concerned with the use of the person as a means (instrumentalism). But as we encountered in the previous section, the use of the body, and how the body is used (functionally or sexually), calibrates the degree of consent-astuteness that we can expect from the user of the body. How the body is instrumentalised changes the moral calculus. It is otherwise tempting to equate instrumentalism ('the conversion of subjects into instruments or tools') with objectification ('refusing to regard subjects as beings with their own feelings and experiences (i.e. as subjective)').[28] When we instrumentalise the person we objectify them, and when we objectify the person we instrumentalise them.

Yet we can do one without the other. As we will discuss here, we are capable of using a person (instrumentalism) without using them as an object (objectification). And as we will discuss in the next essay, we are capable of objectifying a person without instrumentalising them. As far as instrumentalism without objectification is concerned, consider the following examples:

> You lie to your partner in order to conceal the details of a surprise birthday party for your partner.
>
> You obtain a booking at a restaurant by mentioning (unbeknown to them) that your friend, a famous musician, will be in attendance.
>
> You convince a purchaser of the merits of an expensive oven that is superfluous to their needs.
>
> You are elected to public office by promising harsher criminal sentencing by an electorate who is fearful of violent crime statistics when you know the statistics to be misleading.

In each of these instances, you have used another *person's emotional or rational capacities* (their trust/reputation/naivety/fear) in order to secure your own ends (party planning/dinner reservation/appliance sale/public office) without affording the other person(s) the opportunity to agree to, or share in, your own ends. The instrumentality may not be the only wrong in some of these examples; there might be some dishonesty and conceit too. We can nonetheless see how the two wrongs—dishonesty or conceit (such as relying on misleading crime statistics) and instrumentality (using a constituency's emotional response of fear)—compound the wrongdoing.

The point of contrast is that when it comes to objectification, one person uses another's *physical or embodied* capacity to secure their own ends. This contrast can explain the triviality of 3a. In the scenario, Lucy used Peter's relationship status to be with him in the hospital ward, without affording Peter the opportunity to agree to the use of him. It was a relatively trivial feature (Peter's relationship status) that was instrumentalised by Lucy, rendering a trivial wrong

[28] Nussbaum (n 13) 257.

(less serious, for example, than her dishonesty to Jack in circumstances that required candour, and less serious than her breach of Peter's family's trust). It would, in comparison, be a serious wrong if

> 3(b) Lucy sustained the misunderstanding in order to obtain a sperm 'donation' from a comatose Peter.

In 3(b), we encounter another instance of the instrumentalism of the body, which (as we have discussed) triggers a duty of astuteness, where the content of the duty will be calibrated by a feature of the person that is being instrumentalised (where it may be possible to discharge the duty of astuteness for the posthumous or comatose donation of sperm in favour of genuine procreative relationships).

When it comes to sex, however, the use of the person will always involve the use of the person's body. Separating instrumentalism from objectification may then seem redundant. As we will see here, and in the following essay, we nonetheless have two main reasons to pull apart the concerns. First, to understand the wrongfulness of 2(a) the 'pure case of rape' is to appreciate the compounding impact of instrumentality and objectification, *together* (rather than one being an instance or subset of the other). Second, just as we can encounter instrumentality without objectification, we can also encounter objectification without instrumentality. I will introduce this with reference to 2(c) but then explain it fully in Essay 2.

Let us start with the compounding impact of instrumentality and objectification. I suggest that we can best understand the wrong in 2(a) the 'pure case of rape' with reference to the compounding impact. But, first, consider some other compelling accounts of the wrong. Shute and Gardner explain the wrongfulness of 2(a) in the following way:

> This is a kind of use of a person, a kind of *objectification* of a subject. That a rapist objectifies his victim by treating her as a mere repository of use-value is what is basically wrong with rape.
>
> ...
>
> Rape, in the pure case, is the sheer use of a person. . . . Rape is terrifying and humiliating even when unaccompanied by further affronts, because the sheer use of a person, and in that sense the objectification of a person, is a denial of their personhood. It is literally dehumanizing.[29]

[29] Gardner and Shute (n 3) 204, emphasis added.

This echoes Carolyn Shafer and Marilyn Frye's account:

> [H]e is using her in furtherance of ends other than hers. Moreover, the ends for which he is using her body are ends which are contrary to hers, given that her ends include the maintenance of her bodily integrity and health. The use of a person in the advancement of interests contrary to its own is a limiting case of disrespect. It reveals the perception of the person simply as an object which can serve some purpose . . . it conveys to her that she is seen as an object with a sexual function.[30]

As well as Lynne Henderson's:

> [R]ape denies that you are a person, that you exist. . . . When a woman's existence just does not matter, intercourse becomes rape. Thus, the important factor is non-existence. . . . Thus I also disagree with theorists who see rape as an invasion of bodily integrity or privacy or personal autonomy. It is those things, too, but it is more.[31]

Rape (as in 2(a)) is the use of the person whilst denying personhood. And although Shute and Gardner's account equivocates between instrumentality and objectification, these explanations rely upon the compounding effect of both. For Shute and Gardner, the rapist uses his victim 'as a mere repository of use-value' (instrumentalism) by denying or subtracting 'their personhood', leaving in place only their body as an object (objectification). For Shafer and Frye, the rapist is 'using her in furtherance of ends other than hers' (instrumentalism) by using 'the person simply as an object which can serve some purpose' (objectification). And for Henderson, rape is the invasive use of the body (instrumentalism) whilst denying the existence of the person in favour of the body (objectification). Neither instrumentalism nor objectification alone captures the wrong in 2(a) the 'pure case of rape'.

For completeness, we can also isolate objectification without instrumentality. To do so, consider Gardner's variant on the pure case of rape:

[30] Carolyn M Shafer and Marilyn Frye, 'Rape and Respect' in Mary Vetterling-Braggin, Fredrick Elliston and Jane English (eds), *Feminism and Philosophy* (Littlefield, Adams and Co 1977) 341.

[31] Lynne N Henderson, 'What Makes Rape a Crime' (1987) 3 Women's LJ 193, 226–27.

2(c) *Gardner's variant*: '[a woman] wants her lover' to have penetrative sex 'while she's out cold, "just like the imaginary woman in the Shute-Gardner article I was reading today" she tells him'.[32]

We can note here that no instrumentalism arises here. Beyond agreeing to the treatment of her, the woman here is orchestrating her treatment (and her lover has been asked to follow her script and stage direction). She is nonetheless being used as if she was an object, 'as if she were a kind of super-realistic inflatable doll',[33] as a prop in her own pornographic fantasy. We will return to this in the next essay. For now, it is enough that one can occur without the other (objectification without instrumentalism in 2(c) *Gardner's variant*, and instrumentalism without objectification in 3(a) While You Were Sleeping), and, more importantly, that one can compound the other (2(a) the 'pure case of rape').

We have been able to explain the triviality of 3(a) by pulling apart instrumentalism and objectification. The wrongfulness of the instrumentalism will depend upon the person's capacity that is being instrumentalised; whilst it may be wrong to use a person's trust, fear, reputation, or relationship status, instrumentalising a person's body (without regard for them as a person) is a distinct wrong that is captured by the overlap of instrumentalism and objectification. Sexual offences represent the compounding wrong of using a person (as a means) whilst reducing the person (to an object).

1.5

We might think we have already explained why the harmless instrumentalism in 2(a) the 'pure case of rape' was serious. As above, all instances of instrumentalism of the person as a sexual object, without consent-astuteness, amount to serious wrongs. What remains to be explained, however, is the relationship between the *harmlessness* of the instrumentalism and the *wrongfulness* of the instrumentalism in 2(a) the 'pure case of rape'. There is also a methodological explanation that remains outstanding. A concern that has no doubt been lingering is that 2(a) the 'pure case of rape' sanitises rape; it removes all the (albeit contingent) features that make rape (and other sexual offences) violating, traumatising, and dehumanising. This is the main methodological concern

[32] John Gardner, 'Reasonable Reactions to the Wrongness of Rape' (2017) 29 Denning LJ 3, 15.
[33] Gardner (n 32) 15.

introduced at the beginning of this essay. In this section, I will try to both address this methodological concern and complete the explanation of the wrongfulness of 2(a) the 'pure case of rape'.

When it comes to Shute and Gardner's 'pure case of rape', we might object that the scenario is a cold, unemotional abstraction that 'does not accord with reality as perceived in our everyday lives by most, or all, of us'.[34] Moreover, by essentialising the wrong in terms of the breach of the duty of consent-astuteness (as I have done), 2(a) forces us to bracket other features of rape, sexual violation, and sexual offences that other commentators take to be central, or essential, to our understanding of these wrongs. Hence, the methodological objection is that the hypothetical represents a deliberate sidelining of features that some consider to be essential to our understanding of the wrong.

There is a lot to consider when it comes to the features and characteristics of sexual wrongs that have been bracketed here. To start, by considering the 'pure case of rape', we have already sidelined (by way of construction) the moral potence of a person's actual consent to the treatment of them, and the wrongfulness of acting contrary to their consent. If Peter Westen is right, and 'the primary harm of rape is a function of a putative victim's mental state',[35] then the analysis here has bracketed 'the primary harm of rape'. In addition, by bracketing consent in fact, we have also shelved consideration of how consent can (ever) function in a social context of pervasive power disparities. For Catherine MacKinnon, '[l]ack of consent is redundant and should not be a separate element of [rape]'.[36] In the place of lack of consent, rape should be defined as 'sex by compulsion'.[37]

We also overlook whether force or violence, whilst being definitionally inessential, nonetheless construct a 'real rape stereotype' that may continue to ground a set of assumptions about the wrongs that we have come to associate with rape and sexual offences.[38] These implicit assumptions can inform debates about the criminal law as well as application of the criminal law. Equally, the 'pure case of rape' also overlooks the sexual character of the wrong, as 'a corporeal encounter involving genitalia or a socially and culturally coded expression of sexual desire',[39] or as a socially coded expression of control or male

[34] Bob Watt, 'The Story of Rape: Wrongdoing and the Emotional Imagination' (2014) 26 Denning LJ 46, 46.

[35] Westen (n 9) 151.

[36] Catharine A MacKinnon, *Toward a Feminist Theory of the State* (Harvard UP 1989) 245.

[37] MacKinnon (n 36) 245.

[38] Helen Reece, 'Rape Myths: Is Elite Opinion Right and Popular Opinion Wrong?' (2013) 33 OJLS 445, 455.

[39] Conaghan (n 1) 166.

dominance, which may be essential to locating the wrong of rape and sexual assault as distinct from other assaults on bodily integrity. Moreover, we have further been blinkered from the social and cultural milieu which enables these wrongs. That is, we sideline or marginalise what Nicola Gavey describes as the 'everyday taken-for-granted normative forms of heterosexuality [that] work as a cultural scaffolding for rape'.[40]

Perhaps most worryingly, Shute and Gardner's 'pure case of rape' seems to elide into Louise du Toit's 'simple case of rape' without physical violence or trauma.[41] The 'simple case of rape' is used by du Toit to illustrate that if rape amounts to the use of the body without permission, then the 'simple rape seems relatively trivial'.[42] It is trivial in the way that we might regard the harmless appropriation of another's property to be trivial.[43] By bracketing the harms suffered by victims, and the experiences endured by victims, both the 'pure case of rape' and the 'simple case of rape' are neglectful of the 'true nature' of rape as 'the violent erasure of a woman victim's sexual subjectivity'.[44] To make matters worse, the 'pure case of rape', by bracketing the harms suffered, effectively *erases* (in the analysis of rape) *the erasure* of subjectivity (in instances of rape).

The 'pure case of rape'—as with the 'simple case of rape'—seems carelessly neglectful, in a number of ways, of the true nature or phenomenology of rape. It might seem like an objectionable way to start an analysis of sex, consent, and the criminal law.

Whilst we might be uneasy with the 'pure case of rape' scenario, let us not dismiss it (and its implicit methodology) too hastily. Recall the initial encounter with 2(a) the 'pure case of rape'. Whilst being abstracted and sanitised, note how 2(a) the 'pure case of rape' does invoke in us an outrage, a 'disgust', and 'an inward shudder for the victim'.[45] Both impulses—the *unease* (with the abstract hypothetical) and the *disgust* (at the content of the hypothetical scenario)—were impulses solicited by the authors of the 'pure case of rape'. They wanted

> the imaginary rape . . . to stir up strong feelings in our readers even though (by hypothesis) there could be no feelings at all about the rape on the part of anyone *inside* the imaginary world in which it happened, for in that world (by hypothesis) the rape went entirely undetected.[46]

[40] Nicola Gavey, *Just Sex? The Cultural Scaffolding of Rape* (Routledge 2005) 3.
[41] Louise du Toit, *A Philosophical Engagement with Rape: The Making and Unmaking of the Feminine Self* (Routledge 2009) 43–45.
[42] Conaghan (n 1) 175.
[43] Du Toit (n 41) 43–45.
[44] Du Toit (n 41) 33.
[45] Watt (n 34) 49.
[46] Gardner (n 32) 5–6.

They wanted to stir feelings of trauma about a scenario that is sanitised of trauma in order 'to test . . . the relative moral importance of trauma in rape cases', and confirm that 'an undetected rape, hence a rape giving rise to no trauma, is still very seriously wrong'.[47] Whilst rape and sexual assault can amount to

> the death of a liberal and individualistic conception of subjectivity: there can be no sense of self-possession when the self has been invaded by the desires, pleasures, wills, and actions of another,[48]

the seriousness of the wrong exists independently of 'the death of subjectivity'. If an undetected rape is still a serious wrong in this way, then we might be sympathetic to the view that rape can be an 'horrific' and 'a direct violation of the victim's body and selfhood' and seek to account for the 'destruction, damage, or the crossing of the will of the victim in a way that impacts directly on the victim's selfhood',[49] without having to explain the wrongfulness of rape *in terms of* the damage or destruction of personality and selfhood. John Stanton-Ife is right, that to 'reject "consent" as the answer to why rape is wrong' is 'to sell its moral importance short'.[50] To answer 'why it is so grave'[51] concerns how the wrong 'impacts directly on the victim's selfhood'.[52]

The explanation for this distinction begins with the relationship between responses and reasons. Recall, again, your own response to 2(a) the 'pure case of rape'. We were uneasy with the hypothetical because we wanted the scenario to acknowledge the harm, pain, erasure, or trauma that victims of rape and sexual offences suffer. We wanted the scenario to acknowledge the harmfulness of the reduction of a person to a sexual object that occurred (albeit undetected) in the scenario. When a hypothetical fails to acknowledge these phenomena, we resist its premise, and we instead empathically project a response that we think the victim would adopt were the rape be discovered. The point here is that our own response to the hypothetical and the hypothetical response that we project on to the hypothetical person are nonetheless reason-based.

47 Gardner (n 32) 6.
48 Robin West, *Caring for Justice* (NYU Press 1997) 104.
49 John Stanton-Ife, 'Horrific Crime' in RA Duff and others (eds), *The Boundaries of the Criminal Law* (OUP 2010) 157, 162.
50 Stanton-Ife (n 49) 162.
51 Stanton-Ife (n 49) 162.
52 Stanton-Ife (n 49) 157.

That is, *we had good reasons* to respond in that way. The fact that 'a victim's personality would or might be destroyed by rape (if and when that is true)'[53] provides for us reasons to respond to the hypothetical; it provides us reasons to

> abhor rapists and relish their getting their comeuppance, to be saddened by the human capacity for evil, to be anxious or alarmed for the victim, to feel vengeful or heartbroken on her behalf, and more generally, in a suitably empathetic way to share the victim's pain.[54]

The point of the 'pure case of rape' was to illustrate that we cannot explain the wrongfulness of rape in terms of the harm and trauma suffered by the victim (the phenomenology of the wrong) alone, in either the hypothetical 'pure case of rape' or the 'true nature' of rape cases. Were the victim to learn of the rape in 2(a), she may feel violated, traumatised, dehumanised, or erased. Whatever the response, the victim is 'still capable of asking what it is about the rape that makes her feel as she does'.[55] The answer to that question cannot, itself, lie in the harm and trauma. The phenomenological response cannot 'bottom out' in experiences themselves.[56] Instead, if the victim feels violated, then it is because the rapist used her as an instrument and an object; if the victim feels erased, then it is because the rapist showed complete disregard for her as a person; if the victim feels dehumanised, then it is because of the rapist's use of her body as an object, in a manner that is inconsistent with her humanity. Shute and Gardner's account of the 'pure case of rape' can provide the reasons a person might be traumatised, without having to build the trauma into the wrong itself. That is also true of the 'true cases'. What makes (du Toit's) 'simple case of rape' and (Shute and Gardner's) 'pure case of rape' *non-trivial* is that, in all cases, it is capable of non-trivial harm; it is capable of harmful ways of erasing a person's subjectivity. However the harm manifests, and whatever a victim's response to the wrong, the instrumentalism and objectification that they endured explain the harm, and provide reasons for their phenomenological response.

In this way, instrumentalism and objectification are essential to our understanding of the wrong. Whilst being essential to our understanding, instrumentalism and objectification do not exhaust the moral coverage of the wrongs that can occur. Violence, injury, fear, trauma, intimidation, abuse of power, betrayal of trust, embarrassment, denigration, and so on may be experiences that

[53] Gardner (n 32) 9.
[54] Gardner (n 32) 9.
[55] Gardner (n 32) 10.
[56] Gardner (n 32) 10.

feature predominantly for the victim. These can be wrongs in themselves, and they can also serve to aggravate the instrumental and objectifying use of the person. The point here is that a serious wrong nonetheless pertains even in the absence of these phenomena.

If the instrumental use of the body is essential to our understanding of sex, and of the wrongfulness of rape, then it ought to be able to explain other putative 'essential' or central features of 'real rape'. I suggest that it can. If the instrumental use of the body triggers the duty of consent-astuteness, then we should be—in all instances—concerned about compulsion and coercion, since manipulating another's reasons for action is the antithesis to being astute as to their reasons for action. Compulsion, by itself, without the consent-astuteness or consent in fact motivating our concern for it, has no moral traction. If a cultural scaffolding of misogyny and sexualisation pervades all instances of sex, which conditions men to expect woman to be objects for their use, then this is problematic because it artificially dilutes what they think the duty of consent-astuteness requires of them. If sex is used to express a social and cultural code of subordination and domination, as deliberating inverting the subject–subject relationship into a subject–object relationship, then it is because social and cultural codes calcify around the essential properties—instrumentalism and objectification—of sex. By relying on a distinction between wrongfulness and harmfulness, we can nonetheless say that all instances of *rape are capable of* these harms, without having to explain the wrongfulness in terms of these (contingent) harms. In doing so, we can preserve the claim that the wrongfulness of rape *can be explained* in terms of the instrumental use of the body.

Recall the approach taken here: to isolate the morally relevant, and essential, properties of sex. If I have succeeded in doing so, and if an essential property of sex is that it instrumentalises another person's body, then we would expect a range of our experiences of sex to derive from these essential features. The experiences may be positive and affirming, where one embodied person becomes the focus of sexual desire and attraction where they intend (want) the other person's intent (desire). The experiences may be negative and dehumanising, where a person is reduced to an object, at the expense of their personhood. The instrumental use of the body—the compounding impact of both instrumentalism and objectification—is capable of this erasure, and it is this erasure that can explain the moral content of a catalogue of harms.

Allow me then to directly address the methodological concern with the approach taken here. Conaghan opined that '[a]bstract reasoning around competing moral values too often leads to the excision of concepts from their context',[57] and, to be clear, the abstract reasoning in this essay has deliberately excised the concepts of instrumentalism and objectification from their context. We should, therefore, expect normatively inert concepts as a result of our abstract reasoning. Rather, what we have seen is how by isolating the morally relevant and essential properties, we have been able to explain how sex—all sex—is capable of engaging a range of normative concepts and endangering a range of important values. Our concern for compulsion, misogyny, and subordination all stem from an essential property of sex, namely, the instrumental use of the body.

We can now conclude by solving the puzzles we started with. Martha used her lover benignly because she performed her duty of consent-astuteness, a duty that we can take as being the primary way of avoiding the wrong of instrumentalising another person. Lucy committed a trivial wrong because she instrumentalised a trivial feature of Peter. In comparison to both 1(a) Martha's Pillow and 3(a) While You Were Sleeping, sex is instrumentalising the other in a far more morally hazardous way. In contrast to 3(a) what makes using a person for a sexual end particularly morally hazardous is that it instrumentalises the body: a compounding wrong of instrumentalism and objectification. In comparison to 1(a), sex is morally hazardous because it risks inverting the subject–subject relationship that sex is capable of sustaining.

Scenario 2(a) the 'pure case of rape' represented two parallel puzzles. I have suggested here that the wrongfulness of the rape can be explained in terms of the instrumental use of the body, and that this wrong can explain a catalogue of harms that can be inflicted. In parallel, I have also suggested here that 'abstract reasoning around moral values' can explain the moral content of a catalogue of contextual concerns, as they arise in 'real' cases. In defence of this analytical methodology, I have also grounded a general feature of sex: that all sex is the use of another person's body as a means to an end. As well as a general ameliorative principle, if A is to instrumentalise B, then A must have reasons to believe that B would agree to A's treatment of B. So far—we might want to say—Conaghan is right, this approach has yielded an 'impoverished account of the operational parameters' of the concepts of sex and consent. In particular, if A must act on 'reasons' (to ameliorate A's instrumentalism of B), then the 'reasons' that A must act on are abstracted from the context and conditions in which they apply. The essays that follow seek to render what those reasons are. In the next essay, I start with the question of whether those reasons extend beyond the fact of B's consent, to include B's reasons for consenting.

[57] Conaghan (n 1) 180.

2

A Prop in Someone Else's Fantasy

2.1

'Often', Jordan Pascoe observes, 'one does not know, when one consents to sex, that one has agreed to be a prop in someone else's pornographic fantasies'.[1] Given how routinely 'a pornographic artifact is used in place of a human sexual partner', it may be just as routine 'that a human sexual partner is used as if she were a pornographic artifact'.[2] Even if a person were to know they were being used as a pornographic prop, knowing may not make it any less concerning. That is, of course, assuming that 'being used as a prop' is something that should concern us. After all, for Nussbaum, objectification 'might be a wonderful part of sexual life'.[3] The foreground purpose of this essay is to find the resources to explain why being a prop should concern us (whilst holding onto the counterintuition that objectification 'might be a wonderful part of sexual life'). This requires us to return to two ideas from Essay 1—instrumentalism and objectification—to explore how to ameliorate the problems we associate with the latter.

As we know from the previous essay, as a general principle, we ought not to *use* a person (merely as a means to an end) ('the instrumentalism principle'). We can avoid 'using a person' when we ensure that they accept or agree to our treatment of them. Hence, the duty of consent-astuteness (discussed in the previous essay) ameliorates the instrumental use of a person. Whilst there is plenty of work still to do in elucidating what it means to discharge the duty of consent-astuteness, we might think that the requirement of consent exhausts our moral inquiry.

I suggest, instead, that there is a further principle—'the objectification principle'—which requires that we ought not to use a person as a thing

[1] Jordan Pascoe, 'Beyond Consent: On Setting and Sharing Sexual Ends' (2023) 8(2) Philosophies 21, 26.

[2] Rae Langton, *Sexual Solipsism: Philosophical Essays on Pornography and Objectification* (OUP 2009) 317.

[3] Martha C Nussbaum, 'Objectification' (1995) 24 Philos Public Aff 249, 274.

Sex and Self-Ownership. Jesse Wall, Oxford University Press. © Jesse Wall 2025.
DOI: 10.1093/9780191987809.003.0002

(objectification). The broad contention in this essay is that even when our interactions with another are consensual, we may still be using them 'as a thing'. To ameliorate the problem of objectifying another person, we need to discharge a further duty, the duty of motivational-astuteness: the requirement that we respond to, or share in, the reasons for the person's agreement to the treatment of them.

In the discussion that follows, I consider a weak and a strong formulation of the objectification principle. According to the weak formulation, 'we ought not to use a person in their capacity as a thing'. Whilst the 'objectification' here might map—more generally—onto sexual practice, it not obvious how the weak objectification has any moral content (to generate the 'ought not to'). We encounter the inverse problem with the strong objectification principle. This principle provides that 'we ought not to use a person as if they were a thing'. Here, it is easier to locate the moral content of the strong objectification principle (the 'ought not to'), but is more difficult to accept that sex—in general—offends against the principle. In this essay I will provide an account of

1. the moral content of the weak objectification principle,
2. the generality of the strong objectification principle,

and provide

3. the solutions to the problems that both principles identify.

In the background of this discussion is an account of how our views or attitudes towards consensual sex may be morally mismanaged views or attitudes. Whilst we may not deny the general (instrumentalism) principle—that the consent of the other person is necessary to our permissible use of them—our understanding of sex (sex-as-we-know-it) may enable a moral outlook that is inconsistent with duties of consent-astuteness. In the background of this essay is an account of how

4. sex (as-we-know-it) may be 'conceptually unrelated to any and all person-related characteristics' of the person with whom we are having sexual relations.[4]

[4] Melinda Vadas, 'The Manufacture-for-use of Pornography and Women's Inequality' (2005) 13 J Polit Philos 174, 190.

The point that will eventually emerge (in subsequent essays) is that while the criminal law accommodates this moral mismanagement as being exculpatory, it ought not to.

For now, the heavy lifting here is lifting more Kantian baggage. In addition to the Kantian instrumentalism principle, we encounter at 2.2 Kant's claim that 'as soon as a person becomes an Object of appetite for another' then 'all motives of moral relationship cease to function'[5] (the objectification principle). At 2.3, I examine how a person might 'become an object' by considering a weak and a strong interpretation of Kant's claim, and then consider what it might mean for 'all motives of moral relationship [to] cease to function'. I explain (at 2.4) how Kant's own solution to the objectification problem (the legal institution of marriage) can be reinterpreted to provide the solution to the moral hazards that the weak and strong objectification principles identify. I then conclude (at 2.5) by considering the relationship between the general instrumentalism principle and the objectification principles whilst also solving the puzzles that preoccupied this discussion.

2.2

We are familiar with a general prohibition, courtesy of Kant, not to use a person ('the instrumentalism principle'). This 'Formula of Humanity' requires us to

> act that you use humanity, whether in your own person or in the person of any other, always at the same time as an end, never merely as a means.[6]

To illustrate the general principle, Kant then explains how it generates a duty not to make false promises:

> [H]e who has it in mind to make a false promise to others sees at once that he wants to make use of another human being merely as a means, without the other at the same time containing in himself the end. For, he whom I want to use for my purposes by such a promise cannot possibly agree to my way of behaving toward him, and so himself contain the end of this action.[7]

[5] Immanuel Kant, *Lectures on Ethics* (Louis Infield tr, Harper and Row 1963) 163.

[6] Immanuel Kant, 'Groundwork of the Metaphysics of Morals' in Mary Gregor (ed), *Practical Philosophy* (Mary Gregor tr, CUP 1996) 80.

[7] Kant, 'Groundwork of the Metaphysics of Morals' (n 6) 80.

If the problem with false promises is that the other person 'cannot possibly agree to my way of behaving' then the solution is to require that the other person be able to agree or consent to 'my way of behaving'. More broadly then, to treat another person as an end, and not merely as a means, requires from us that we seek their consent for our use of them. When it comes to sex, if sex is the use of the person for our own ends, then the consent of the person is enough to satisfy the general principle. The moral inquiry might end there, and consensual sex might be otherwise insulated from any further moral concern or critique.

Kant, however, had more to say. When it came to sex, adherence to the general principle was not enough. Even when we are not using a person as a mere means, we are still using a person as an object. As he explains:

> Sexual love makes of the loved person an Object of appetite; as soon as that appetite has been stilled, the person is cast aside ...
>
> ... Taken by itself [sexual love] is a degradation of human nature; for as soon as a person becomes an Object of appetite for another, all motives of moral relationship cease to function, because as an Object of appetite for another a person becomes a thing and can be treated and used as such by every one.[8]

I will suggest here that we should follow Kant on this point and consider how our use of a person's body engages two different principles. We ought not to *use a person* (as mere means to our ends) and, in addition, we ought not to *use a person as a thing.*

To help isolate the two principles from one another, consider the following scenario:

> 1. *Friends*: A and B are friends who recently had a series of casual sexual encounters ('casual' in the sense that neither expected long-term romantic engagement). B was having sex for pleasure. A was having sex to become pregnant; she wants to have a child (but not a partner or a father for the child). Whilst both parties were aware that no contraceptive measures were used, B was unaware of A's productive aims. That is, until a mutual friend informs B of A's aims. B feels 'used' by A. The feeling, for A, is reciprocal.

[8] Kant, *Lectures on Ethics* (Infield tr) (n 5) 163.

I am interested in how we understand this claim that *A used B*, and the counter-claim that *B used A*. In particular, if these claims have any moral content, I am interested in whether we need recourse to more than 'the general principle' (instrumentalism) to understand their moral content.

There are three ways in which we might respond to this scenario. The first is to say that 1(a) *They knew what they were doing*. Whilst A was using B as a means to an end (pregnancy) and B was using A as a means to an end (sexual pleasure), neither of them was using the other merely as a means to their own ends. The sex between A and B was consensual; A and B allowed each other to pursue the other's own ends. It was their own choice to pursue sex with one another, and the general principle requires that we leave these choices up to each person. We are no longer treating a person as a mere means when we make use of the person whilst also allowing them to make their own choices and pursue their own ends.

This first response relies upon an account of consent where consent represents a set of attitudes (of willingness, acceptance, or agreement) towards a proposed act. Consent, on this standard account, is about the *what*, and not the *why*. Hence, on this standard account, B was not used by A. A was pursuing her own ends (reproduction), but she did so with B's consent, to the extent that B freely chose to engage in an act whilst being informed of all the physiological risks and consequences of the act. His ignorance of A's motivations did not undermine the quality of his consent.

We might feel that the first response misses something. We might want to say that 1(b) *A wrongfully used B* on the basis that using someone for reproductive ends requires more than their consent to the sexual intercourse. If consent represents an avenue for 'sharing in the ends' of the other person, then in this scenario, B was afforded no opportunity to 'share in' A's reproductive ends. He was given no way to 'possibly agree to her treatment of him as a mere dispensary of semen'. The suggestion here is that sex with a procreative aim forms a special case, where having an aim to have a child triggers a special obligation to disclose this aim or motivation. It would follow, on this second response, that B's consent was somehow vitiated. B was misled by A's failure to disclose information that was relevant to his decision. In this way, *B was used by A*.

It is difficult, however, to ground the special obligation. We can assume that B was not misled as to the use of contraceptive measures, nor had he any reasonable expectation of contraceptive measures; we can assume that B was aware of the risks of pregnancy that follow from unprotected penetrative vaginal sex; we can assume that B knew that he would have no decision-making authority over B's reproductive choices if she became pregnant. All of the information that goes to the possibility that A would become pregnant was already part of (or, at least, could have been part of) B's decision-making process. *At best*, B could complain that he had reasons to presume that the casual sex with A was mutually motivated by physical attraction and desire for sexual pleasure. And, unbeknown to him, A withheld her motivations.

But if B's best-case grievance relies upon pulling motivations into the conditions for permissible use of the person, then why stop there?

`On a third account, 1(c) *A used B and B used A* (both in problematic ways). This is on the basis that using a person's body for your own ends requires more than the other person's consent to the sexual intercourse. As I will explain here, A used B's body as an instrument for her own ends (procreation) and 'bracketed' B's own reproductive desires, wishes, and intentions. He was used *as a thing*, and the provision of his consent cannot ameliorate the harm. At the same time, B used A's body as an instrument for his own ends (sexual pleasure), bracketing A's own desires, wishes, and intentions; she was used *as a thing*, and the provision of her consent cannot ameliorate the harm.

In the discussion that follows, I wish to develop the moral resources to ground the following claims about A and B:

> The first response (1(a) *They knew what they were doing*) overlooks a morally relevant principle (the objectification principle).
>
> The second response (1(b) *A wrongfully used B*) attempts to engraft an arbitrary set of motivational concerns (which are concerns addressed by the objectification principle) on to the general principle.
>
> The third response (1(c) *A used B and B used A*) is sound but relies upon the objectification principle (as a standalone moral principle or one that is engrafted on to the instrumentalism principle).

To do so, we need to consider Kant's 'objectification principle' and then consider how his own solution (the 'unity of the will') addresses the problem of objectification. As we shall see, A and B objectified one another without a 'unity of wills'.

2.3

Back to Kant. Recall that, on his account of sex, adherence to the general principle was not enough for sex to be permissible. This is because:

> [i]f a man wishes to satisfy his desire, and a woman hers, they stimulate each other's desire; their inclinations meet, but their object is not human nature but sex, and each of them dishonors the human nature of the other.[9]

Even consensual sex 'dishonors the human nature of the other' by treating the other as an object of sexual desire. For Kant, being used as a sexual means is unlike the other uses that we can make of people, where in the latter instances: '[a] [m]an can certainly enjoy the other as an instrument for his service; he can utilize the other's hands or feet to serve him, though by the latter's free choice'.[10] Sex is different; it involves 'allowing someone else to make direct use of my body for their own ends' and not merely 'granting another a right against me for the use of my skills or my time'.[11] Elsewhere Kant describes sex as 'cannibalistic',[12] where

> in this sort of use by each of the sexual organs of the other, each is a consumable thing with respect to the others, so that if one was to make oneself such a thing by contract, the contract would be contrary to law.[13]

As Pascoe explains further, when it comes to sex 'my body is being used by another to fulfil their ends: by body is being used according to someone else's will'.[14] We can agree to forgoing our own use of our time, energy, or skills in favour of someone else, but we cannot agree to forgo the use of our own body in favour of someone else.

Hence, we can locate a principle that reaches beyond the general principle:

> Objectification principle: we ought not to use a person as a thing (for sexual desire).

We need to clarify what this principle might require. To start, we need to resolve the ambiguity that lies in the preposition 'as'. Specifically, the ambiguity in the comparison or contrast between 'person' and 'thing' that the 'as' is intended to create. There are two possible interpretations. On a weaker interpretation,

[9] Kant, *Lectures on Ethics* (Infield tr) (n 5) 163–64.

[10] Immanuel Kant, *Lectures on Ethics* (Peter Heath and JB Schneewind eds, Peter Heath tr, CUP 1997) 155.

[11] Pascoe, 'Beyond Consent' (n 1) 4.

[12] Immanuel Kant, 'Metaphysics of Morals' in Mary Gregor (ed), *Practical Philosophy* (Mary Gregor tr, CUP 1996) 495.

[13] Kant, 'Metaphysics of Morals' (n 12) 495.

[14] Pascoe, 'Beyond Consent' (n 1) 4.

using the body of a person as a thing brackets the incorporeal aspects of personhood (their will or subjectivity), leaving only their corporeal existence (their body or objectivity) to direct ourselves towards. On this (weaker) interpretation, 'as a thing' means 'using the person *in their capacity as* a thing'. In contrast, on a stronger interpretation, using a person 'as a thing' reduces the person to their corporeal aspects, as if they have no incorporeal aspects to their being. On the stronger interpretation, 'as a thing' is taken to mean 'the use of a person *as if they were* a thing'.

Let us try and understand the first, weak, interpretation of the objectification principle. There are a range of reasons why we might love another person and why we might be attracted to them. Most, by far, are incorporeal. We might love their intellect, their sense of humour, their earnestness, their optimism, their cynicism, their patience, their confidence, their convictions, and so on. A closeness, familiarity, and affinity with them can be built upon shared experiences, a shared outlook, and a shared set of values or commitments. These are, again, all incorporeal. We can use physical affection to express the love and admiration that we have for them. We can touch and embrace the other and express our love for them. The body is the medium of our social experience, and here, the body mediates loving expression between *subjects*: between two embodied persons each trying to reach beyond their own body and beyond the body of the other person.

For Kant, sex takes a different turn. Since '[he] thought that sex was about the heedless pursuit of pleasure',[15] acting on one's own sexual desire is a departure from the above forms of loving affection, towards the pursuit of sexual pleasure. The 'moral difficulty' that Kant encounters when it comes to sex lies in the fact that 'sexual interest in another is not interest in the other as a person'. For Kant:

> The desire which a man has for a woman is not directed toward her because she is a human being, but because she is a woman; that she is a human being is of no concern to the man; only her sex is the object of his desires. Human nature is thus subordinated.[16]

Sexual interest in a person, then, is a pivot away from the incorporeal person, towards the corporeal. After all, as Barbara Herman explains:

[15] Jordan Pascoe, 'I Hunger for You: Kant and Kinky Sex' in Sharon M Kaye (ed), *What Philosophy Can Tell You About Your Lover* (Open Court 2012) 33.

[16] Kant, *Lectures on Ethics* (Infield tr) (n 5) 163–64.

> [i]t is a little odd to imagine sexual arousal at a moral deed—perhaps a bit less odd to be turned on by a quality or virtue, though some more than others: courage more easily than kindness (a cynic might see the marks of virility or maternity as the object here).[17]

Erotic attraction—unlike love, admiration, or fondness—is directed towards the body of another person. It may not be just any person (it is the person we love and admire), but the erotic attitude is still directed towards the body of the person, and the desire is about the use of that body for our own pleasure. It is in this way that the other person becomes an object of sexual desire. This attention—this erotic attitude that is directed towards us—might be sought after. We might want to be an object of sexual desire for another person.

It is therefore difficult, at this point, to appreciate the 'moral difficulty' that Kant encounters. This is, in part, because on Kant's own account, when a person becomes an object of sexual desire, their 'human nature' is (only) '*subordinated*'. When desire is 'directed towards' the woman's body as an object, she is being used 'in her capacity' as an object of sexual desire. That is to bracket or suspend her 'human nature'. It is not—by itself—to deny or erase it. As we can appreciate, if 'bracketing' is not 'erasure', this first interpretation softens the objectification principle, and softening of the principle makes substantiating the moral content of the principle more challenging. Nonetheless, for Kant, the bracketing of a person's human nature or subjectivity is incompatible with the relationship we ought to have with another as a relationship between moral subjects.

Bracketing the incorporeal aspects of someone's personhood in favour of their corporeal ones (the weak objectification principle) may not, at this point, raise much moral concern (if at all). There is, however, a stronger interpretation available to us. On the stronger interpretation of Kant's objectification principle, using a person 'as a thing' can then be understood as being *reductive*, where one person 'regards the other as a mere body, for physical gratification';[18] a *terra nullius* that can be occupied by the will of another. It could also be understood as being *invasive*, where one person 'regards the other as a person, but one to be annexed, taken over',[19] where one will can be replaced in favour of another. These are bolder claims that make the moral content of the

17 Barbara Herman, 'Could It Be Worth Thinking About Kant on Sex and Marriage?' in Louise Antony and Charlotte Witt (eds), *A Mind of One's Own: Feminist Essays on Reason and Objectivity* (Westview Press 1993) 62.

18 Langton (n 2) 327.

19 Langton (n 2) 327.

principle easier to substantiate. But they also make the principle more difficult to apply in general. In other words, using a person 'as if they were a thing' is easier to accept as morally objectionable than using a person 'in their capacity as a thing', but, as Langton contends, '[n]either description is plausible, as a description of the essential and inevitable character of sexual relationships'.[20] Hence, it is more difficult to suggest that this is a characterisation of sex that holds in all cases.

We have so far struggled to locate the moral content of the weak objectification principle. We might think that it can be found in the moral sting of Kant objectification claim, that 'as soon as a person becomes an Object of appetite for another, *all motives of moral relationship cease to function*'.[21] It might be that the problem with sexual desire lies in the displacement of the reasons that ought to motivate our interactions with others. Hence, Kant could be taken to be suggesting that one motive (sexual desire) can *preclude or exclude* other motives and reasons for acting. However, he does not go that far. Rather, Kant's suggestion is that sex is objectifying because our love and affection for a person (our 'human love') stands apart from, and cannot 'enter into', our sexual desire for that person ('sexual love'). As he explains:

> [H]uman love is good will, affection, promotion of happiness of others and finding joy in their happiness. But it is clear that when a person loves another purely from sexual desire, none of these factors enter into love.[22]

It follows that Kant accepts that these reasons or motivations (human love and sexual love) can sit alongside one another:

> [S]exual love can of course be combined with human love and so carry with it the characteristics of the latter, but taken by itself and for itself, it is nothing more than appetite.[23]

Kant is making two claims. Sex, 'by itself', is the desire for the person as an object (where 'affection' cannot 'enter into' motivations for sexual love). It is possible, nonetheless, to love a person (have affection for them) and objectify them (have desire for them) concurrently. Note how this interpretation softens the objectification claim even further. It maintains the claim that sexual desire

[20] Langton (n 2) 327.
[21] Kant, *Lectures on Ethics* (Infield tr) (n 5) 163.
[22] Kant, *Lectures on Ethics* (Infield tr) (n 5) 163.
[23] Kant, *Lectures on Ethics* (Infield tr) (n 5) 163.

can only be about the person as an object, without implying that sexual desire precludes the other reasons that we might have to be physically intimate with a person.

This concurrency, however, is no escape route out of the problem. As Barbara Herman notes, the language of 'carry with it' 'is not the language of transformation'.[24] If the 'human love' (affection) that we have for another runs parallel with our 'sexual love' (desire) for a person as an object, then affection and desire coexist without resolving or ameliorating the concerns that we have with objectifying a person. The moral content of the weak objectification principle remains elusive.

There are, however, motivations or reasons for acting that do *preclude* or *exclude* the motives of moral relationship. For instance, the objectification principle can be reanimated if we replace 'desire' with a different motive or reason for acting: dominance. As Andrea Dworkin explains in her seminal work:

> There is a deep recognition in culture and experience that intercourse is both the normal use of a woman, her human potentiality affirmed by it, and a violative abuse, her privacy irredeemably compromised, her selfhood changed in a way that is irrecoverable, unrecoverable . . .
>
> It is especially in the acceptance of object status that her humanity is hurt. . . . In becoming an object so he can objectify her so that he can fuck her, she begins a political collaboration with his dominance; and then when he enters her, he confirms for himself and for her what she is: she is something, not someone; certainly not someone equal.[25]

Herein lies an important contrast: unlike 'desire', the ends of 'dominating' the person—of affirming their inferiority—*do* displace or exclude other motives or reasons. If we assume that the 'motives of moral relationship' include a motive of equal moral standing between persons, then using a person as a thing to be dominated is incompatible with the relationship of equal moral standing. In this way, 'motives of moral relationship cease to function', and the strong objectification principle retains robust moral content.

There is a further implication. In the use of the person as a thing to be dominated, we no longer have available to us the soft interpretation of the preposition 'as' to mean 'in their capacity as'. To use a person as a thing to be dominated is to be reductionist or invasive. It cannot merely mean focusing their corporeal

[24] Herman (n 17) 64.
[25] Andrea Dworkin, *Intercourse* (Free Press 1987) 140–41.

existence whilst bracketing their incorporeal existence; rather, to 'affirm their inferiority' means to deny the equality of their will or subjectivity.

Now, this is bleak. We might not accept—or we might not want to accept—that all sex is domination (and political collaboration in domination). Whilst we might have been willing to grant Kant the premise that all sex is about the pursuit of sexual desire, we might be less willing to accept the alternative claim that all heterosexual sex is about male dominance. However, these are different types of claims. The first claim (that all sex is about desire) is an analytical claim about sex *per se*. It is a claim about the morality of the necessary elements of sex, independent of any contingent features. The second claim (all heterosexual sex is about male dominance) is a critical claim about sex in context. It is a claim about the morality of sex, taking into account—contingent—social features and lived experiences.

With regards to the second (critical) claim, to say that the features are 'contingent' is not to deny that they are general or universal. For instance, when Catharine MacKinnon characterises heterosexual sex as 'male dominance', the dominance is

> not an artificial overlay upon an underlying inalterable substratum of uncorrupted essential sexual being. . . . It has no basis in anything other than the social reality its hegemony constructs. The process that gives sexuality its male supremacist meaning is therefore the process through which gender inequality becomes socially real.[26]

In this way, 'male supremacy is largely universal, if always in specific [cultural] forms'.[27] Sex being about dominance might be a contingent and yet universal feature of sex-as-we-know-it. In comparison, Dworkin herself entertains the possibility that some of the 'fundamental questions about intercourse' might be 'intrinsic' in the sense that '[h]is dominance over her is expressed in the physical reality of intercourse'.[28] Hence, sex *per se* might be about dominance, and even if sex is not irreducibly and fundamentally about the use of a person as a thing to be dominated, 'sexual practice expresses objectifying social structures' so that it is inescapable that sex is about the use of a person as a thing (to be dominated).[29]

[26] Catharine A MacKinnon, *Toward a Feminist Theory of the State* (Harvard UP 1989) 173.
[27] MacKinnon (n 26) 151.
[28] Dworkin (n 25) 136.
[29] Herman (n 17) 63.

Pornography is an obvious example of something that preconditions sexual practices to express objectifying social structures. As Vadas explains, 'where pornography is manufactured-for-use, men's sexual relations with women are conceptually unrelated to their female partner's personhood'.[30] It then follows 'that men's sexual relations with women will, under these conditions, be conceptually unrelated to any and all person-related characteristics or abilities their female partners might have'.[31] Moreover, if we accept that sex-as-we-know-it is sex with people without the person-related characteristics of people, then we are under a duty to escape this web of social structures. Laughton echoes Kant in explaining how this 'sexual solipsism' is

> the life of one who 'must shut himself up in himself', who must remain 'completely alone with his thoughts as in a prison'—a prison from which [Kant] says it is our duty, epistemic and moral, to escape.[32]

Whether there is an escape route (out of the sexual solipsism) is a question that we confront below (at 2.4). For now, we can note the two different iterations of the objectification principle. First, for Kant:

> sex [*per se*] is the use of the body of a person [in their capacity] as a thing [to be desired].

As we have discussed, what still remains unaccounted for is why this principle has any moral content (ie why this weak form of objectification should concern us). We will not get a sense of the problem that the weak objectification principal highlights until we get a sense of the solution (in the next section).

In comparison, a strong interpretation represents the moral rebuke that

> sex (as a social practice) is the use of the body of a person as (if they were) a thing (to be dominated).

It is a bold claim, but it is one that relies upon the entrapment of the moral agent in a social web of 'objectifying social structures'. Unfortunately, it is an entirely plausible web of social structures that we might find ourselves in. There *might* be a solution. In the next section, we will turn to consider Kant's own antidote

[30] Vadas (n 4) 190.
[31] Vadas (n 4) 190.
[32] Langton (n 2) 345.

to the problem of objectification. This will also afford us the opportunity to consider the moral content of the weak objectification principle and to assess the inescapability of the strong form of objectification.

2.4

Kant's own solution to the problem of objectification was the legal institution of marriage, where marriage represents

> an agreement between two persons by which they grant each other equal reciprocal rights, each of them undertaking to surrender the whole of their person to the other with a complete right of disposal over it.[33]

Whilst the idea, by itself, 'seems significantly flawed',[34] feminist interpreters of Kant have nonetheless tried to rescue the idea from being 'an embarrassment to moral philosophers and philosophers of law alike'.[35] The reconstruction starts with drawing out the elements of equality and reciprocity in Kant's account of marriage. This then helps us unpack what it might mean to have a 'unity of will', where the 'unity of will' represents the conditions under which sex can be both objectifying and respectful.

To explain Kant's notion of 'equal reciprocal rights' that marriage represents, Herman provides a helpful analogy:

> Suppose I give you every pencil I own or will come to own knowing that (or on condition that) you will give me every pencil that you own or will come to own. One could say that we thereby create a community of pencil ownership—a unity of will about pencils.[36]

When it comes to sex and objectification, I am permitted to *use the body of another other*, and the other person is permitted to use my body, by way of ownership, with there being no loss of ownership or control over ourselves, since, through a reciprocated surrender, we can retrieve ourselves. As Kant explains:

[33] Kant, *Lectures on Ethics* (Infield tr) (n 5) 167.

[34] Donald Wilson, 'Kant and the Marriage Right' (2004) 85 Pac Philos Q 103, 112.

[35] Susan Mendus, 'Kant: "An Honest but Narrow-Minded Bourgeois"?' in Howard Lloyd Williams (ed), *Essays on Kant's Practical Philosophy* (University of Wales Press 1992) 175.

[36] Herman (n 17) 66.

> [I]f I yield myself completely to another and obtain the person of the other in return, I win myself back; I have given myself up as the property of another, but in turn I take that other as my property, and so win myself back again in winning the person whose property I have become. In this way the two persons become a unity of will.[37]

The language of property and ownership might be a distraction. This is in part because it requires us to think about ourselves being the owned *thing* and the *owner* at the same time (even Kant thought it 'impossible to be a person and a thing, the proprietor and the property').[38] It is then easier to think of 'two persons becoming a unity of will' in terms of decision-making authority rather than ownership. Hence, on this interpretation of the 'unity of will':

> spouses engage in shared deliberation and decision-making. Each spouse is able to make decisions for the other spouse and to direct his or her conduct. Since each spouse has the right to direct the conduct of each, they must now make their decisions together.[39]

The 'unity of will' can therefore represent a shared decision-making authority over the sexual interaction that involves the two bodies. Like Kant's account of marriage, and Herman's sharing of pencils, the unity of will is predicated on the values of equality and reciprocity, where each person has equal authority in the decision-making process, and each person reciprocates the surrendering of sole authority. Critically, it requires not merely a sharing of rights to use in the body but also *the sharing of the ends* that the use of a body enables for that person. It is a unity of the *what* and the *why*. Needless to say that this relationship of a unified will occurs beyond the social and legal institution of marriage, and beyond Kant's narrow confinement to the heterosexual.[40] Even on Kant's own account, the unity of will 'is still more perfectly present' in friendship where there is 'more equality, than in marriage'.[41]

The requirements of the unified will reach beyond the requirements of consent. As Pascoe explains, the unified will 'is importantly different from how we align our ends through contract'; whilst 'I may agree to the activity, or even to

[37] Kant, *Lectures on Ethics* (Infield tr) (n 5) 167.
[38] Kant, *Lectures on Ethics* (Infield tr) (n 5) 165.
[39] Lina Papadaki, 'Kantian Marriage and Beyond: Why It Is Worth Thinking about Kant on Marriage' (2010) 25 Hypatia 276, 284.
[40] Papadaki, 'Kantian Marriage and Beyond' (n 39) 288.
[41] Kant, *Lectures on Ethics* (Heath tr) (n 10) 413.

your ends' this 'is not the same thing as taking your ends as my own'.[42] Herein lies an important contrast: consent or agreement represents a willing acceptance of another's rights of use (for their own ends); a united will represents a sharing of ends. Hence, the 'sharing' here consists of sharing in the ends (the *why*) and not just sharing in the means (the *what*). In this way, the 'unity of will' relies upon an 'epistemological duty',[43] since it requires a 'respect for the ends that another has set for themselves—which means, of course, knowing the ends another has set for themselves'.[44]

It is this 'sharing of ends' (that marriage or mutual ownership represents) that provides a solution to the objectification problem. I am not being treated as a thing for someone else's ends when I share in those ends with the other person. I do not merely agree to the use of me; I am part of a decision-making process where I control *the reasons* for the use of me. As Papadaki explains in terms of Kant's marriage solution:

> [N]either the husband nor the wife is in danger of being turned into an object as a result of their mutual ownership of each other. They, rather, become this larger agent: the couple. And as parts of this agent, they are both autonomous and in control of their shared lives.[45]

The key point is that to address the objectification problem, something beyond another person's consent (or agreement) is required.

Now, to illustrate the value of the 'something *beyond* consent', consider the moral hazards of sex where consent is present but the unity of will is absent. The problem that Robin West has highlighted is that sole reliance on the 'ethic of consent' means that 'sex is now widely insulated from criticism, so long as it is consensual, regardless of the *motive* that triggered the consent'.[46] The focus on consent in demarcating what is morally permissible or otherwise morally hazardous overlooks the choices that motivate consent:

> So, not only sex for pleasure but also . . . sex for survival, sex for exercise, sex for money, sex for diversion, sex for release from stress, sex as entertainment,

[42] Pascoe, 'Beyond Consent' (n 1) 7.
[43] Pascoe, 'Beyond Consent' (n 1) 7, citing Lois Pineau, 'Date Rape: A Feminist Analysis' (1989) 8 L & Phil 217.
[44] Pascoe, 'Beyond Consent' (n 1) 7, citing Christine M Korsgaard, *Creating the Kingdom of Ends* (CUP 1996) 192–93.
[45] Papadaki, 'Kantian Marriage and Beyond' (n 39) 284.
[46] Robin West, 'Consent, Legitimation, and Dysphoria' (2020) 83 MLR 1, 19.

> sex as an expression of friendship, or sex as expressive of any other impulse is all equally insulated from critique so long as it is consensual.[47]

It is sex for reasons other than sexual pleasure that creates the problem of (what she terms) 'hedonic dysphoria'.[48] This is a harm inflicted where

> many women and girls and some boys and men likewise ... often or routinely consent to sex when they neither desire, want, welcome, or ultimately find it to be physically pleasurable.[49]

According to West, this amounts to an 'alienation from the hedonic self'.[50] Simone de Beauvoir identified the same problem, where a woman

> wants to remain subject whilst she is made object . . . she retains her subjectivity only through union with her partner; giving and receiving must be combined for both. If the man confines himself to taking without giving or if she bestows pleasure without receiving, the woman feels that she is being maneuvered, used; once she realizes herself as the Other, she becomes the inessential other.[51]

Here we encounter the harms of consensual sex without a 'unified will'. It is an 'alienating' phenomenon of 'being maneuvered, used' (being a prop in someone else fantasy). It is the use of the body of a person for the sexual ends whilst bracketing the sexual ends that they have made for themselves. Note that the problem still occurs even when sexual desire can coincide with, and sit alongside, other motivations (such as affection). Where the motivations for the use of the body are not shared—and where the epistemic duty has not been performed to 'know the ends another has set for themselves'—a person is being used unilaterally for another's end, and the person's will (their subjectivity, their hedonic self) is bracketed. In this way, under the weak objectification principle, the person becomes an object; she becomes 'the inessential other'. The solution, or antidote, is the 'unified will': If sex (*per se*) is the use of the body of a person as a thing to be desired, then sharing in, and reciprocating,

[47] West (n 46) 19.
[48] West (n 46) 5.
[49] West (n 46) 5.
[50] West (n 46) 5.
[51] Simone de Beauvoir, *The Ethics of Ambiguity* (first published 1948, Bernard Frechtman tr, Citadel Press 1976) 397.

the motivation (desire) is a sharing of the ends that each person is using the other's body for.

Whereas the unified will can address the weak objectification principle, it might not provide a solution to the strong iteration of the principle. Recall that the strong principle differed in two main ways: it concerned sex *as a social practice*, and it concerned the use of the body of a person as a thing *to be dominated*. This changes how the solution might work. On the one hand, if sex is objectifying *as a social practice*, then the 'unity of the will' might enable two people to separate or distance themselves from the social practice. On the other hand, if it is not possible for people to partition their sexual practices from sex as it is socially constituted, then 'the unity of the will' cannot address the objectification problem, as the domination of one person by another person's will is the antithesis of equality and reciprocity (a shared will).

Let us start with the antithesis between domination and the unified will. As we have seen, the 'unified will' can address Kant's version of objectification, even Kant's 'cannibalistic' account of sex (where we make use of each other bodies as a 'consumable thing'). Provided that the other person shares in these motives, desires, and reasons for acting (and not merely agree to the action itself), the hazards of objectification can be addressed (or at least 'quarantined').[52] As Pascoe explains, 'cannibalistic sex' can be 'humanized':

> my vampiric desire to consume my partner becomes a moral desire to love, respect, and enjoy my partner. The idea is that sexual desires themselves are transformed so that my tendency to objectify my partner is checked by the deep respect that our loving, committed relationship has instilled in me.[53]

Domination, however, differs from even the most heedless pursuit of sexual desire. Domination is a denial of a person's will (their choices, desires, or experiences) in favour of another person's will; it is to dominate or control another as an inferior. As we have seen, it is a reduction of a person so that their will is absent, or an invasion of a person so that their will is displaced. One person 'dominating' another precludes the possibility of sharing in each other's ends (or motives) because it negates the equality and reciprocity that the 'unified will' is predicated upon.

However, if 'using a person as a thing to be dominated' is a social construction, it is tempting to suggest that the social meaning that sex conveys—the

[52] Pascoe, 'I Hunger for You' (n 15) 33–34.
[53] Pascoe, 'I Hunger for You' (n 15) 29–30.

confirmation of inferiority—can be opted out of. It might seem plausible that two people can, between themselves, build a 'society of two'[54] where they remain outside the cultural and political milieu, 'secluded in its intimacy, its dual solitude'.[55] For example, it is plausible that two people may display a painting of the Virgin Mary at their home for solely aesthetic reasons, independent of the religious, social, or cultural meaning assigned to the image. It might be less plausible that two people can display the Confederate flag in their home in a way that is somehow insulated from its historical association with racism and slavery. Similar to the painting and the flag, it is not clear whether two people can engage in a sex act that they know to be associated with dominance or misogyny without also expressing or affirming the inequality that the act is taken to represent.

It is a question of whether we have the 'generative freedom' to transcend the social constructs that ingrain patriarchal meaning (the 'given') in heterosexual sex,[56] where we can 'surpass the given toward an open future'.[57] This requires, according to Simone de Beauvoir, each person to 'freely [recognize] the other, each regarding himself and the other simultaneously, as object and as subject in a reciprocal manner'.[58] In other words, the 'generative freedom' is predicated upon, as a starting point, a Kantian unity of will. Yet, as we have seen, Catharine MacKinnon denies that there exists an 'uncorrupted essential sexual being' that can be found beneath the layers of social meaning. And even if we sought to build a 'society of two', without there being an 'uncorrupted essential sexual being' found beneath the covers, we may then struggle to 'go beyond recapitulating identifications in experience that are already socially constructed under patriarchal terms'.[59]

Varden's reconstruction of Kant on sexual desire provides one way through this tension.[60] To start with, Varden acknowledges that our sexual desires, identities, and orientations are neither reflectively and freely chosen nor are they scientifically predetermined.[61] Sexual desires are 'given', in the sense that

[54] Diane Perpich, 'From the Caress to the Word: Transcendence and the Feminine in the Philosophy of Emmanuel Levinas' in Tina Chanter (ed), *Feminist Interpretations of Emmanuel Levinas* (Pennsylvania State UP 2001) 44.

[55] Claire Katz, 'Levinas Between Agape and Eros' (2007) 11 Symposium 333, 337.

[56] Valerie Giovanini, 'Alterity in Simone de Beauvoir and Emmanuel Levinas: From Ambiguity to Ambivalence' (2019) 34 Hypatia 39, 43.

[57] De Beauvoir, *The Ethics of Ambiguity* (n 51) 91.

[58] Simone de Beauvoir, *The Second Sex* (first published 1949, HM Parshley tr, Vintage Books 1989) 140.

[59] Giovanini (n 56) 49.

[60] Helga Varden, 'Kant on Sex. Reconsidered—A Kantian Account of Sexuality: Sexual Love, Sexual Identity, and Sexual Orientation' (2018) 4(1) Fem Philos Q 1, 16.

[61] Helga Varden, *Sex, Love, and Gender: A Kantian Theory* (OUP 2020) 125; Varden, 'Kant on Sex. Reconsidered' (n 60) 13.

they are experienced first-hand as socially and culturally mediated forms of interaction. Yet, we nonetheless retain

> reflective self-consciousness and abstract conceptual reasoning powers [that] enable us to have a certain distance from our sexual desires such that we can develop, transform, and enhance them, including through a playful, aesthetic game of concealing and revealing our bodies to each other.[62]

As Varden explains, Kant's account starts with the fig leaf (in the story of Adam and Eve), where the concealment demonstrated an attempt to 'make an inclination more inward and enduring by its withdrawing its object from the senses' and 'an inclination by good conduct to influence others to show respect for us'.[63] According to Kant, this illustrates 'the consciousness of some dominion of reason over impulse'.[64] Some capacity, that is, to adopt an attitude towards, to reason about, and to share our sexual desires and impulses.

More broadly—beyond clothing ourselves—we retain the reflective ability to consider which desires and impulses we identify with, as part of our general capacity to 'develop, transform, and integrate all of aspects of our being', including the sexual desires and motivations that we act on, into 'the particular beings that we are'.[65] This reflective and integrative capacity includes the sexual ends that we set for ourselves, and which sexual desires we identify with, that form part of our 'practical identity' (the corollary being that having these sexual ends—desires, identities, and orientations—that we set for ourselves being bracketed or ignored is again the reduction of the person to the 'inessential other'). The existence of our reflective capacity does not dissolve the critical claim that all heterosexual sex is about male dominance. The point here is that whilst the 'uncorrupted sexual being' may not be possible, we nonetheless have some reflective capacity to position ourselves closer to sex *as it should be*, and further away from sex *as it is*. And the exercise of this reflective capacity requires the sharing of sexual ends.

The potential path out of the problem here is the generative freedom to recognise a sexual partner 'as object and as subject in a reciprocal manner' in a way that moves beyond the social embeddedness that ingrains patriarchal

[62] Varden, *Sex, Love, and Gender* (n 60) 119.
[63] Immanuel Kant, 'Conjectural Beginning of Human History' in RB Louden (ed), *Anthropology, History, and Education* (RB Louden tr, CUP 2007) 112-13; Varden, 'Kant on Sex. Reconsidered' (n 60) 13.
[64] Kant, 'Conjectural Beginning of Human History' (n 63) 112-13.
[65] Varden, *Sex, Love, and Gender* (n 61) 44.

meaning in heterosexual sex. This path, however, may be a *cul de sac*. If we are interested in how sex conveys a social meaning (sex-as-we-know-it), then any alternative meaning that we might try and attribute to it may be just as susceptible to other—potentially, equally patriarchal—social forces. Moreover, at this point, it is a methodological *cul de sac*: when we catalogue the ways that sex is socially understood to be objectifying, we do so by assuming that there is some neutral standpoint from which we can identify and assess the social understanding. But if the social embeddedness is all-pervasive, then there is no neutral standpoint. We might be asking questions that cannot be answered by presupposing a standpoint that does not exist.

2.5

But we nonetheless have enough moral tools to solve the puzzles that we started with. Starting with A and B, recall that there were three responses to the allegation that one *used* the other:

1(a). *They knew what they were doing.*
1(b). *A wrongfully used B.*
1(c). *A used B and B used A.*

The first (1(a)) was to suggest that consent was enough and that neither A nor B had reason to feel used by the other. The purpose of this discussion has been to show that consent is not enough and that the general (instrumentalism) principle does not exhaust the moral inquiry. The problem that the first response overlooks is the problem of 'the inessential other' that occurs when a person is used as a thing, meaning that the treatment of a person is directed towards a person's corporeal being and the bracketing of their incorporeal being denies the relevance of the sexual ends that they set (and can reset) for themselves.

The second response (1(b)) was to suggest that A's procreative aim generated a special duty (to disclose reproductive ends) that could be engrafted on to the general principle. Whilst it is true that B did not share in A's ends for her use of his body, both failed to disclose their own ends, discover the others, and ensure that they shared in each other's ends. Hence, the second response struggles to explain why one motivation ought to be discoverable, whilst the other need not be.

Nonetheless, we can appreciate that it is both tempting and possible to collapse the (weak) objectification principle into the general principle. If the general (instrumentalism) principle asks whether another person 'can possibly agree to my way of behaving towards them', then—*in some contexts*—'my way of behaving towards them' can encompass my motivations for my behaviour. What we owe one another, by way of consent and ends-sharing, may be context-specific. For instance, if lost teenagers discreetly follow an experienced hiker out of the woods, they are using the hiker as a means to an end without affording her the possibility of agreeing to their way of behaving towards her. They do so without offending our moral sensibilities. This is because the hiker in this scenario 'has no "right"' to choose whether she is discreetly followed out of the woods (and otherwise not disturbed).[66] In other contexts, our manner of behaving towards another person will require agreement to the act. If I am buying something that belongs to you, it matters that we agree to the exchange (of 'rights'), but we can nonetheless be indifferent as to each other's motivations. In some other contexts, such as our embodied interactions, for someone to agree to 'our manner of behaving towards them' might require consensus as to the act and its underlying motivation.

The point is that the general principle can be calibrated to address the concerns that we housed under the objectification principle, if we want to work within a broad but singular moral principle. In this way, 'consent' can have a narrow or broad meaning; it is a concept

> which we can fill with either narrow liberal values, based on the idea of the subject as an individual atomistic rational choice maker, or with feminist values encompassing attention to mutuality, embodiment, relational choice, and communication.[67]

The danger, however, of collapsing the objectification principle into the general instrumentalism principle is that it risks overlooking the magnitude of the *wrong* of doing an act without consent (in the narrow sense) when compared to the *endangerment* of harm when consensual sex (in the narrow sense) remains objectifying and alienating.

The third response (1(c)), which I take to be sound, makes use of the weak objectification principle (as a standalone principle, or as a concern properly engrafted on to a broad general principle, as above). A used B *in his capacity as a thing* for the purpose of her ends of becoming pregnant. A did not enable B

[66] Lina Papadaki, 'Treating Others Merely as Means: A Reply to Kerstein' (2016) 28 Utilitas 73, 80.

[67] Sharon Cowan, 'Freedom and Capacity to Make a Choice: A Feminist Analysis of Consent in the Criminal Law of Rape' in Vanessa Munro and Carl Franklin Stychin (eds), *Sexuality and the Law: Feminist Engagements* (Taylor & Francis 2007) 53.

to share in her motivational ends (or, in terms of a broad general principle, did not provide the possibility for B to 'agree to her way of behaving towards him'). And *vice versa*: B used A *in her capacity as a thing* for the purpose of his ends of sexual pleasure, and B did not enable A to share in his motivational ends (or did not provide the possibility for A to 'agree to his way of behaving towards her'). They both used (objectified) each other.

So, does consenting to being a prop in someone else's pornographic fantasies offend against a moral principle? It follows from the discussion here that *wanting* to be a prop (*willing* another person's use of us as a thing) does address or ameliorate objectification concerns. Short of being a prop, wanting to be an object of sexual desire for another person, and that person treating you as an object of sexual desire 'might be'—as Nussbaum suggests—'a wonderful part of sexual life'.[68] We encounter, again, the value of reciprocated intentions, where we intend for another person to intend the same thing.[69]

That said, we might be concerned that even when both people want one person to be used as an object of sexual desire, they are being complicit in expressing the inferiority of that person (and the category of persons the object is taken to represent). If sex-as-we-know-it has become sex with persons without 'person-related characteristics', then merely 'sharing ends' may not be an escape route out of the objectification problem. It may be that, short of conjuring enough 'generative freedom' to escape, our social understanding of sex may have become so solipsistic and morally mismanaged that our sexual partners have become an 'inessential other'. At the very least, we can appreciate that there are instances where one person's attitude towards another, as an object, is a morally mismanaged one, and the question that we will eventually encounter is whether the moral mismanagement is exculpatory or inculpatory.

As a result of these two essays, we now arrive at two moral principles that govern sexual conduct. To avoid instrumentalising a person, we are under a duty of consent-astuteness (to have reasons to believe that the person would agree to the treatment of them), and to avoid objectifying a person, we are under a duty of motivational-astuteness (to know, appreciate, and share in the reasons for the person's agreement to the treatment of them). Whilst we might accept that the criminal law has a role in enforcing the duty of consent-astuteness, we might doubt that the law should concern itself with the duty of motivational-astuteness. In the next essay, I displace some of that doubt.

[68] Nussbaum (n 3) 274.

[69] Roger Scruton, *Sexual Desire: A Moral Philosophy of the Erotic* (Free Press 1986) 18.

3
Choice Under Pressure

3.1

'On pain of declaring all bad choices nonautonomous', warns Heidi Hurd, 'one must be cautious about declaring plaintiffs insufficiently autonomous when they are prepared to sacrifice important interests to avoid trivial losses'.[1] Hurd has in mind '[a] woman who acquiesces to sex because she fears that she will not be asked out on another date, or because she seeks to avoid embarrassment'.[2] In this way, a person may be autonomous in making a good, or poor, choice between imperfect or unappealing options. Their exercise of a choice, however, does not shield the person who manipulated the options that the autonomous person had to navigate from criticism. This essay will explore how coercion or pressure can be blameworthy and, in some instances, wrongful, without a choice being coerced.

Our blame or criticism aside, it is otherwise only when the alternatives are so unappealing as to be practically unavailable—where a person no longer has a practical choice to refuse sex—that we deem the choice to be no longer an autonomous one. There is, therefore, a narrow legal category of *forced sex*, where threats of physical force or violence, for instance, present no reasonable choice to the victim. Forced sex vitiates the consent provided by the victim and clearly renders criminal wrongdoing. As Stuart Green explains, the Model Penal Code 'makes it a crime to cause another person to engage in an act of sexual penetration "by using or threatening . . . to use physical force . . . or inflict serious bodily injury on that person or anyone else"'.[3] Equally, 'consent to intercourse is presumed not to exist' under the Sexual Offences Act 2003 (UK) if the defendant 'us[ed] violence against the complainant or [caused] the complainant to fear that immediate violence would be used'.[4]

[1] Heidi M Hurd, 'The Moral Magic of Consent' (1996) 2 Legal Theory 121, 143.
[2] Hurd (n 1) 143.
[3] Stuart P Green, *Criminalizing Sex: A Unified Liberal Theory* (OUP 2020) 118, citing American Law Institute, 'Model Penal Code: Sexual Assault and Related Offenses, Council Draft No. 7' (20 December 2017) s 213.1(1).
[4] Green (n 3) 118; citing Sexual Offences Act 2003 (UK), s 75(2)(a).

Sex and Self-Ownership. Jesse Wall, Oxford University Press. © Jesse Wall 2025.
DOI: 10.1093/9780191987809.003.0003

This essay, however, is not concerned with *forced sex*. Instead, it is focused on the broader category of *pressured sex*, where the putative victim is presented with unappealing options that fall short of threats of violence. Whilst '[o]btaining sex by threats of violence has always been a crime; obtaining sex by threats of nonviolence traditionally was not'.[5] At best, 'sex obtained by means of a nonviolent threat is best understood as an "emerging" offence',[6] with proposed crimes of compelling a person to have sex where the non-violent threat 'would prevent resistance by a [person] of ordinary resolution'.[7] Under these emerging offences, the non-violent threat, like the violent threat, has the practical effect of removing the choice that consent is meant to represent.

Outside of these proposed reforms, the orthodoxy is that pressured sex does not vitiate consent, is nonetheless morally blameworthy, but otherwise does not concern the criminal law. The foreground purpose of this essay is to affirm the first two implications of pressured sex and to resist in some instances the third implication. Hence, when it comes to the category of pressured sex, I will defend five broad propositions:

1. pressured sex does not remove choice;
2. pressured sex therefore does not vitiate consent;
3. pressured sex is nonetheless blameworthy;
4. some instances of pressured sex transgress normative phenomena; and
5. pressured sex that transgresses normative phenomena ought to concern the criminal law.

These propositions turn on three distinctions that I will carve out, and rely upon, in this essay. The first is the distinction between 'a coerced choice' (that vitiates consent) and 'coercive conduct' (that does not, by itself, vitiate consent). This distinction can be located in the concept of coercion itself. On the one hand, a finding of coercion can defeat 'the typical normative results of [the] choice' that was coerced (a coerced choice).[8] On the other hand, a finding of coercion can 'determine whether A's conduct is at least prima facie wrongful or . . . blameworthy' (coercive conduct).[9]

[5] Green (n 3) 199.
[6] Green (n 3) 199.
[7] American Law Institute, 'Model Penal Code: Sexual Assault and Related Offenses, Council Draft No. 6' (15 September 2017) s 213.3(1)(a)(i) and (ii).
[8] Kimberly K Ferzan, 'Consent and Coercion' (2018) 50 Ariz St LJ 951, 968.
[9] Mitchell N Berman, 'The Normative Functions of Coercion Claims' (2002) 8 Leg Theory 45, 49.

The second distinction is between 'blameworthiness' (as a vague form of responsibility) and 'accountability' (as a form of relational responsibility). Here, 'blame' is a 'reactive attitude' that we can appropriately adopt towards a person who acted contrary to moral reasons,[10] implying that the person ought to respond, in some way, to the moral reasons they did not adhere to. We can say that a person is blameworthy if they ought to be the target of this reactive attitude. 'Accountability', in comparison, is a more demanding 'relational' or 'interpersonal' response. 'Accountability' specifies how a person ought to be responsible: a person ought to account for the moral reasons they did not adhere to, to a person who has the right or duty to hold them to account.[11]

The third distinction is between moral reasons and normative phenomena. Simply put, (undefeated) moral reasons determine what ought to be done (by a given agent, in each situation). Normative phenomena are a set of deontic moral ideas—obligations, demands, permissions, rights, wrongs, and so on—that structure a normative relationship (between right-holder and duty-bearer, permission-granter and permission-holder, wrongdoer and wronged party, and so on). In relying on these distinctions, the central contention that will be developed here is that whilst all coercive conduct is blameworthy insofar as it is contrary to moral reasons, coercive conduct triggers accountability when it transgresses normative phenomena.

In the foreground of this essay, the concept of coercion is being broken apart and put back together, in order to understand the relationship between coercion and criminalisation. In the background of this essay, the concept of consent is also under similar critical pressure, and will be fractured (in this essay) and put back together (in the next essay). As we will eventually see, the lines of fracture are the same: consent represents a choice (that coercion can remove), consent generates a permission (that coercion can vitiate), and consent is an expression of interests (that coercion estops reliance upon).

This essay will start (at 3.2) by substantiating the distinction between 'coerced choice' and 'coercive conduct', and then will introduce the problems of thresholds and implications that we encounter in both concepts. I then suggest (at 3.3) that the implications of 'coercive conduct' are that the coercive person cannot rely on the consent of another person as an expression of their interests. It then becomes a question of whether 'coercive conduct' is criminalisable conduct. I consider (at 3.4) that if we are concerned with harms and moral reasons,

[10] Peter Strawson, 'Freedom and Resentment' in Gary Watson (ed), *Free Will* (2nd edn, OUP 2003) 61.

[11] RA Duff, *Answering for Crime: Responsibility and Liability in the Criminal Law* (Hart Publishing 2007) 25.

then it is criminalisable conduct, but then argue (at 3.5) that criminal responsibility is a normative implication that presupposes normative phenomena. This explains why some instances of coercive conduct, which transgress normative phenomena, ought to be considered a crime.

3.2

You may recall that, in Essay 1, I drew a distinction between different 'entry points' into the same inquiry. If we are interested in the moral duties that govern our sexual conduct, then the principles of consent-astuteness (to avoid instrumentalising a person) and motivational-astuteness (to avoid objectifying a person) ought to be our focus. If we follow this thread and focus on these principles, then we can appreciate how coercion is contrary to these principles on the basis that coercion either aims to remove choice or aims to manipulate the reasons that motivate a choice. Such conduct is inconsistent with the principles of consent- and motivational-astuteness, which require attentiveness to a person's choices and their reasons for their choices.

We could, however, take the sexual autonomy of each person as our entry point. If so, then it is the effect of coercion on a person's sexual autonomy that ought to be our focus. If being autonomous means that we are entitled to choose between a range of worthwhile options, and coercion has the practical effect of removing the worthwhile options, then coercion undermines the moral quality of the choice being exercised. We can say that apparent consent is vitiated, and, as a result, the apparent consent is not capable of performing the moral work that we assign to consent.

In this way, coercion leads a double life, or 'serve[s] two normative functions'.[12] Coercion can be about choice, and coercion can be about manipulative conduct. On Berman's account, one of the normative functions of coercion is to 'determine whether A's conduct is at least prima facie wrongful or whether A is blameworthy'.[13] By isolating this normative function we can consider whether someone's conduct, itself, is blameworthy independently of the impact the conduct had on the choices of another person. '[W]e need', in other words, a standard of coercion to tell us 'when . . . the coercer's behavior is wrongful and condemnable' even if the coercion does not undermine the normative power of consent.[14]

[12] Berman (n 9) 49.
[13] Berman (n 9) 49.
[14] Ferzan (n 8) 957.

For Berman, the second function of coercion is to 'determine whether B is excused for conduct that would otherwise warrant blame'.[15] Here the focus is directed towards the choices being made by person B in light of coercive pressure being applied to them by person A. With regard to the second normative function, the suggestion that when someone is coerced, they are 'excused' for their conduct is too narrow. As Ferzan explains, it is better to say that coercion defeats 'the typical normative results of [the] choice' that was coerced.[16] When it comes to B's wrongdoing that was coerced by A, the finding of coercion excuses B or their wrongdoing; when it comes to B's promise that was coerced by A, the promise does not generate an obligation on B to perform the promise; and when it comes to consent, the expression of B's consent that was coerced by A does not generate the permission for A to interact with B. In all these instances, the normative force that the wrongdoing, promise, or consent would otherwise have (to generate blame, obligations, or permission) is vitiated; it no longer has normative power.

Note how the second function of coercion (coerced choice) is tightly knitted together by three strands. Since 'coerced choice' is concerned with the normative results of choice, it is predicated upon a person's choice being able to change a normative situation. Moreover, if a coerced choice changes the normative results of choice, then coercion defeats the normative results of the expression of consent. It then follows that a rape, sexual violation, or a sexual assault has occurred. This is because these are wrongs that are understood in terms of the absence of valid consent. Here, the three threads—the normative power of consent, how the power can be vitiated, and the implications of vitiated consent to sex—are tightly knitted together. In comparison, when it comes to 'coercive conduct', the threads are much more open-ended. Coercive conduct does not undermine consent or the moral quality of choice, it remains nonetheless a source of blameworthiness or wrongfulness, and it is not clear what follows from identifying blameworthy or wrongful instances of coercive conduct. The main task of this essay is to tighten these loose threads.

For now, it is enough to appreciate how the dual function of coercion—blaming the coercer and vitiating the choice of the coerced—enables us to isolate different aspects of coercion. In light of this duality, consider scenarios 1, 2(a), and 3 (with scenarios 2(b)–(d) to follow):

[15] Berman (n 9) 49.
[16] Ferzan (n 8) 968.

1. *Violent threat:* A instructs B that unless she has sex with him, A will injure B. B then agrees to the sex.
2(a). *Non-violent threat (audition):* A (an executive producer) informs B (an actor) that unless she has sex with him, A will prevent B from having a callback audition. B then agrees to the sex, in order to have the audition.
3. *Harassment*: At A's apartment after a date with B, A (a celebrity) repeatedly petitions B (a non-celebrity) to have sex with him (through physical advances and direct verbal requests), despite B's 'physical and verbal cues that she [does] not want to'.[17] A persists until B—'annoyed, exhausted, disappointed'[18]—consents to sex with A.

As a rough cut, we might say: in (1) *Violent threat*, A was being coercive, B was coerced, and B's consent was vitiated; in 2(a) *Non-violent threat (audition)*, A was being coercive, but B was not coerced, at least not to the extent that the 'coercion' vitiated her consent; and in (3) *Harassment*, A was applying pressure that fell short of being coercive conduct, and B was not coerced.

Our rough cut, however, assumes answers to two types of initial questions: threshold questions and implication questions. (1) *Violent threat* represents an easy case; the relevant threshold is clearly satisfied and the implications are clear. In (1) *Violent threat*, A caused B 'to fear that immediate violence would be used' and, in doing so, 'structur[ed] [B's] options . . . such that she prefers sexual intercourse to the alternatives she fears she will otherwise suffer'.[19] As a result, the ostensible consent is no consent at all, and the wrong that was committed was a serious wrong, which can be appropriately defined with reference to the absence of consent.

In comparison, 2(a) *Non-violent threat (audition)* and (3) *Harassment* both test the limits of the threshold and implication questions. It is not immediately obvious whether A's pressure in 2(a) *Non-violent threat (audition)* was *enough* to be considered 'coercive conduct', and it is unclear whether B's choices were constrained or manipulated *enough* to have been coerced. Moreover, even if we accept that some kind of threshold has been satisfied—so that we can say that 'there was coercion'—it is also unclear what ought to follow from these

[17] Ferzan (n 8) 955, referencing Katie Way, 'I Went on a Date with Aziz Ansari. It Turned into the Worst Night of My Life' (*BABE*, 13 January 2018) <https://babe.net/2018/01/13/aziz-ansari-28355> accessed 1 December 2024.

[18] Ferzan (n 8) 974.

[19] Kimberly Kessler Ferzan and Peter Westen, 'How to Think (Like a Lawyer) about Rape' (2017) 11 Crim Law Philos 759, 776.

findings. These two questions—thresholds and implications—are related, and we will come to that momentarily (at 3.3).

Before we worry about 'coercive conduct', let us start by focusing on 'coerced choice' and consider the initial difficulty of locating a threshold for coerced choice. At the very least, we know that B's choice in (3) *Harassment* was not a coerced choice. There was pressure, but not enough pressure to remove B's choice and vitiate B's consent. The difficulty that we encounter with *coerced choice* is that it requires a threshold condition to be satisfied, to identify whether the pressure that was applied to solicit consent was sufficient to undermine the moral quality of the consent.

We could, by following Pallikkathayil, explain a coerced choice in terms of being deprived of an option that a person would otherwise be entitled to pursue. On this account, one person coerces another when the coercer 'impermissibly constrains another's options when its potential to influence the recipient depends on denying her a moral veto'.[20] A finding of coercion rests upon isolating the choices that a person has a right of 'moral veto' over.[21] An adjacent formulation, by Wertheimer, suggests that a person is coerced if the proposal makes that person worse off relative to an appropriate baseline if the person does not acquiesce.[22] For Wertheimer, the 'normative baseline' is explained in terms of the person's rights so that the proposal makes the person 'worse off than she has the right to be'.[23] Similar to Pallikkathayil, the Wertheimer threshold or baseline for coercion relies upon isolating a normative position that the coerced person has a right to occupy.

On these accounts, what makes 2(a) *Non-violent threat (audition)* fall below this threshold is the fact that B is not being denied a right or moral veto, nor is she worse off than she has a right to be, because she has no right or entitlement to the callback audition. Similarly, with (3) *Harassment*, B has no right for her date with A to go well, nor even an entitlement that A be civil. Notice, again, how both these accounts delegate explanatory work to normative phenomena—specifically, rights (B's right or entitlement of a moral veto, 'worse off than [B] has the right to be'). Once these normative phenomena are in play, we can then locate more straightforward instances of non-violent coercion, such as:

[20] Japa Pallikkathayil, 'The Possibility of Choice: Three Accounts of the Problem with Coercion' (2011) 11 Philos' Impr 1, 14.

[21] Pallikkathayil (n 20) 12.

[22] Alan Wertheimer, 'Consent to Sexual Relations' in Franklin Miller and Alan Wertheimer (eds), *The Ethics of Consent: Theory and Practice* (OUP 2009) 198.

[23] Wertheimer, 'Consent to Sexual Relations' (n 22) 200.

2(b). *Non-violent threat (immigration)*: A (an immigration official) informs B that unless she has sex with him, A will change B's immigration status and remove her right to reside in the given county. B then agrees to the sex, in order to retain her right to reside.

2(c). *Non-violent threat (employment)*: A (the employer) informs B (the employee) that unless she has sex with him, A will fire B. B then agrees to the sex, in order to retain her employment.

2(d). *Non-violent threat (privacy)*: A (the ex-boyfriend) informs B (the ex-girlfriend) that unless she has sex with him, A will distribute intimate images of B (that B shared with A when they were in a relationship). B then agrees to the sex, in order to retain her privacy.

These scenarios satisfy the Pallikathayill–Wertheimer threshold. As Pallikathayill explains with reference to circumstances akin to 2(c) *Non-violent threat (employment)*:

> [O]n the veto conception of constraint, this announcement constrains the employee's options. In order to determine whether this constraint is impermissible, the impaired normative authority account begins by asking whether the employer may permissibly fire the employee.[24]

Pallikathayill notes that, beyond the 'institutional or contractual obligations in this case', the employee is otherwise entitled to veto any such 'abrupt and radical change in the job description', such as requiring an employee to 'now also act as a prostitute'.[25] The same account can explain the coercion in 2(b) *Non-violent threat (immigration)* and 2(d) *Non-violent threat (privacy)*: B is entitled to veto any arbitrary change to her immigration status, just as B is entitled to control intimate images of herself, and the coercion in both cases removes the power of veto.

Yet the finding that A coerced B (in *immigration*, *employment*, and *privacy*) is predicated upon the Pallikathayill–Wertheimer accounts, setting a relatively low threshold for finding a decision was coerced ('veto that B is entitled to exercise'/'worse off than B has the right to be'). Alternatively, we might set the threshold higher and say with Conly that

[24] Pallikkathayil (n 20) 18.
[25] Pallikkathayil (n 20) 19.

> [f]or a choice to be coerced . . . it is necessary that the person doing the choosing has no reasonable choice between doing what the coercer wants and the bad option which the coercer has introduced.[26]

In assessing whether a person had 'a reasonable choice', we could consider whether the pressure 'would prevent resistance by a woman of ordinary resolution'.[27] If the threat or pressure would cause a person of reasonable firmness to consider themselves to have no practical alternative but to acquiesce to the demand, only then would the high threshold for coerced choice be satisfied.

The difference between the standards is material. On the higher threshold, the non-violent threats may not amount to coercion. The coerced person B in the non-violent threat scenarios had a practical alternative to acquiescing to the demand for sex: 2(a) B could forgo the audition opportunity, 2(b) B could challenge the arbitrary change of immigration status, 2(c) B could challenge the unlawful dismissal, and 2(d) B could lawfully prevent the disclosure of the image. The hard-line position here is that

> [o]ur legal system is designed to provide remedies for (some) private wrongs. If one decides to forgo what is an adequate remedy, it is arguable that society has done all it needs to do.[28]

It is a choice between very unappealing options, but arguably a choice nonetheless, and the practical availability of choice precludes (on the higher threshold) the allegation of a coerced choice. On the lower threshold, the non-violent threats (that pertain to rights, in 2(b)–(d)) amount to coercion because, although there was a choice, it was a choice between different ways of forgoing a right of veto (or a choice between different ways of being in a worse position than the person had the right to be in).

Ultimately, we will be able to say that the non-violent threats (that pertain to rights, in 2(b)–(d)) amount to coercion. But to do so, we need an account of coercion that does not rely on the high threshold of 'no reasonable choice between doing what the coercer wants and the bad option which the coercer has introduced'. The point so far is: whether consent is vitiated by a non-violent threat depends on a threshold for when coercive conduct can be said to vitiate consent. Both thresholds delegate work to normative phenomena, either in the

26 Sarah Conly, 'Seduction, Rape, and Coercion' (2004) 115 Ethics 96, 106.
27 American Law Institute, 'Model Penal Code: Draft No. 6' (n 7) s 213.3(1)(a)(i) and (ii).
28 Alan Wertheimer, *Coercion* (Princeton UP 1987) 35.

form of rights or entitlements or focus on the practical capacity to exercise a *right* to choose. It is the presence or absence of normative phenomena that differentiate cases of coerced choice (violent threat and non-violent threats (that pertain to rights)) from pressure that does not coerce a choice (2(a) *Non-violent threat (audition)* and (3) *Harassment*). As I will explain in the next section, we rely upon threshold conditions to shape some degree of proportionality between the wrong and its implications. The next point being: any given answer to the threshold question requires—or, at the very least, presupposes—an answer to the implications question.

3.3

We have so far encountered threshold conditions in coerced choice because, when we approach coerced choice, we do so with the normative implications of coerced choice always ready in mind. We know that coercion can invalidate the granting of a permission. If consent can grant permission by waiving or suspending an obligation not to do something, then vitiated consent fails to suspend or waive that obligation. In this way, we can anticipate that coerced consent to sex will amount to a sexual act in the absence of consent. If the implication of identifying coerced consent is rape, for instance, then the threshold for coercion is high: a threat of force or physical violence or a non-violent threat that leaves 'no reasonable choice'. We employ a high threshold in order to ensure some proportionality between the gravity of the wrongdoing and the weight of its implications. Even if we accept a lower threshold (such as the threshold of 'worse off than she has the right to be'), where a person is forced to forgo one right (to residency, to employment, or to privacy) at the expense of another right (to bodily integrity), the implication that the 'consent' to sex is vitiated *arguably* retains some proportionality.

Scenario (3) *Harassment*, however, seems clearly different. We can dismiss the conduct in (3) *Harassment* from being coercive because we have implications vaguely in mind. Let me provide an example of this relationship between the threshold condition and normative implication when it comes to coercive conduct in circumstances more akin to (3) *Harassment*. Conly relies on the following analogy: when 'Cousin Beau' asks you to invest in a business opportunity and 'stresses his own suffering, hearkens back to the many times he's helped you, and suggests he can't possibly feel the same in the future if you don't do this little thing', he has not committed a wrong.[29] That is, he has

[29] Conly (n 26) 114.

not committed wrongs of theft or extortion, because he has not gone 'beyond [his] rights', since he is 'allowed' to use 'the strength of family ties to [his] own ends'.[30] By analogy, there is no wrong in (3) *Harassment*, since A had not gone beyond his rights to use emotional and social pressure to pursue his own ends.

The analogy seems right, and this is because the analogy sets up a disconnect between threshold conditions and assumed normative implications. In particular, Conly's explanation works because of the categories of wrongdoing that the account presupposes. Note how Cousin Beau's conduct was viewed in light of criminal categories: theft or extortion. We might approach (3) *Harassment*, and perhaps 2(a) *Non-violent threat (audition)*, in the same way and make a similar assumption: we consider whether the pressure amounts to coercion in the shadow of a sexual offence, such as rape, sexual violation, or sexual assault—namely, categories defined with reference to the absence of consent. The point is that one (the implication of wrongdoing) informs the other (threshold condition for the wrongdoing). We set high threshold conditions for the pressure or threats that vitiate consent because we assume that the implication is vitiated consent.

In comparison, consider the implications (so far) of 'coercive conduct': blameworthiness. An inquiry that is only burdened by implying blameworthiness can identify, with ease, that A is generally blameworthy in 2(a) *Non-violent threat (audition)* and (3) *Harassment*, although the degree of blameworthiness varies. At the same time, identifying a general or 'free-floating' blameworthiness is unhelpful. We want to know what *ought* to happen to A if A is 'blameworthy'. It is clear that A ought to, somehow, respond to (and account for) his coercive conduct. It is clear that A should regret the conduct, and B can resent A for the conduct. But what else? Is A blameworthy enough to lose his career? Is he blameworthy enough to be prosecuted and censured by public officials? The point here is that for 'coercive conduct' to perform a 'normative function',[31] it ought to have identifiable normative implications: something (beyond a reactive attitude) that follows from the finding of coercion.

Ferzan provides a helpful account of the normative implications of 'coercive conduct'. In circumstances akin to (3) *Harassment*, the choices of B were not coerced, so there is no rape, but there remains a distinct wrong in A 'availing himself of a benefit that he obtained through his wrongful conduct'.[32] Ferzan reasons by analogy: in the same way that legal doctrines of entrapment prevent

[30] Conly (n 26) 114–15.
[31] Berman (n 9) 49.
[32] Ferzan (n 8) 984.

law enforcement agencies from benefitting from their wrongdoing, and in the same way that principles of restitution prevent a claimant's recovery where the claimant's own 'inequitable conduct in the transaction . . . is the source of the asserted liability',[33] so too a coercer ought to be prevented from benefitting from his own coercion.

From the analogy emerges a principle. Ferzan's principle provides that 'as a result of the coercer's wrongdoing, [A] is not entitled to avail himself of the consent'.[34] The principle, however, contains an important ambiguity: there are different ways to benefit from a wrong. When a public official entraps a private individual, the benefit the public official obtains is a *practical* one—say, an evidence or a confession. It is a *practical* benefit that the official must then forgo. When a transaction calls for restitution, it is a *material* benefit that the claimant is attempting to recover for themselves and that the principle prevents them from recovering. When it comes to consent, when one person coerces another person, the coercer obtains a *permission* (the waiver of an obligation that would otherwise apply).

Now, if we are to apply this iteration of Ferzan's principle, we collapse the two functions of coercion and arrive at a conclusion that we then want to avoid. If A benefitted from B's permission (*waiver* of an obligation), and if we are willing to *rescind this normative benefit of the waiver*, then we find ourselves in the shadow of a serious sexual offence, since we are viewing the interaction in terms of the absence of consent. Yet that mischaracterises the wrong in (3) *Harassment* and 2(a) *Non-violent threat (audition)*.

The fundamental problem here stems from how 'the moral magic' of *consent as an attitude* has dominated the commentary.[35] The underlying assumption so far has been that the sole function of consent is to express a choice, so either the coercive conduct undermines the moral quality of that choice (as in 1 and 2(b)–(d)) or it does not (as in 2(a) and 3). Whilst consent does function to express a choice, it is not the only function. Consent also represents an evaluation of interests. Consent enables A to believe that when B agrees to do θ, B considers doing θ to be in B's interests. As Michelle Madden Dempsey explains, when it comes to B:

> This is B's decision. He's an adult and can decide for himself whether he thinks the risk is worth it. In considering what to do, I will assume that his

[33] American Law Institute, *Restatement (Third) of Restitution and Unjust Enrichment* (American Law Institute 2011) s 63; Ferzan (n 8) 986.
[34] Ferzan (n 8) 981.
[35] Hurd (n 1) 124; Larry Alexander, 'The Moral Magic of Consent (II)' (1996) 2 Leg Theory 165, 166.

> decision is the right one for him. After all, he is in a better position than I to judge his own well-being.[36]

All things going well, when another person consents to an interaction, we can take their consent as indication that the interaction is (in their assessment) in their best interests. All things going well, their consent is a sufficiently accurate proxy for their best interests. Which means, all things going well, there is no need to look behind their consent and consider their interests. Epistemically, we can say their consent is enough.

When a person applies pressure on another, however, all things are *not* going well. In applying Ferzan's principle, coercive conduct rescinds the benefit of consent, but the *epistemic* benefit (not the normative benefit). Coercive conduct takes away from the coercer the defence that 'there was no need to look behind consent and consider the coerced person's interests'. To continue the analogies with private law doctrines, it estops reliance on (the epistemic function of) consent. But we can go further. Beyond estopping reliance, we can also easily infer that the applier of pressure (A) *knows* that the decision by the coerced person (B) is contrary to B's interests.

Hence, in the context of 2(a) *Non-violent threat (audition)*, the implication of A applying pressure on B through a non-violent threat is that A has no reason to believe that the sex is in B's interests. Instead, A knows that he is requiring B to act contrary to her interests (either B engages in unwanted sex or B forgoes a career opportunity). Scenario (3) *Harassment* differs slightly. The implication of A's pressure is that A has created a real risk that the sex was not in B's interests. This explains our reactive attitude of blame directed towards A in 2(a) *Non-violent threat (audition)* and (3) *Harassment*. In 2(a) *Non-violent threat (audition)*, A knows that he is requiring B to act against her own interests, and the usual device for A to assume 'that B's decision is the right one for her' (consent) has been rescinded by the pressure applied on B. In (3) *Harassment*, A *should* know that he is pressuring B to act against her own interests, and consent as a device for expressing one's own interests is (arguably) also rescinded by the pressure applied on B.

We therefore have the different functions of coercion aligning with different functions of consent. One function of coercion is to identify results of a choice. In this way, thresholds for 'coerced choice' are concerned with rescinding the normative benefit of the choice. The normative benefit is the waiver of an

[36] Michelle Madden Dempsey, 'Victimless Conduct and the Volenti Maxim: How Consent Works' (2013) 7 Crim Law Philos 11, 20.

obligation (permission), and whilst a coerced person may express consent, the coercion undermines the moral quality of the permission. Another function of coercion is to identify conduct that is blameworthy. 'Coercive conduct' is blameworthy so far as it amounts to knowingly requiring a person to act contrary to their own interests.

3.4

'Coerced choice' has a direct path to accountability: if A interacts with B, without B's permission (since the consent expressed by B was coerced by A), then A is accountable for his wrongdoing: namely, the breach of the obligation to obtain permission. We can then accept (with ease) that a public official has the right to hold A to account for his wrongdoing. Hence, following (1) *Violent threat*, we would expect a criminal trial to ensue from the events. 'Coercive conduct', in comparison, has no such path. This is because we have still only located a 'free-floating' blameworthiness. We can say that in 2(a) *Non-violent threat (audition)* and (3) *Harassment*, A is blameworthy (A is an appropriate target for our reactive attitude or blame) for knowingly or carelessly requiring B to act against her own interests. But this does not necessarily imply that another person can hold A to account for knowingly requiring B to act against her own interests.

To put the same point more broadly: if 'coercive conduct' is to perform a putative *normative* function, coercive conduct then ought to have *normative* implications. What is missing from our account of coercive conduct, so far, is normative phenomena: the rights that are infringed, and obligations that are breached, which then generate wrongs. Recall how coerced choice was predicated on the normative phenomena of rights, either by delegating the threshold condition to whether a *right* of veto has been removed, making the coerced person worse off than she has a *right* to be, or—more fundamentally—by removing the practical capacity for choice, forgoing the *right* to refuse what the coercer wanted. As we have seen, by latching upon the normative phenomena of rights, we are able to make sense of the concept of coercion in the *Non-violent threat* scenarios 2(b)–(d), not as the removal of the right to choose, but as coercive conduct that forces a person to forgo a right that they are entitled to exercise.

In comparison, 2(a) *Non-violent threat (audition)* suffers from the lack of normative phenomena. Whilst A may be blameworthy for knowingly requiring B to act contrary to her interests, B has no right that her interests be promoted in her interaction with A, and A is under no obligation to promote or advance B's interests. No doubt, A's conduct is blameworthy conduct that we should attend to, without necessarily criminalising the conduct. In other words, there may be moral reasons that A ought not to coerce/pressure B—in 2(a) *Non-violent threat (audition)* and (3) *Harassment*—without the conduct transgressing normative phenomena. If so, there are no *normative* implications of A applying coercive pressure on B in these two scenarios.

This might seem to be coming from an unhealthy obsession with the deontic form (the form of rights, wrongs, and obligations). Moral reasons, we could say, explain obligations. Sufficiently, important interests, we could also say, sit behind rights. Acting contrary to any of them is then *wrongful* (in a broad sense). Hence, in response, we could solve this puzzle of 2(a) *Non-violent threat (audition)* by executive fiat. That is, posit that 'A is under an obligation not to knowingly require B to set back her interests', and then back-fill the obligation with reference to the harms caused to B, by A.

We can do so because coercive conduct that requires a person to act contrary to their interests is harmful. It is harmful on more than one measure. One way to substantiate 'harm' is with reference to 'interests', so that a harm is a 'thwarting, setting back, or defeating of an interest'.[37] Part of the ambiguity, however, that follows from substituting one vague term (*harm*) for another (*interests*) derives from the different ways in which interests can be set back or thwarted. We could view interests hedonistically (and subjectively) in terms of preferences or 'desire fulfilment', or objectively in terms of the 'certain things [that] are good or bad for people'.[38] In the context of sex and sexual desire, the two views can often converge. It is objectively good for a person when their own preferences and sexual desires are fulfilled in sexual intercourse, and a person's (hedonic and objective) interests are set back when the sexual intercourse is unwanted or undesired.[39] But there are plenty of instances of divergence where a person's own assessment of their interests differs from our objective assessment of their interests. Hence, in scenarios akin (3) *Harassment*, when a woman 'acquiesces to sex because she fears that she will not be asked out on another date, or because she seeks to avoid embarrassment', we might want to say—with Hurd—that she was 'prepared to sacrifice important interests to avoid trivial losses'.[40] But we can only say this by valuing one interest

[37] Joel Feinberg, *The Moral Limits of the Criminal Law Volume 1: Harm to Others* (OUP 1987) 33.
[38] Derek Parfit, *Reasons and Persons* (Clarendon Press 1984) 499.
[39] Robin West, 'Consent, Legitimation, and Dysphoria' (2020) 83 MLR 1, 5.
[40] Hurd (n 1) 143.

(sexual choice) and devaluing another interest (a second date) differently from the woman herself.

Another way of substantiating 'harm' is with reference to a setback to autonomy, where autonomy is understood as the ability to choose between a range of worthwhile options (and the capacity to a make a choice, independently of others).[41] We can therefore appreciate that each person ought always to be entitled to choose whether they engage in a sexual interaction with another, and that being denied the ability to choose is a central case of harm to autonomy. In this way, if autonomy is the ability to pursue a range of worthwhile options, if harm occurs when this ability is set back, and if coercion amounts to being deprived of a choice between worthwhile options, then coercion is harmful *par excellence.*

However, the same tension arises as to whether an option is sufficiently worthwhile to count as something that an autonomous person would choose to pursue. If 'our concern for autonomy is a concern to enable people to have a good life', then our concern 'furnishes us with reason to secure that autonomy which could be valuable'.[42] Protecting worthwhile options secures the exercise of autonomy whilst 'protecting bad options does not enable one to enjoy valuable autonomy'.[43] What counts as a worthwhile option, as against a bad option, requires the same type of assessment that we encountered above, in order to separate the 'certain things that are good or bad for people' from the 'bad options' a person might want to pursue.

Now, these interest-based and autonomy-based formulations of harm can explain how coercion *that removes the capacity for choice* is directly harmful. If sexual autonomy is the exercise of choice as to when, with whom, and under what conditions we engage in sexual acts, then a direct harm is suffered when we are deprived of this choice. In addition, these formulations of harm can also explain how coercive conduct that requires a person to act contrary to their interests is also harmful. This 'further' harm follows from two observations. The first observation is that sexual autonomy also requires that our sexual choices further our hedonic interests (where the pursuit of our own sexual desires and preferences is objectively valuable). Unwanted and undesired sex is a setback to this objective interest. Recall (from Essay 2) the harm of 'hedonic dysphoria'[44] where

[41] Joseph Raz, 'Autonomy, Toleration, and the Harm Principle' in Ruth Gavison (ed), *Issues in Contemporary Legal Philosophy: Influence of HLA Hart* (Clarendon Press 1987) 327.
[42] Joseph Raz, *The Morality of Freedom* (OUP 1986) 412.
[43] Raz, *The Morality of Freedom* (n 42) 412.
[44] West (n 39) 5.

> many women and girls and some boys and men likewise . . . often or routinely consent to sex when they neither desire, want, welcome, or ultimately find it to be physically pleasurable.[45]

The second observation is that the decision to engage in a sexual act may be a choice between options where the alternative option may also be contrary to our objective interests. In such instances, a person is unable to choose between a range of worthwhile options since both options are contrary to their objective interests. This is a 'further harm' to sexual autonomy, where sex is chosen but the choice is between two different ways of setting back one's own interests.

3.5

So far, so good. It seems that we can recognise normative phenomena—namely, the *obligation* not to knowingly require a person to act contrary to their own interests—and justify the prohibition with reference to harm. If we accept that 'establishing that an action is wrong . . . is indispensable to justifying its prohibition' and that 'there are harm-based constraints on state intervention to regulate wrongs',[46] then we are well on our way to criminalising 'coercive conduct' as a standalone wrong. After all, if we grant the first move (if we recognise the obligation not to knowingly require a person to act contrary to their own interests), it then follows that acting contrary to the obligation is both wrongful and harmful.

However, in doing so, the solution by executive fiat evades a fundamental question about responsibility. 'To be responsible', according to Antony Duff, 'is to be answerable; answerability is to a person or body who has the right or standing to call me to account'.[47] Duff's 'answerability' is a form of relational responsibility. Relational responsibility differs from the broader, or more basic, notion: 'an ability to respond' where '[t]here is nobody to whom it is owed'.[48] A person is responsible when they are able to respond to their failure to adhere to moral reasons that applied to their moral situation. In comparison, a person

[45] West (n 39) 5.

[46] AP Simester and Andreas von Hirsch, *Crimes, Harms, and Wrongs: On the Principles of Criminalisation* (Hart Publishing 2011) 21.

[47] Duff (n 11) 23–25.

[48] John Gardner, 'Relations of Responsibility' in Rowan Cruft, Matthew H Kramer and Mark R Reiff (eds), *Crime, Punishment, and Responsibility: The Jurisprudence of Antony Duff* (OUP 2011) 87.

is accountable (or 'relationally responsible') when another person can require them to respond to their failure.

Now, in all the scenarios that we have considered so far, A is responsible in the basic or vague sense. In (3) *Harassment*, A sought to structure B's options so that B might act in A's interests, and contrary to her own interests. To the extent that we have moral reasons to share in (rather than manipulate) another's motivations to consensual interaction (see the principle of motivational-astuteness at 2.5), A acted contrary to those reasons, and A is 'responsible' for doing so. First and foremost, B has reasons to *resent* A's conduct. This is a 'reactive attitude[] that result[s] from one's seeing in another's actions evident . . . ill will toward one[self]'.[49] B has reasons to adopt this attitude (resentment) towards A. In addition, A has reasons to *regret* his conduct. A's actions manifest a disregard for B's interests at the expense of his own. These reactive attitudes—of resentment and regret—are apt. This ability to respond (with reactive attitudes) is relational, but only in the weakest sense: insofar as we attach importance to 'the attitudes and intentions toward us of those who stand in these relationships to us' then we are 'prone' to these reactive attitudes.[50] In this way, we might also have reasons to attend to A's manipulative conduct (we can be concerned by, be critical of, and write blogposts and newspaper articles about it). We do not, however, have a right or duty to hold him accountable for the conduct. It is *not* that it is 'none of our business' but instead 'one's reason to attend is insufficient to give one a right or a duty to do so'.[51]

Moreover, to the extent that we can be attentive to A's *blameworthy* conduct, we have 'the full ledger of moral responsibility' to attend to. If '[m]oral appraisability has to do with that type of inward moral praising and blaming that constitutes making a private judgment about a person', then '[s]omeone is blameworthy if he is deserving of such blame; that is, if it is correct, or true to the facts, to judge that there is a "debit" in his "ledger"'.[52] In formulating our judgement about a person, we have open access to the full range of moral reasons that they ought to have adhered to.

The criminal law has a much narrower focus. To start with, it represents a specific context where one person (a public official) does have a right or duty to hold another person responsible for that person's conduct. It is, in other words, a particular form of relational responsibility. Moreover, the criminal law is not

[49] John Deigh, 'Reactive Attitudes Revisited' in Carla Bagnoli (ed), *Morality and the Emotions* (OUP 2011) 201.
[50] Strawson (n 10) 76.
[51] Gardner (n 48) 92.
[52] Michael J Zimmerman, *An Essay on Moral Responsibility* (Rowman and Littlefield 1988) 38.

concerned with the full moral ledger. Instead, it is concerned with normative phenomena. The claim here is that what bridges the gap between basic responsibility (blameworthiness) and relational responsibility (accountability) is normative phenomena. As Darwall explains:

> Deontic terms like 'required', 'obligatory', 'prohibited', 'wrong', 'permissible' ... occupy a different conceptual space than do those concerning what reasons favor, support, or justify, since they distinctively concern accountability.[53]

To be concerned with accountability is to adopt the standpoint or perspective that 'you and I take up when we make and acknowledge claims on one another's conduct'.[54] We cannot understand 'accountability', according to Darwall, in terms of 'the balance of moral reasons'.[55] Rather, recourse to these deontic concepts is necessary in order to adopt the standpoint of accountability or relational responsibility.

At face value, principles of criminalisation already commit us to this view. If 'any prohibition of •-ing can be justified only when •-ing is a morally wrongful action'[56] (Simester and von Hirsch's 'Necessity Thesis'), then our concern for normative phenomena—the wrongful actions, the breach of obligations, and infringement of rights that wrongs represent—has been hiding in plain sight. The claim here, however, might be more contentious than a commitment to the 'Necessity Thesis'. It is the suggestion that we cannot understand criminal responsibility (as a form of accountability or relational responsibility) without recourse to deontic standards and normative phenomena.

Moreover, even with recourse to deontic standards, criminalisation goes beyond a concern for wrongdoing. Criminal responsibility, as opposed to other forms of relational responsibility, concerns an even narrower set of normative phenomena. The criminal law enables the state to remove options by prohibiting categories of conduct, whilst enabling public officials to exercise powers of investigation and public prosecution in order to impose punitive and stigmatising sanctions. I have unpacked these implications of criminalisation elsewhere.[57] The point here is that an account of criminal responsibility—as

[53] Stephen L Darwall, 'What Are Moral Reasons?' (The Amherst Lecture in Philosophy, 2017) 7.
[54] Stephen L Darwall, *The Second-Person Standpoint: Morality, Respect, and Accountability* (Harvard UP 2006) 12.
[55] Darwall, 'What Are Moral Reasons?' (n 53) 7.
[56] Simester and von Hirsch (n 46) 22.
[57] Jesse Wall, 'Public Wrongs and Private Wrongs' (2018) 31 CJLJ 177, 183–95; Jesse Wall, 'The Margins of Private Law' in Kate Falconer, Kit Barker and Andrew Fell (eds), *Life and Death in Private Law* (Bloomsbury Publishing 2024) 47.

a particular form of relational responsibility—needs to be able to explain these implications of criminalisation. There are a number of possible explanations for these implications. For Edwards and Simester, 'officials have a right to call such wrongdoers to answer for their wrongs' when 'public officials are well placed to get answers from those wrongdoers on behalf of beneficiaries'.[58] For Marshall and Duff, when public officials 'take seriously the wrong [the victim] has suffered' and 'respond . . . to [the defendant's] wrongdoing' in order to censure the wrong,[59] they are doing so in the 'public interest in the sense that it properly concerns all members of the polity'.[60] Akin to reliance on the harm principle and the wrongfulness principle alone, Edwards and Simester's proceduralism and Marshall and Duff's shared and mutual concern are all over-extensive. At best, they capture and explain a set of moral wrongs that are also legal wrongs, without accounting for the full set of features that are distinct to the criminal law.

We need, therefore, a further constraint on criminalisation. Ultimately, we need to come to terms with two related questions. One asks: 'why is the *ex ante* issuance of morally-loaded, prohibitory norms itself one of the state's proper functions?'[61] The other asks: if '[p]unishment is only justified when and to the extent that it is deserved',[62] what conduct deserves punishment? One way to answer these questions, and to account for the full set of implications of criminalisation, is to accept that if the state is responsible for promoting a set of values, then the state can punish conduct that is antithetical to a value that the state is responsible for promoting.[63] 'Antithetical conduct' is conduct 'that manifests a *disrespect* for the interest or value that has been violated' by demonstrating an unwillingness to be guided by the appropriate interest or value.[64] It follows as a necessary condition of criminalisation that 'any serious violation of a value that the state is responsible for supporting is a candidate for criminal punishment'.[65] To the extent that the state is responsible for supporting the ends-setting capacity of each person, then the criminal law 'treats as a wrong any action that manifests disrespect for the capacity to choose ends'.[66]

[58] James Edwards and Andrew Simester, 'What's Public About Crime?' (2017) 37 OJLS 105, 132.
[59] SE Marshall and RA Duff, 'Criminalization and Sharing Wrongs' (1998) 11 CJLJ 7, 16.
[60] RA Duff and SE Marshall, 'Public and Private Wrongs' in James Chalmers, Fiona Leverick and Lindsay Farmer (eds), *Essays in Criminal Law in Honour of Sir Gerald Gordon* (Edinburgh UP 2010) 71.
[61] Simester and von Hirsch (n 46) 17.
[62] Douglas Husak, *Overcriminalization: The Limits of the Criminal Law* (OUP 2008) 82.
[63] Wall, 'Public Wrongs and Private Wrongs' (n 57) 185.
[64] Grant Lamond, 'What is a Crime?' (2007) 27 OJLS 609, 621.
[65] Lamond (n 64) 626.
[66] Alan Brudner, *Punishment and Freedom: A Liberal Theory of Penal Justice* (OUP 2009) 31.

This can explain why the conduct in *(1) Violent threat* clearly is, and clearly ought to be, a crime. B has a right to refuse a sexual advance, and B has a right not to be injured, and the state is responsible for promoting both iterations of the right to bodily integrity. Being required to choose between two different ways of forgoing the right to bodily integrity is antithetical to exercising the capacity to choose ends. Public officials therefore have the right to call the coercer (A) to account for his wrongdoing, which was not just wrongdoing in the deontic sense (acting contrary to the obligation to obtain consent) but wrongdoing that 'manifests disrespect for [B]'s capacity to choose ends'.

We can also explain why the *Non-violent threats* in 2(b)–(d) ought also to be considered criminal conduct. B has a right to refuse a sexual advance, and B is entitled to retain her right to residency/employment/privacy. However, to explain why, we do not need to rely on the premise that B had no practical choice (the Conly threshold). Instead, we can invoke the notion that coercive conduct can be a standalone wrong. If we accept that the state is responsible for promoting both B's right to bodily integrity and her right to residency/employment/privacy, then A is accountable (relationally responsible) for knowingly requiring B to *forgo a right*—either her right to bodily integrity or her right to residency/employment/privacy. These instances of coercive conduct transgress normative phenomena (the rights to bodily integrity/residency/employment/privacy) that the state is responsible for promoting. By knowingly requiring B to forgo those rights, A manifests a disrespect for such values.

In comparison, 2(a) *Non-violent threat (audition)* is blameworthy but not criminalisable conduct. A is responsible (blameworthy) for knowingly requiring B to act contrary to her interests, which is coercive conduct that is contrary to moral reasons, to which we ought to attend. And yet A is not relationally responsible (accountable). Without normative phenomena to latch on to, we cannot generate the relational accountability needed for a public official to hold A to account for his wrongful conduct. Scenario (3) *Harassment*, too, falls into the same category (blameworthy but not criminal). We can criticise the conduct for being contrary to moral reasons without being able to isolate the wrongdoing for which we can hold a person relationally responsible.

More broadly, beyond solving these puzzles, we have also identified three moving parts in the concept of coercion: (a) coercion removes choice by removing options, (b) coercion invalidates the normative implications of consent, and (c) coercion requires a person to act contrary to their own rights and interests. The task of this essay has been to explain how these parts work together. When it comes to 'coerced choice', it is well established that when (a) coercion removes choice, then (b) the normative, permission-granting, implication of consent is vitiated, and the coercer is accountable for the wrongfulness of instigating sex without valid consent. Beyond 'coerced choice' is the emerging legal category of 'coercive conduct'. The contention here has been that even when the 'coercive conduct' does not remove a choice, it nonetheless (c) requires a person to act contrary to their own *rights*, and in this way, the coercer ought to be accountable for this wrong. As I will consider further in the following essay, we can locate the same lines of fracture in the concept of consent: (a) consent represents an attitude towards an option, (b) consent generates or waives normative phenomena, and (c) consent is a proxy for a person's assessment of their own interests. The task of the next essay is to see how the moving parts of consent also work together.

4

That Was Then, This Is Now

4.1

'The success of the claim "[b]ut that used to be okay!"' in response to conduct that is now considered to be wrongful depends, according to Michelle Madden Dempsey, on 'whether there has been a genuine shift in wrongfulness norms' between now and then.[1] By 'a genuine shift in wrongfulness norms', Dempsey means a shift in the 'line between conduct that is actually wrongful in a given society at a particular time and that which is not wrongful'.[2] Whilst the claim ('but that used to be okay') depends on such a shift, the claim itself is an assertion of ignorance or unawareness of a contemporary wrongfulness norm. If the claim succeeds in excusing wrongful conduct, it does so on the basis of a general exculpatory principle, that a person cannot be held morally responsible for 'failing to respond to a reason he is unaware applies to his conduct'.[3]

To properly understand the claim 'but that used to be okay' is to first understand the relationship between norms (that shift) and reasons (that a person can be unaware of). The first task for this essay, therefore, is to explain the relationship between a change in a normative practice and a person's claim to an unawareness of moral reasons. To do so, I categorise three sets of moral reasons: will-grounded, world-grounded, and practice-grounded reasons. I will explain how a worthwhile social practice can generate moral reasons, and to the extent that social practices can change over time, so too can the moral reasons that the practice generates.

For example, consider the following candidates for 'a genuine shift in wrongfulness norms':

1. *Capacity (then/now):* It was permissible then, but it is impermissible now, for A (a twenty-one-year-old) to have sex with B (a sixteen-year-old) on the basis that B lacks the capacity to consent to sex with A.

[1] Michelle Madden Dempsey, 'Coercion, Consent, and Time' (2021) 131 Ethics 345, 368.
[2] Dempsey (n 1) 368.
[3] Douglas Husak, *Ignorance of Law: A Philosophical Inquiry* (OUP 2016) 152.

Sex and Self-Ownership. Jesse Wall, Oxford University Press. © Jesse Wall 2025.
DOI: 10.1093/9780191987809.003.0004

2. *Power (then/now):* It was permissible then, but it is impermissible now, for A (a university professor) to have sex with B (a graduate student, in the same department as A) on the basis of the power dynamic between A and B.
3. *Silence (then/now):* It was permissible then, but it is impermissible now, for A to take B's silence (motionlessness and lack of objection), alone, in response to a sexual advance to be indicative of consent to sex.

I will advance three main claims with regard to these scenarios:

1. A change in a normative social practice can result in a change in the moral reasons that apply to a given moral situation.
2. A person cannot be held responsible for acting contrary to moral reasons that they were unaware applied to their moral situation.
3. Unless the person was unaware of the moral reasons they acted contrary to as a result of their mismanagement of their moral outlook.

I will contend that these scenarios (*capacity*, *power*, and *silence*) are illustrative of how a normative social practice can generate moral reasons (*now*) that previously did not form part of the moral situation (*then*). However, establishing that a shift in norms generated new moral reasons only enables the claim that A was aware of the moral reasons that A acted contrary to. If we accept, as a general exculpatory principle, that a person can only be responsible for acting against reasons they were aware applied to their situation, then the claim ('but that used to be okay') can work to excuse the moral wrongdoing.

I then will contend that whilst the general exculpatory principle can excuse wrongdoing in historical cases (past conduct in the context of past norms), it does not excuse wrongdoing in contemporary cases (contemporary conduct in reliance on past norms). To affirm this intuition, an inculpatory exception needs to be carved out of the general exculpatory principle. I will suggest here that although a person cannot be held responsible for acting contrary to moral reasons they were unaware applied to their situation, they can nonetheless be held responsible for mismanaging their moral outlook, where that mismanagement resulted in the lack of awareness of the moral reasons they acted against. In such cases—such as the contemporary cases—the claim 'but that used to be okay' fails as an excuse.

This essay will start (at 4.2) by isolating practice-grounded moral reasons (that can change) from will-grounded and world-grounded moral reasons (that cannot). I then return (at 4.3) to the above scenarios to illustrate how practice-grounded reasons can change, and to introduce the intuition that only historical cases of wrongdoing are excused by the general exculpatory principle. I consider (at 4.4) the inculpatory exception to the general exculpatory principle, in terms of both *how* a person may be culpable for acting contrary to reasons that they were unaware applied to their moral situation and *when* the exception applies to render them culpable. The essay concludes at 4.5 with the contention that whilst the claim 'but that used to be okay' can excuse wrongdoing, it is a *contingent* (on a change in social practices), *limited* (to normative wrongdoing), and *qualified* (by the inculpatory exception) excuse.

4.2

We need to start by grappling with the relationship between norms and reasons in order to entertain the idea that moral reasons have the capacity to change over time. Consent forms part of the 'normative phenomena' that we encounter when we consider the permissibility, obligatoriness, or wrongfulness of an act. 'Normative phenomena' include any moral rights a person may have, whatever obligations we may owe them, and the wrongs that we might commit against them. We have some, but not complete, control over the normative phenomena that we encounter. As David Owens explains, 'promising, giving, commanding and consenting are all forms of *normative power*' as 'they are all powers to change the normative situation by declaration'.[4] Specifically, an act of consent can change the normative situation between A and B by suspending or waiving an obligation that would otherwise—in the absence of consent—be wrongful (contrary to the obligation).

Norms can also *act on* moral reasons. It is through the exercise of the normative powers of promising, consenting, and forgiving that we can *generate* moral reasons (to perform a promise), *enable* moral reasons (to do a permitted act), and *disable* moral reasons (to remedy a wrong). In terms of consent, B's consent is enabling in the sense that it allows A to act on reasons that would otherwise be excluded from the moral equation. In this way, consent (as a normative phenomenon) has a transformative effect—it transforms a set of reasons from being excluded (by an obligation) to being 'unexcluded' (by the waiver of the obligation).

None of this, so far, seems amenable to change over time. Consent *then*, just as consent does *now*, transforms the reasons that a person may act upon. The

[4] David Owens, 'The Possibility of Consent' (2011) 24 Ratio 402, 402.

moral calculus should be simple and timeless: either B's consent is (and was) valid to transform the reasons that A may act on, or it is not (and was not). But this does not capture the complexity of the norms and reasons that consent (or any other normative power) governs. The mistake here is to focus too narrowly on only one aspect of consent—consent is a choice—and assume that the exercise of a choice alone can be transformative of normative phenomena.

We have already encountered (in the previous essay) three dimensions of consent: (a) consent represents an attitude towards an option, (b) consents generates or waives normative phenomena, and (c) consent is a proxy for a person's assessment of their own interests. In this essay, we can consider how these dimensions fit together. The dimensions align with three sets of moral reasons that consent, and normative powers more generally, is predicated upon. In brief, these moral reasons are:

> *Will-grounded moral reasons*: B's will (or choice) can trigger a change in the normative situation between A and B, by generating reasons (to perform a promise), enabling reasons (to do a permitted act), and disabling reasons (to remedy a wrong).
>
> *World-grounded moral reasons*: descriptive features of the world aggravate (or mitigate) the moral weight of the normative phenomena (rights, wrongs, and obligations) that arise between A and B.
>
> *Practice-grounded moral reasons*: worthwhile social practices determine the normative phenomena (rights, wrongs, and obligations) that can arise between A and B.

Will- and world-grounded moral reasons can change (but only in a trivial sense): a person can change their mind and the descriptive features of the circumstances can change. It is *how* these reasons determine how we ought to behave that are incapable of change. That is to say, the moral relevance of a person's will (their consent, promise, or forgiveness) is immutable, as is how the descriptive features of the world can aggravate wrongs or strengthen obligations.

When it comes to change *over time*, only practice-grounded reasons are capable of change. If so, then for the excuse '[b]ut that used to be okay!' to be plausible, it needs to be interpreted as a claim about practice-grounded reasons. It is different from 'I did no harm' (a claim about world-grounded moral reasons) or 'but B chose to' (a claim about will-grounded reasons). Instead, the excuse ('but that used to be okay') is a claim about the applicable norms that changed over time and how that change might excuse a person's responsibility for wrongdoing. As we will see throughout this essay, it is tempting to shift our focus away from practice-grounded moral reasons. This is a temptation that we need to resist if we want to understand the excuse '[b]ut that used to be okay!'.

We now need to interrogate the three sets of moral reasons. Let us start with will-grounded moral reasons. One way to explain the moral force of consent is in terms of the *willing attitude* of the consenting person. According to this 'attitudinal view' of consent, the permissibility of an act done to another person is determined by the other person's attitude of willingness, acceptance, or acquiescence towards the specific act.[5] This is the so-called 'moral magic' of consent.[6] It is a person's subjective or internal attitude of willingness, acceptance, or acquiescence that is doing the work of 'transforming' the moral status of the act into an act that is morally permissible.[7] Beyond consent, we might also rely on the exercise of choice, or the will, to explain the moral force of other normative phenomena, such as promise-making and forgiveness.

These will-grounded accounts of normative phenomena encounter the objection that the will itself cannot generate moral reasons. Rather than the will, the 'descriptive features of the world fix what we have reason to do'.[8] It then follows that 'there is no other way to change the normative shape of the situation, than by changing the descriptive shape of the situation'.[9] Hence, the challenge for the attitudinal view is the

> *Challenge of supervening wrongs*: If all moral reasons supervene upon descriptive features of the world, then all wrongdoing derives from descriptive features of the world.

The doubt here concerns how it is then possible for a person's attitude to be transformative—to change the moral status of the act into an act that is morally permissible. If B consents to ϕ (a tattoo) that they will enjoy and cherish over the course of their lifetime, then A (the tattoo artist) has (world-grounded) reasons

[5] Peter Westen, *The Logic of Consent: The Diversity and Deceptiveness of Consent as a Defense to Criminal Conduct* (Routledge 2016) 4–5; Kimberly Kessler Ferzan, 'Consent, Culpability, and the Law of Rape' (2016) 13 Ohio St J Crim L 397, 400.

[6] See Heidi M Hurd, 'The Moral Magic of Consent' (1996) 2 Leg Theory 121, 124; Larry Alexander, 'The Moral Magic of Consent (II)' (1996) 2 Leg Theory 165, 166.

[7] Heidi M Hurd, 'The Normative Force of Consent' in Peter Schaber and Andreas Müller (eds), *Routledge Handbook on the Ethics of Consent* (Routledge 2018) 44, as cited in Ferzan (n 5) 405. See also Larry Alexander, 'The Ontology of Consent' (2014) 55 Anal Philos 102.

[8] Arto Laitinen, 'Normative Powers, Agency, and Time' in Carla Bagnoli (ed), *Time in Action: The Temporal Structure of Rational Agency and Practical Thought* (Routledge 2022) 59.

[9] Laitinen (n 8) 59.

to provide the tattoo. The moral reasons (to ϕ), however, supervene on the descriptive fact that the tattoo is likely to be valued and appreciated. B's consent to ϕ can then be relied upon by A only because there are independent, world-grounded reasons in favour of ϕ. In comparison, if B consents to ϕ* (an ugly tattoo) that will provide momentary joy to B and a lifetime of embarrassment or offence to others, then A does not have sufficient (world-grounded) reasons to provide the tattoo (A would *not* be acting contrary to B's consent—but would still be acting contrary to reasons).[10] The point of the contrast is that B's consent, in either scenario, is not transformative of ϕ/ϕ*; B's consent is merely reporting and anticipating descriptive features of the world. It is these descriptive features—'world-grounded reasons'—that provide A with reasons for action. We may defer to B's own assessment of B's interests when it comes to decisions about B's body, but it is still not B's will or choice that transforms the moral status of the act.

This doubt has a long pedigree. It questions whether 'the mere expression of an individual's will to alter her moral status can be effective in doing so in just the way she intends'.[11] It is 'most mysterious and incomprehensible' for Hume that a 'certain form of words, along with a certain intention, changes entirely the nature of an external object, and even of a human creature'.[12] This challenge from supervenience suggests that 'it should be the world that fixes normative reasons and oughts, not our thoughts'. Contrary to the attitudinal view, consent has moral force from world-grounded moral reasons—'reasons given to us by the way the world is'[13]—and not reasons that a person tries to will into existence. If we accept this scepticism (from the challenge of supervening wrongs), then we arrive at an epistemic view of consent, where the moral force of consent is reducible to the epistemic access it provides to world-grounded moral reasons. When another person consents to ϕ, we can take their consent to ϕ as an epistemically reliable proxy for their best interests, for the descriptive features of the world that make ϕ-ing good for the person.

The 'epistemic view' of consent, however, then attracts the following challenge:

> *Challenge from bare wrongdoing:* Acts can be wrongful without acting against world-grounded moral reasons.

[10] Kent Hurtig, 'Consent and Normativity' in Miguel Garcia-Godinez, Rachael Mellin and Raimo Tuomela (eds), *Social Ontology, Normativity and Law* (De Gruyter 2020) 106.

[11] Seana Valentine Shiffrin, 'Promising, Intimate Relationships, and Conventionalism' (2008) 117 Philos Rev 481, 481.

[12] David Hume, *A Treatise of Human Nature* (LA Selby-Bigge ed, PH Nidditch rev, 2nd edn, OUP 1978) 524.

[13] Ruth Chang, 'Do We Have Normative Powers?' (2020) 94 Proc Aristot Soc Suppl Vol 275, 298.

Consider two examples of bare wrongdoing. In one example, I might make a promise to you that 'I will get you a ticket to the concert'. In this scenario, you have no interest in attending the concert, yet in making such a promise, I have changed the normative situation between you and me; I now owe you a promissory obligation to get you a ticket. If I fail to perform the promise, then I have breached a promissory obligation that is, in terms of your own interests, entirely harmless and inconsequential. In the second example, you email me to invite me to 'use our pool while we are away during the summer'. Unbeknown to you, the email stays in your outbox, unsent. Presumptuously, I use your pool during the summer without your permission, in doing so committing a wrong (acting contrary to an obligation) that does no harm to your interests. In these scenarios, I have acted wrongfully without acting contrary to your will or acting against your world-grounded interests. Now, the moral weight or degree of wrongdoing will vary depending upon the world-grounded interests that have been set back, and when it comes to 'bare wrongs' the harm to you may be trivial. But the wrong (trivial or otherwise) originates from the breach of obligation (a broken promise of concert tickets/a pool used without permission).[14]

There is a risk that the above examples, and the challenge from bare wrongdoing itself, might only be leveraging our intuitions from our experiences of broken promises and presumptuous neighbours. The mere fact that we practise promise-making and permission-giving does not mean that these practices act upon, or give rise to, the moral reasons. The difficulty here is that the bare existences of these normative social practices—of promising, permitting, and forgiving—cannot themselves 'explain how an exercise of normative powers generates normative reasons'.[15] Nonetheless, if a social practice is 'all-things considered desirable',[16] or 'legitimate',[17] then we can explain how that practice can generate normative moral reasons. For instance, for Raz:

> a person's act is an exercise of a normative power if it brings about or prevents a normative change because it is, all things considered, desirable that that person should be able to bring the change about or prevent it by performing that act.[18]

[14] Joseph Raz, 'Is There a Reason to Keep a Promise?' in Gregory Klass, George Letsas and Prince Saprai (eds), *Philosophical Foundations of Contract Law* (OUP 2014) 76.

[15] Chang (n 13) 279.

[16] Chang (n 13) 279, citing Joseph Raz, 'Normative Powers (revised)' (2019) Oxf J Leg Stud Research Paper 36/2019 <https://ssrn.com/abstract=3379368> accessed 1 December 2024.

[17] Chang (n 13) 279, citing Scott Shapiro, 'Law, Plans, and Practical Reason' (2002) 8 Leg Theory 387.

[18] Raz, 'Normative Powers (revised)' (n 16) 2.

To understand how a normative practice can generate moral reasons, we need to consider *why* the practices of promise-marking, permission-giving, and forgiving might be worthwhile and desirable. These normative powers are best understood as social tools for building (or ending) relationships. It is difficult to contemplate a morally sufficient or morally adequate life without the exercise of normative powers that facilitate interactions with others. Without normative powers, we would have no ability to share a physical space whilst retaining control of it, we would be unable to retain decision-making authority over our body whilst we physically interact with another person, we would have no reason to declare our plans or intentions nor any reasons to rely on anyone else's plans, and we would be forced to hold on to resentment beyond its expiry date and to live in the shadow of all of our wrongdoing. A world without normative powers would be an isolating and asocial world. In perfectionist terms, we would have an inadequate range of options through which to live a morally adequate life. As Shiffrin explains, 'the realization of our central autonomous capacities requires a diverse and rich set of meaningful options'.[19] In this sense, normative powers represent the moral tools that we need to live morally worthwhile lives, which nonetheless require us to 'have a certain social reality'[20]—a concretised and shared understanding of the normative phenomena that we encounter in our relational lives.

The notion of practice-grounded moral reasons therefore relies on a distinction between *valuable* or *desirable* normative social practices (that generate reasons) and *valueless* or *undesirable* ones (that do not). This requires an evaluation of the practice. For example, consider a normative social practice (ie a social practice that pertains to normative phenomena) where 'A and B are friends, and A cannot date B's ex-boyfriend without B's permission'. The requirement of B's permission is determined, arguably, by a worthwhile social practice that prioritises solidarity between friends over romantic pursuits. Or, it is, arguably, an unnecessarily constraining practice that devalues individual choice and independence. The point is that it turns on our moral appraisal of the practice: whether, on Raz's criterion, it is 'all things considered, desirable that B should be able to bring the change' in what A can and cannot do with regards to A's social life. If the practice is a worthwhile one, then the requirement of B's permission is predicated upon practice-grounded moral reasons. It may be better—all things considered—for persons to prioritise their close friendships over romance (or it might not). If the conventional practice has

[19] Shiffrin (n 11) 502, citing Joseph Raz, *The Morality of Freedom* (OUP 1986) 369ff.
[20] David Owens, *Shaping the Normative Landscape* (OUP 2012) 9–10.

value, then its value is ultimately grounded in what is worthwhile, or desirable, in moral terms.

The moral significance of normative powers (of consent, promise making, and forgiveness) can then be understood as belonging to a set of social tools that are 'at the outset, morally discretionary', that are 'activated by the happenstance [of] social convention',[21] and that can nonetheless generate or enable moral reasons. Imperfect but still worthwhile practices will still generate or enable reasons.

This 'conventional' account of the normative power of consent attracts one final challenge. Whilst breaching obligations owed to another person can erode a valuable social practice, it is also a wrong committed against the other person. A false promise, a breach of trust or confidentiality, or acting without permission or consent all demonstrate a disrespect for the person to whom the obligation is owed, on the basis that the person could never agree to be misled, chose to disclose information in circumstances of trust and confidence, or did not agree to the act that required permission. As I have explained in Essay 1, wrongfulness of a nonconsensual interaction can only be explained with reference to the disrespect for the person (the instrumental use of the body), where the experiential harms (the phenomenology) aggravate the wrong. We can now add that a concern for sustaining a conventional practice is a trivial concern in comparison to will-grounded and world-grounded concerns. The challenge for the conventional account of consent is:

> *Challenge from pure wrongdoing:* Where an act requires permission and is performed without permission, the wrong is the disrespect of the person (independently of the value of the practice).

To respond to this challenge, we need to return to where we started: the transformative power of the consenting attitude. This is because we still need to account for how a *change* in a normative situation—the generation, enabling, or disabling of reasons—is possible (without a change in the descriptive situation). The change in the normative situation is predicated upon a 'will-grounded reason',[22] where a person will's generated, enabled, or disabled a moral reason. The 'magic' here is more metaphysical than moral. It is this 'freedom to have an active role in determining the reasons we have' that is 'the hallmark of the rational agency that underwrites robust normative powers'.[23] By exercising these

21 Shiffrin (n 11) 483.
22 Chang (n 13) 294.
23 Chang (n 13) 298.

normative powers, 'we have a fundamental say in determining how we should live'.[24] Whilst we have the capacity to commit, to choose, or to will normative phenomena into (or out of) existence, this 'willing' . . . is not itself a choice governed by reasons. It is just something we do.'[25] But to deny a person this capacity (their capacity for choice) is to deny their status as a *person*.

That said, whilst willing is 'just something we do', it is *not* 'something that we do independently'. Agency, choice, or the expression of a will, in itself, cannot determine the obligations that apply to oneself (or another person). To consent, to promise, and to forgive are all interpersonal acts that then change the normative relationship between two people (rights, wrongs, and obligations that exist between two people). These 'normative phenomena'—which bind people together—cannot be unilaterally *willed* into existence (or out of existence) or *created* (or erased) by will-grounded reasons alone. Normative phenomena rely upon normative social practice to curate rights, wrongs, and obligations that exist between two people. Nonetheless, a normative change can be *triggered* by the exercise of the will. In this way:

> *which* reasons you generate by exercising a normative power is not up to you; your reasons are determined by the normative ['conventional'] principle that explains how your willing can generate reasons. You get to choose which principle to trigger, and thus, indirectly, which reasons you generate.[26]

We can now return to the three sets of moral reasons. Willing something into existence—by triggering a conventional practice—does generate or transform a reason. Here, the exercise of the will (choice) explains the change in the normative relationship. The normative phenomenon itself (such as how promises are made, how permission is given, when forgiveness can be expressed, and so on) is determined by social or conventional practices (where the practice is morally worthwhile). Finally, the weight of the normative phenomenon is determined by world-grounded reasons, where a promisee may have relied upon the promise to their detriment, where acting without permission is particularly harmful, or where forgiveness removes burdensome remedial obligations. We need, therefore, all three views of the moral force of consent: the attitudinal view explains how 'will-grounded reasons' are the catalyst for change, the conventional view explains how normative social practices that determine

[24] Chang (n 13) 298.
[25] Chang (n 13) 298.
[26] Chang (n 13) 282.

the normative phenomena can be triggered by will, and the epistemic view explains how acting contrary to these norms can be contrary to 'world-grounded' morals reasons that add weight to the wrongdoing. As we will now turn to consider, it is the normative moral reasons that have the capacity to change, and it is this change over time that the excuse ('but that used to be okay') is predicated upon.

4.3

With these three sets of moral reasons in place, let us now return to the putative shift in moral reasons. The implication from the discussion so far that we will need to latch on to is that

(a) if social practices are capable of generating, enabling, or disabling moral reasons and
(b) if social practices are capable of change over time, then
(c) it is possible for a practice to generate, enable, or disable moral reasons (*now*) that previously did not form part of the moral situation (*then*)
(d) to the extent that a person (*then*) can claim to be ignorant of the moral reasons that did not form part of the moral situation.

The general contention in this section is that our *then/now* scenarios are illustrative of the implications in (c) and (d).

Returning to these scenarios will also afford us the opportunity to encounter a general principle of responsibility. As we will explore in the next section, the general principle suggests that a person can only be held responsible for acting against moral reasons when the person is aware that the moral reasons apply to their moral situation. If this is so, then a person cannot be held to account for moral reasons that previously did not form part of the moral situation in which they acted. In this section, I will introduce the intuition that the principle of responsibility is exculpatory for historical cases but does not apply to contemporary wrongdoing.

This intuition relies upon the distinction between historical and contemporary cases. The claim '[b]ut that used to be okay!' might be asserted in two different contexts. One is where the interaction between A and B occurred in the past, and—according to A's claim—the norms (*then*) permitted the interaction, thereby excusing the wrongdoing ('historical cases'). The other context is where the interaction is a contemporary event, and the claim ('but that used to be okay') is an assertion that A acted on a (genuinely held, but false) belief—based on past norms—that the interaction was permissible ('contemporary cases').

Let us therefore return to those scenarios. Recall that in *capacity (now and then)*, Adult A (a twenty-one-year-old) had sex with Young Person B (a sixteen-year-old). Michelle Madden Dempsey explains that the sex, *now*, would be 'wrong according to contemporary wrongfulness norms'.[27] Yet, if, back *then*, 'sixteen-year-olds were . . . regarded as having sufficient maturity for a range of practices involving the giving of consent', then 'we may have a case where the wrongfulness norms have shifted'.[28] This may be because we, *now*, have a better understanding of the cognitive and emotional capacities of sixteen-year-olds, and the impact that age differentials can have on decision-making in an intimate context, that is reflected in a norm that renders the sex (*now*) to be wrongful.

Back *then*, in comparison, Adult A had not acted contrary to the norm, since (back *then*) the normative practice was such that Young Person B had capacity to consent to sex with Adult A. Back *then*, B's capacity was a practice-grounded reason for A to take her consent as permitting him to act on reasons (which he would otherwise be precluded from acting on)—except we know *now* that it is a practice-grounded reason that is not, all things considered, worthwhile or desirable. Hence, there has been a shift in the normative practice, and the moral reasons that the practice generates have changed.

Note that these practice-grounded reasons form only part of the moral situation. The remaining features of the moral situation remain constant between *now* and *then*. First, in both instances (*now* and *then*), Young Person B willed the sex, and sought to trigger a norm where her consent permitted the interaction. The implication being that B cannot *will* out of existence the norm that now renders her expression of consent to be non-permission-giving. She cannot consent to her consent being valid. Not *then*, and not *now*. Second, in both instances, the descriptive features of the world—how the sex impacted upon B's interests—remained the same. To that end, the suggestion that A did not act wrongfully (contrary to a norm) in *capacity (then)* does not imply that A did not harm B in *capacity (then)*.

It is hard not to maintain some attention towards the harm that Adult A may have caused Young Person B. Recall the distinction between blame and accountability drawn in Essay 3. If we are interested in blaming Adult A for

[27] Dempsey (n 1) 352–53.
[28] Dempsey (n 1) 353.

the *harms* that they have caused Young Person B—in fully accounting for the 'debit' in his 'ledger'[29]—then the harms caused by Adult A remain in our moral frame. In contrast, to hold a person accountable (I have suggested) relies upon finding the relevant normative phenomena to latch onto.[30] To that end, the claim 'but that used to be okay', as a claim about accountability and normative phenomena, has limited moral relevance. 'It may have been permissible', we might want to say in retort, 'but it was harmful'. If, however, we are interested in holding people accountable for failing to respond to normative phenomena (the obligations we owe, the rights we hold, and the wrongs we need to remedy), then the shift in norms, and the claimed ignorance of the reasons that the norms generate, makes the excuse 'but that used to be okay' a plausible way of excusing wrongs. It is enough here to note here that the excuse narrows our attention to normative phenomena (a narrowing that we sometimes want to resist). For some (such as those who are interested in the full moral ledger), the narrowing is myopic; for others (who are interested in moral and legal obligations), the narrowing is unproblematic.

If we can narrow our attention to norms and obligations, then the excuse can invoke the principle that a person can be blameworthy for acting contrary to (normative) moral reasons only if they were aware of the (normative) moral reasons. When we view the scenarios as historical cases, we can begin to appreciate how the principle of responsibility can be exculpatory. In *capacity (then)*, the normative practice (*then*) provided that Young Person B had capacity, and B's capacity was a practice-grounded reason for Adult A to take Young Person B's consent as permitting Adult A to act on reasons (that would be otherwise excluded).

Similarly, in *power (then)*, there was no normative practice that prohibited Professor A from having a sexual relationship with Graduate Student B, thereby no practice-grounded reasons against Professor A engaging in the relationship. There were no will-grounded reasons against the relationship, only world-grounded reasons against the relationship. Whilst Professor A cannot deny these harms, he could also plead an unawareness of these harms (world-grounded reasons) and engage the same exculpatory principle.

As for *communication (then)*, if A was to be mistaken as to B's consenting attitude, 'the reasonableness of his mistaken belief turns on whether, in each social context, people in [B]'s position typically do communicate consent in that way'.[31] To put it into the scheme of this essay, A's claim to be unaware of a

[29] Michael J Zimmerman, *An Essay on Moral Responsibility* (Rowman and Littlefield 1988) 38.
[30] Stephen L Darwall, 'What Are Moral Reasons?' (The Amherst Lecture in Philosophy, 2017) 7.
[31] Dempsey (n 1) 357.

will-grounded moral reason (that B did not consent) relies upon a practice-based reason to take silence and the absence of objection as an expression of consent. The excuse might work if we assume that, back *then*, if anyone in B's position sought to consent to sex, B merely needed to allow A's sexual advances in order to trigger the consent. Given the assumption, it is possible that 'an honest and correct understanding of how people actually communicated consent in the past could ground a slightly modified defense' that 'it used to be okay'.[32]

The further context of contemporary wrongdoing might strike us as significantly different. Here the excuse is doing different work, suggesting that A cannot be blameworthy on the basis that he was not aware of the practice-grounded reasons that are generated by a contemporary social practice. The excuse ('but that used to be okay') in this context ought to be met with scepticism.

Consider, for example, the contemporary wrongdoing in *power (now)*. We would, *now*, consider the sex between Professor A and Graduate Student B to be wrongful (contrary to a norm). The contemporary norm generates moral reasons for Professor A not to engage in a sexual relationship with Graduate Student B. There may be sufficient reasons for why the new norm is a worthwhile social practice. Graduate students interact with their professors within an institution that is structured towards their (the professors') authority, along with an in-built admiration and deference we afford to those who excel at our chosen discipline. In some instances (from which the norm generalises to govern all instances), a graduate student may pursue a sexual relationship with a professor that is motivated (in part) by the institutionalised admiration and deference for the professor. When it comes to her personal life, it may not be in the graduate student's interests to act on the institution-given admiration for, and deference to, the professor. Robin West expresses concern for the graduate student's role within the relationship, and within the institution, in the following way:

> [H]ot desired sex between a graduate student and professor might lock a girl into first an eroticized, but eventually a dreary . . . role. Rather than become a teacher, scholar, . . . that graduate student who was so taken by her teacher might instead become a lover . . . which might be just great, or it might ultimately prove to be tedious, boring, unchallenging, and not hot at all.[33]

[32] Dempsey (n 1) 358.

[33] Robin West, 'Sex, Law and Consent' in Franklin Miller and Alan Wertheimer (eds), *The Ethics of Consent: Theory and Practice* (OUP 2009) 237.

In this way, West explains, the sex 'might be eventually harmful over the long haul . . . even if fully desired by both parties'.[34] If the sex is consensual, the 'harmful sex is clearly not rape. If the sex is welcome it is not sexual harassment either'.[35] It is, nonetheless, contrary to a norm that has been introduced to the moral situation. That being said, only worthwhile normative practices generate moral reasons (recall the above discussion of the *ex-boyfriend rule*). Professor A might *deny* the wrongdoing by denying the premise that the contemporary normative practice generates reasons against the relationship.

If, however, A acknowledges the practice-grounded reasons, the response—'but that used to be okay'—may still excuse the wrongdoing. It can be exculpatory if Professor A was unaware of the norm and the reasons it generates. But even if Professor A's lack of awareness was genuine, we might wonder how Professor A managed to be unaware of the changes in his moral situation. As we shall see in the next section, if Professor A *mismanaged* his moral outlook in *power (now)*, then the claim 'but that used to be okay' becomes hollow, devoid of any exculpatory reasons. The same can be true of *capacity (now)*; if A can be blamed for relying on outdated capacity norms, then we may be able to sustain our moral criticism of the relationship even when A was unaware of contemporary capacity norms. Equally, with regard to *communication (now)*, if A is to claim a belief in consent on the capacity of outdated normative practices, then for A to be excused, A's belief cannot be the result of his failure to attend to communicative practices.

4.4

In this section we will consider an exception to a general principle. As we have just seen, the moral relevance of the claim 'but that used to be okay' relies upon a general principle of responsibility: that 'no rational person can be faulted for failing to respond to a reason he is unaware applies to his conduct'.[36] This is on the basis that

> judgments of moral responsibility should require an internal assessment of the reason-responsiveness of agents, that is, should proceed from the subjective perspective of the agents themselves.[37]

[34] West (n 33) 237.
[35] West (n 33) 237.
[36] Husak (n 3) 152.
[37] Husak (n 3) 154.

The general principle is exculpatory; when it applies, it works to excuse wrongful behaviour. But as we have also encountered in the previous section, we want to carve out an exception to the general principle, to account for some circumstances where a person may be morally responsible for behaviour even when they were unaware of the moral reasons that they acted contrary to. For example, in response to *capacity (now)*, *power (now)*, and *communication (now)*, we might want to carve out a 'wilful ignorance' exception, where a person might suspect the truth of a moral proposition (p) but he nonetheless

> (wilful ignorance) fails to pursue reliable, quick, and ordinary measures that would enable him to learn the truth of p, and . . . has a conscious desire to remain ignorant of p in order to avoid blame or liability in the event the truth emerges.[38]

In such instances of wilful ignorance, the general exculpatory principle is displaced, and the person is considered responsible for acting contrary to the moral proposition that they were ignorant of. In Husak's example, a person who accepts payment to drive a car across an international border without checking the contents of the car ought to be criminally responsible for importing the illegal drugs contained in the car, because his ignorance was 'wilful' (in the above sense) and therefore provides no excuse. Given the right additional facts, *capacity (now)*, *power (now)*, and *communication (now)* might also amount to instances of wilful ignorance. The point, for now, is that the exception (here, 'wilful ignorance') to the general exculpatory principle is *inculpatory*; it works to allocate responsibility to a person for conduct that otherwise would be covered by the exculpatory principle of responsibility.

Husak's wilful ignorance exception is a narrow one. Having a 'conscious desire to remain ignorant' is just one way in which an exception to the general exculpatory principle can be carved out. We should therefore consider, as our starting point, a more general exception:

> *Culpable ignorance*: A person is responsible for acting contrary to moral reasons (that they were unaware applied to their moral situation) only if (and because) the person is culpable for the ignorance from which he acted.

As a preliminary matter, we also need to consider what is inculpatory about the inculpatory exception. In other words, we need to identify what we are holding

[38] Husak (n 3) 220.

a person responsible for when we carve out an exception to a general exculpatory principle. Consider three claims about responsibility, where the first is a false claim:

1. Culpability *despite* ignorance: A person is culpable for the wrongful conduct done whilst being ignorant.[39]
2. Culpability *for* ignorance: A person is culpable for being ignorant of what was wrongful about their conduct.
3. Culpability *through* ignorance: A person is culpable for the wrongful conduct whilst being ignorant 'only in virtue of being blameworthy for the ignorance'.[40]

The first claim is false because it is squarely contrary to the general exculpatory principle. The second claim is consistent with general exculpatory principle, but the claim implies a much lesser form of responsibility. On the 'culpability *for* ignorance' account, a person's wrongful action (coupled with an unawareness of the moral reason they acted contrary to) is not, itself, the basis of responsibility. We can instead hold a person responsible for the behaviour that resulted in their unawareness of their moral situation. They are then responsible (only) for their false moral belief (in the permissibility of their actions). In this (lesser) way, a person is responsible *for* being ignorant of the reasons they acted contrary to (but not responsible for acting contrary to them).

It is the third claim that should interest us here. So far, the inculpatory exception provides that if the exception applies, then we might hold A responsible for behaviour that was contrary to the reasons that applied to his moral situation. The third claim (culpability *through* ignorance) provides that the responsibility is *derivative*, in the sense that the responsibility for the original wrong is derived from the blameworthy behaviour that rendered the person ignorant of the applicable moral reasons.[41] The same point can be made (with a different direction of travel): a person can be responsible for acting against reasons, and the accompanying blameworthy ignorance of moral reasons works *to sustain* their responsibility for their actions, only if (and because) they are culpable for the ignorance *from* which they act. On either account, the wrongdoer is nonetheless connected to the original wrongdoing *through* their culpable ignorance, and not merely culpable *for* being ignorant.

[39] Elizabeth Harman, 'Does Moral Ignorance Exculpate?' (2011) 24 Ratio 443, 445.
[40] Harman (n 39) 445.
[41] Gideon Rosen, 'Skepticism about Moral Responsibility' (2004) 18 Philos Perspect 295, 300.

The distinction between the second (culpability *for* ignorance) and third (culpability *through* ignorance) claims is important, as it generates a weak or strong basis of responsibility. For instance, in terms of *capacity (now)*, if the exception concerns culpability *through* ignorance, then A can be viewed as responsible for having sex with B whilst B lacked the capacity to consent (since the failure to attend to capacity norms sustains A's culpability). This represents a significant wrong that rightfully attracts significant criticism and censure. If, however, the exception concerns culpability *for* ignorance, then A can be viewed as blameworthy for his failure to attend to contemporary capacity norms. The criticism here is directed towards a person for being ignorant. These are distinct bases of criticism and blame, which are channelled through different accounts of the relationship between ignorance and responsibility.

We ultimately do not need to choose between the two iterations of the inculpability exception (but we will return to the distinction in subsequent essays). To the extent that the claim ('but that used to be okay') is asserted as an excuse for the wrongful behaviour, then we ought to focus here on culpability *from* ignorance (whilst noting that an argument for culpability *for* ignorance remains available). But in focusing on responsibility for the wrongdoing (culpability *from* ignorance), we raise the stakes of the game. If the inculpatory exception is going to *sustain* A's responsibility for the wrongful behaviour, even when A was unaware of the moral reasons that render the behaviour wrongful, then we would expect to find some moral failing in a person's practical reasoning (other than being aware of the reasons that they are acting contrary to). I will return to this point again soon.

Apart from our initial consideration of 'wilful ignorance' as an example of an inculpatory exception, what is missing from the discussion so far is the content of the inculpatory exception itself. There are different ways of formulating the exception. They vary in terms of what needs to be satisfied before we can say that a person is culpable for acting contrary to moral reasons even when they were unaware the reasons applied to the moral situation. In other words, they vary in terms of how a person can be blameworthy for acting on an (honestly held but) false moral belief in the permissibility of their conduct. I will briefly survey here three tests—procedural failings, moral mismanagement, and substantive failings. We can consider these three tests in light of the intuition that A ought to be held responsible for the contemporary wrong (in *capacity (now)*, *power (now)*, and *communication (now)*) even when A was acting on a false moral belief in the permissibility of his conduct.

On Gideon Rosen's account of moral responsibility, a person is responsible for acting on a false moral belief only if he has behaved in ways that constitute a violation of his *procedural epistemic obligations* (and this behaviour resulted in his acting on a false moral belief).[42] It follows from this proceduralist formulation that a person may be culpable for failing to '*do*... certain things: to ask certain questions, to take careful notes, to stop and think, to focus one's attention in a certain direction'.[43] On this standard, for instance, an ancient slaveholder (when slaves were those who were captured in battle) is not culpable for his false belief in the permissibility of slavery since the ancient slaveholder 'doesn't ignore arguments against slavery: none are offered to him'.[44] A procedural epistemic obligation is not, Rosen explains, an obligation 'to know or believe this or that'; it is, instead, 'an obligation to *take steps* to ensure that when the time comes to act, one will know what one ought to know'.[45] Hence, one standard for the inculpatory exception suggests:

> *Procedural epistemic failings*: A person is blameworthy for acting contrary to reasons that they were unaware applied to their moral situation where their unawareness is a result of a failure to perform their procedural epistemic obligations to understand their moral situation.

We can accept that, to the extent that it is an obligation, a failure to perform a *procedural epistemic obligation* can be a source of responsibility. A failure to *take the rights steps* can, in this way, be blameworthy in the lesser sense, where the blameworthiness attaches to the ignorance or unawareness itself. However, to sustain (or derive) culpability for the original wrongdoing itself through procedural failures renders (what lawyers might call) a 'strict' form of culpability. This is where a person is culpable for their (two-fold) conduct—the initial conduct plus the procedural failing—without having a blameworthy attitude or morally problematic orientation towards the world. To sustain culpability for the wrongdoing, we need some kind of failing in a person's practical reasoning about the world—their attitude towards their moral circumstances—and not merely procedurally incomplete conduct. Otherwise, without some kind of failing in a person's practical reasoning, the inculpatory exception cannot properly engage with, and carve out an exception to, the general exculpatory principle that is based on the 'subjective perspective of the agents themselves'.[46]

[42] Rosen, 'Skepticism about Moral Responsibility' (n 41) 301–03.
[43] Rosen, 'Skepticism about Moral Responsibility' (n 41) 301.
[44] Harman (n 39) 447; Gideon Rosen, 'Culpability and Ignorance' (2003) 103 Proc Aristot Soc 61, 64–66.
[45] Rosen, 'Skepticism about Moral Responsibility' (n 41) 301.
[46] Husak (n 3) 154.

Procedural failings can nonetheless be a symptom of the disease, where the disease (and the source of responsibility) represents a moral failing to orientate oneself properly towards moral reasons. To explain, let me try to first separate the symptom from the disease. We can be critical of a person acting on an (honestly held but) false moral belief even when they have completed the procedural checklist. For instance, a business owner might close a business with devastating effects on the employees of the business. He might deliberate on business ethics and discuss his business practices with his critics but nonetheless honestly believe (the false moral belief) 'that by pursuing what is in the best interest of his shareholders, he is playing a valuable role in the economy'.[47] For Rosen, the business owner cannot be blameworthy because he satisfies his procedural epistemic obligations and nonetheless arrived at a false moral belief.[48] As FitzPatrick explains, the false moral belief may be the result of a moral attitude or outlook, perhaps a myopic corporate dogmatism or self-interest in the outcome, that makes the business owner unresponsive to reasons. Perhaps the business owner 'never . . . really grasped the importance of putting oneself in others' shoes or considering an impartial perspective in the course of deliberation'.[49] It follows that the business owner 'is not completely amoral, but his reflection is stunted in certain ways'.[50] The unresponsiveness of the business owner, like the overriding loyalty of a Mafia-style family member, and the unshakeable faith of a religious acolyte, can represent an unwillingness to be open to 'truth- and value-related considerations' that we expect of persons.[51] For Montmarquet, when a person is 'not open to this', that person 'may be blameworthy precisely for that failure'.[52] Where the business owner mismanages his moral beliefs, by having a stunted or maladjusted moral outlook, he can be considered responsible for acting contrary to reasons that he was unaware applied to him, where the unawareness of the reasons follows from the mismanagement.

A mismanaged moral outlook can often explain why a person failed in their procedural epistemic obligations, *and* then explain why the mismanaged moral outlook can sustain the culpability for the original wrongdoing. There are a range of moral failings and vices, such as 'overconfidence, arrogance, dismissiveness, laziness, dogmatism, incuriosity, self-indulgence, contempt, and

[47] Harman (n 39) 457.
[48] Rosen, 'Skepticism about Moral Responsibility' (n 41) 308.
[49] William J FitzPatrick, 'Moral Responsibility and Normative Ignorance: Answering a New Skeptical Challenge' (2008) 118 Ethics 589, 601.
[50] FitzPatrick (n 49) 601.
[51] James Montmarquet, 'Zimmerman on Culpable Ignorance' (1999) 109 Ethics 842, 845.
[52] Montmarquet (n 51) 845.

so on'.[53] For example, a person may be motivated to avoid information, bypass critical reflection, or give inadequate attention to others' viewpoints because the person benefits from the false moral belief that their actions are permissible. Here, the responsibility attaches to the self-interest that motivated the procedural failure. This might explain why Husak builds both procedural failings and a blameworthy attitude into his 'wilful ignorance' exception. The source of moral responsibility, I suggest, nonetheless lies at the blameworthy attitude or orientation (the 'conscious desire to remain ignorant' of a relevant moral proposition), and the failure to discharge the procedural epistemic obligations (the 'reliable, quick, and ordinary measures that would enable him to learn' the relevant moral proposition) evidences the blameworthy attitude.

An account of the inculpatory exception that follows from this suggests:

> *Moral mismanagement*: A person is blameworthy for acting contrary to reasons that they were unaware applied to their moral situation where their unawareness is a result of the mismanagement of their moral outlook.

If so, then this account can affirm the *that was then, this is now* intuition. When it comes to historical cases, if A acted on a false moral belief (that B had capacity, he was in a relationship of equality with B, that B was communicating consent), where there was no normative social practice to falsify that moral belief, nor any steps that could have been taken to falsify the belief, then the general exculpatory principles applies (and A cannot be blamed for acting contrary to reasons that he was unaware applied to his moral situation).

When it comes to contemporary cases in *capacity*, *power*, and *communication*, even if A acted on a false moral belief, consideration of contemporary social practices could have counteracted that belief, and it is easy to speculate that there would have been steps that A could have taken to learn of the moral reasons he acted contrary to. More importantly, it is also easy to speculate that A may have been wilfully blind to concerns of capacity, power imbalance, and the communication of consent; A may have been too self-interested, arrogant, or self-entitled to attend to these moral reasons that have (now) a concretised social reality; or A may have otherwise discounted the (now) concretised moral reasons. The point is that the moral mismanagement view of the inculpatory exception aligns with the intuition that the general exculpatory principle applies to historical cases of wrongdoing (*then*) but does not apply to contemporary cases of wrongdoing (*now*).

[53] FitzPatrick (n 49) 605.

We might, however, want to resist, rather than affirm, the intuition. We can resist the intuition, and resist the application of the general exculpatory principle to historical cases, if we carve out a broader inculpatory exception to the general principle. Consider how Elizabeth Harmon offers a much broader inculpatory standard. According to Harmon:

> *Substantive failings*: 'one can be blameworthy for having false moral beliefs although one has not been in any way irresponsible in the management of one's opinion ... [where] one has violated some moral norms that apply to *beliefs* themselves, not the management of one's beliefs'.[54]

Harmon grounds this standard in an account of blameworthiness, where 'an action is blameworthy just in case the action resulted from the agent's caring inadequately about what is morally significant'.[55] The obligation here is a strict one, 'to believe the moral truth'.[56] The implication being that a person who discharged their procedural obligations (to ask the right questions, and so on) and was not informed by a mismanaged evaluative attitude (motivated ignorance, arrogance, and dogmatism), and was unaware of the moral reasons that they acted contrary to, is still culpable for their wrongdoing. In the same way that a '1950's American father who doesn't save to send his daughter to college but does save to send his sons' and has an 'implicit moral belief that his actions are permissible' is still not justified in his false moral belief;[57] the false moral belief in historical cases will also fail to excuse the wrongdoing in *capacity (then)*, *power (then)*, and *communication (then)*. Back *then*, Adult A did not adequately care about Young Person B's capacity to evaluate her own interests; back *then*, Professor A did not adequately attend to B's personal and professional interests; and back *then*, A did not adequately care about how B expressed her consent to sex. The moral relevance of the claim 'but that used to be okay' dissolves entirely.

We return, again, to the same siren song, if we can consider a person blameworthy in light of the full array of moral reasons they acted contrary to, and then sustain our criticism on the basis of inadequate care about what is morally significant. This is, again, the full moral ledger view. And again, on the full moral ledger view, the claim 'but that used to be okay' has much less relevance. On the assumption, however, that the claim ('but that used to be okay') has the

[54] Harman (n 39) 459.
[55] Harman (n 39) 460.
[56] Harman (n 39) 459.
[57] Harman (n 39) 457.

potential scope to excuse wrongdoing (and avoid accountability), then we can narrow our focus on the normative phenomena and the practice-grounded reasons that a person may be aware or unaware that they are acting contrary to. Given the narrow focus on wrongdoing—and armed with the moral mismanagement version of the inculpatory exception—we can then accept that the general exculpatory principle applies to historical cases, without having to accept that the exculpatory principle also applies to contemporary cases of assertions of ignorance.

4.5

In the foreground of the discussion here is an attempt to make sense of an excuse for wrongdoing that takes the casual form 'but that used to be okay'. I have suggested here that whilst the claim 'but that used to be okay' can excuse wrongdoing, it is a *contingent*, *limited*, and *qualified* excuse. It is *contingent* upon a change in a normative social practice, it is *limited* to accountability for wrongdoing, and it is *qualified* by the inculpatory exception to the general exculpatory principle. These are significant limitations on the scope and relevance of the excuse, and illustrate how it should be meet with scepticism and never accepted uncritically. As I have sought to illustrate here, for anyone who asserts the claim, the burden is on them to show a genuine shift in normative practice, to show that their ignorance or unawareness of the moral situation was not a result of their own mismanaged moral outlook, and to accept that they may have nonetheless acted harmfully.

In the background of the discussion has been the development of our understanding of responsibility. From the previous essay, I have carried over the assumption that to rely on a concept of accountability (or relational responsibility), we need to develop an understanding of the normative phenomena of 'obligation, duty, right, and wrong' that can ground our reasons in to hold another person to account for their wrongdoing. In this essay, I have argued that any such normative phenomenon (right, wrong, and obligation) needs to be augmented in a social reality. The claim here has been that worthwhile social practices generate normative phenomena (rights, wrongs, and obligations) that embody practice-grounded moral reasons. What makes those practices worthwhile may be built around will-grounded or world-grounded reasons, but a source of wrongdoing is located in acting contrary to a norm (infringing a right or neglecting an obligation). The further aspect of responsibility under consideration here has been the assumption that responsibility requires an awareness of the reasons that a person is acting contrary to. As we encountered here, an honestly held but false belief in the permission may be generally exculpatory. And yet, the instinct has been to carve out an inculpatory exception to the general principle. I have contended here that where the ignorance of reasons is the product of a person's mismanagement of their moral outlook, the ignorance of their wrongdoing does not sever their culpability for their wrongdoing.

In the essays that follow, we return to these background ideas. First, in the next essay, we will encounter the claim that sex, itself, is a *pro tanto* wrong (contrary to a *pro tanto* obligation). The forthcoming contention is that it is a worthwhile social practice to treat consent as being the waiver of a general obligation not to apply force to a person's body. We will encounter the second background idea in Essay 8, where I will argue that a person's mismanaged moral outlook towards the 'alterity' of another person can sustain their culpability for being mistaken as to the consent of the other person.

5

General Reasons Not to Have Sex

5.1

'Those who think that, in the law of rape, sexual intercourse *tout court* should be regarded as the real offence and consent as the defence had best', according to John Gardner, 'be able to identify a general reason not to have sexual intercourse, such that one needs a defeating reason in favour before one should engage in it'.[1] This essay takes up this challenge. I will argue here that there are general reasons not to engage in penetrative sex. If there are such reasons, and if a qualifying criterion for the elements of a criminal offence is that the conduct is generally wrong, then I am able to refute the predominant justification for the current drafting of the crimes of rape[2] and assault by penetration.[3] The implication here is that for such crimes,[4] the provision of consent ought to be available as a justificatory defence rather than the absence of consent being an element of the offence.

There are two theses in contention here. The first is a moral claim associated with the seminal work of Michelle Madden Dempsey and Jonathan Herring. This is the

> *Pro tanto* moral wrong thesis: Penetrative sex is a moral wrong that calls for an explanation.

In accepting one aspect of the Dempsey and Herring moral thesis, I construct here a further claim, one about the criminal law:

> *Pro tanto* legal wrong thesis: Penetrative sex is a criminal wrong that requires a justification or excuse.

[1] John Gardner, 'Fletcher on Offences and Defences' (2003) 39 Tulsa L Rev 817, 820.
[2] Sexual Offences Act 2003, s 1.
[3] Sexual Offences Act 2003, s 2.
[4] Perhaps also for sexual assault (Sexual Offences Act 2003, s 3) if we were to broaden the analysis beyond penetrative acts.

Sex and Self-Ownership. Jesse Wall, Oxford University Press. © Jesse Wall 2025.
DOI: 10.1093/9780191987809.003.0005

My construction of the *pro tanto* legal wrong thesis depends on three main claims that are substantiated in this essay. These claims are:

1. the elements of an offence represent an act that is *pro tanto* wrongful in all instances;
2. a general feature of penetrative sex is the application of force to a person's body; and
3. the application of force to a person's body is wrongful insofar as it is contrary to a person's right to self-ownership.

The first claim (which we encounter at 5.2) relies upon the Campbell–Gardner criterion for the offence–defence distinction. According to this criterion, the difference between the elements of an offence and the elements of a justificatory (or exculpatory) defence is based upon the difference between general reasons against performing an act and specified reasons in favour of performing the act.

The second claim is developed out of engagement with the *pro tanto* moral wrong thesis (at 5.3). Whilst aspects of the Dempsey and Herring thesis struggle to capture the generality of reasons that the Campbell–Gardner criterion demands, I nonetheless adopt their claim that a general feature of penetrative sex is the application of force to a person's body (such as force to the vagina or anus). This claim explains how the application of force to a person's body is contrary to the right of self-ownership. The implication is that there are general reasons not to engage in penetrative sex on the basis that the application of force that is required to achieve penetration is an infringement of a person's rights of self-ownership.

The third main claim concerns the right to self-ownership itself. The right to self-ownership is a means of respecting the non-use value of each person. At 5.4, I argue that Stephen Shute and John Gardner, who were concerned with the non-use value of each person, nonetheless mischaracterise the right to self-ownership (when they dismiss the infringement of the right to self-ownership as an explanation for the wrongfulness of rape).[5] I contend here that protecting the right to self-ownership, and the exclusionary boundary that it draws around the body, is a worthwhile conventional practice that can generate general reasons against penetrative sex.

[5] Stephen Shute and John Gardner, 'The Wrongness of Rape' in John Gardner (ed), *Offences and Defences: Selected Essays in the Philosophy of Criminal Law* (OUP 2007).

The development of these three claims reveals the choice between two conventional practices. If there are *no* general reasons not to engage in penetrative sex, then we can presume that a person exercises their rights of control over their body in favour of sexual activity, unless they object to the use (the 'no means no' convention). If there *are* general reasons not to engage in penetrative sex, then there is an obligation not to touch or apply force to another person's body, unless the person waives the obligation (the 'yes means yes' convention). The *pro tanto* legal wrong thesis amounts to the claim that the criminal law ought to adopt the 'yes means yes' convention. I then conclude (at 5.5) by responding to five of the main objections to the *pro tanto* legal wrong thesis.

5.2

To help us think about consent and the distinction between the elements of a criminal offence and the elements of a criminal defence, consider the following contrast:

> *Room 1 in L'Hôtel de l'information imparfaite*: Two people enter Room 1, and after some time, one of them emerges from the room with bruising around their eye socket.
>
> *Room 2 in L'Hôtel de l'information imparfaite*: Two people enter Room 2, and after some time, one of them emerges with vaginal (or anal) bruising.
>
> We know very little about the events that occurred in both rooms except that the bruising was caused by the actions of the other person in the room.

In most jurisdictions, the criminal law would treat the events in Room 1 differently from the events in Room 2. The events in Room 1 would satisfy the elements of the offence of assault occasioning actual bodily harm.[6] In the absence of being able to justify the application of force to the eye socket, the applier of the force would be liable for an offence against the other person.

Room 2 is different. To find that a sexual offence was committed, we would need to establish that the vaginal (or anal) penetration was nonconsensual.[7] In the absence of being able to establish that the penetration was nonconsensual,

[6] Offences Against the Person Act 1861, s 47.
[7] Sexual Offences Act 2003, ss 1(1)(c) and 2(1)(c).

we would be unable to establish that a sexual offence had occurred. Curiously, given the vaginal (or anal) bruising, we would be able to establish that a crime had occurred if the events in Room 2 were viewed as an offence against the person (assault occasioning actual bodily harm) rather than a sexual offence (rape or assault by penetration). Sexual offences are somehow different from other offences against the person.

This is not the case in all jurisdictions. If the events took place in *Hotell med ofullständig information* instead, Rooms 1 and 2 would be treated the same. 'According to the conventional structure of Swedish criminal law', Andrew Simester explains, 'justifications are treated as part of the offence definition'.[8] It is possible, too, for the common law to treat defences as 'merely elements of every actus reus which, because of their generality, are not always specified'.[9] Doing so, however, dissolves 'the normatively significant distinction' between '(i) the *pro tanto* wrong, designated by an actus reus–mens rea combination' and '(ii) the wrong *simpliciter* that is perpetrated when, additionally, no justification is available'.[10] Moreover, as I will explain in the following essay, to justify or excuse a *pro tanto* wrong, after (i) establishing the actus reus–mens rea combination, requires its own combination of explanatory and guiding reasons, to resist the move from (i) *pro tanto* wrong to (ii) wrong *simpliciter*. The distinction, therefore, between the elements of an offence and the component parts of a defence is a 'normatively significant' one.

The above scenarios help illustrate how different criminal offences have a different set of minimal conditions. For sexual offences, the absence of consent forms part of the set of minimal conditions of an offence. In comparison, an offence against the person can be established without establishing the absence of consent. Rather, for offences against the person, establishing that the contact or injury was consensual may satisfy a justificatory defence.

According to Kenneth Campbell, there is a conceptual distinction between the elements of an offence and the elements of a (justificatory) defence.[11] Given all the aspects of an actor's conduct, some aspects of the actor's conduct will constitute an offence, whilst other aspects may negate liability by justifying the commission of the offence.[12] The way in which a particular crime is divided

[8] AP Simester, *Fundamentals of Criminal Law: Responsibility, Culpability, and Wrongdoing* (OUP 2021) 425.

[9] Simester (n 8) 426.

[10] Simester (n 8) 426.

[11] Kenneth Campbell, 'Offence and Defence' in Ian Dennis (ed), *Criminal Law and Justice: Essays from the W.G. Hart Workshop, 1986* (Sweet and Maxwell 1987). See also George P Fletcher, *Basic Concepts in Criminal Law* (OUP 1998); Gardner (n 1) 817–18; cf Glanville Williams, 'The Logic of Exceptions' (1988) 42 CLJ 261.

[12] Peter Westen, 'Offences and Defences Again' (2008) 28 OJLS 563, 570.

up into the elements of the offence itself and the elements of a (justificatory) defence will depend on the underlying distinction 'between reasons against doing something and reasons in favour'.[13] According to Campbell, out of the set of rules that 'completely defines the incidence of liability in respect of any act' we can create a 'subset' of rules that defines the scope of the offence.[14] This offence subset defines an action that *we have general reasons not to perform.* The remaining subset represents a set of conditions that, if satisfied, can justify or exonerate an action that would otherwise be a criminal wrong.

To demonstrate this conceptual distinction, Campbell provides an example of a legislator creating an offence of 'operating a radio receiver without a radio licence'. Campbell asks whether the offence is that of 'operating the radio' (with the 'possession of a licence' being available as a defence) or whether 'both elements are within the offence part'.[15] According to Campbell, the answer will turn on whether 'the legislator regards there as being *prima facie* reason against all instances of operating a radio receiver' or takes the view that 'there is reason against operating a radio receiver only if one does so without a licence'.[16]

Campbell's radio licence example highlights two important aspects of the offence–defence distinction. The first is that the general reasons not to perform an action depend on how the action is viewed. How the law against 'operating a radio without a licence' is divided up between the offence and the defence subsets of rules turns on whether the legislator views there being reason against all instances of operating a radio, and, as Campbell recognises, 'there could, according to circumstances, be different answers to this'.[17] In other words, the distinction turns on an evaluation of a social practice. The circumstances may be such that the wrong is viewed as 'depriving the state revenue' or as 'using Western-invented technology'. The distinction between offences and defences is therefore a distinction as to how the component parts of the prohibited action are viewed.

The second aspect of the conceptual distinction worth highlighting is that the general reasons not to perform an action are *general* reasons insofar as they apply to 'all instances' of the action.[18] There may be various wrongful ways to operate a radio, or various wrongful circumstances in which to operate a radio, yet 'operating a radio' only ought to be an offence if there are general reasons

[13] Gardner (n 1) 819.
[14] Campbell (n 11) 75.
[15] Campbell (n 11) 80–81.
[16] Campbell (n 11) 80.
[17] Campbell (n 11) 80.
[18] Campbell (n 11) 81.

that apply to operating a radio *per se* (or operating a radio *in all instances*). The conceptual distinction forces us into an all or nothing categorisation.

We can therefore say that where there are general (but defeasible) reasons not to perform an action, the components of that action will form the elements of an offence. The general reasons not to perform the action are defeasible insofar as they are not conclusive reasons not to perform the action. In this way, the wrong is a *pro tanto* wrong; it is wrong to the extent that it is contrary to a general reason. We may recognise instances where the performance of the action is nonetheless justified (or excused), and, in such instances, the criminal law may provide a defence. When the elements of a justificatory defence are satisfied, the defendant is acquitted, since the reasons in favour of performing the action 'prevail' over the reasons against.[19] If, however, the elements of the defence cannot be satisfied, we can then view the action as being contrary to *indefeasible* reasons, and view the action as a wrong (or wrong 'all things considered').

As we have seen, consent appears in the defence subset of rules that governs offences against the person. The rules that govern sexual offences are different. To satisfy the elements of the offence of rape, sexual penetration, or sexual assault, it is necessary to establish that penetration or touching was nonconsensual. The orthodox explanation for why sexual offences are defined with reference to the absence of consent contends that there is only a general reason not to engage in a sexual act where the penetration or touching is nonconsensual. In other words, the minimal set of conditions for there being general reasons not to engage in a sexual act with another person necessarily includes *the absence of consent*. There is otherwise *no* general reason not to engage in a sexual act with another person.

Hence, when Campbell considered an alternative definition of rape, as 'sexual intercourse by a man with a woman where the consent of the woman is available as a defence', he found the alternative definition to be 'strange'.[20] As he explains:

> The reason why this statute would be so odd is that it implies that the legislator takes the view that there is some reason against all sexual intercourse.[21]

[19] Gardner (n 1) 819.
[20] Campbell (n 11) 82.
[21] Campbell (n 11) 82.

A number of commentators have since explained why the absence of consent to sexual activity falls within the subset of rules that defines the offence by applying the same reasoning. According to Gardner:

> Actual bodily harm is *per se* an unwelcome turn of events, even when consensual; sexual intercourse is not *per se* an unwelcome turn of events, but only becomes one by virtue of being non-consensual.[22]

Stephen Shute agrees:

> If there were always a reason against having sexual intercourse, the offence element of rape should be defined as 'engaging in sexual intercourse'...
>
> However drafting a statute in this way seems wrong. The reason is that it reflects a morality that is foreign to us. We simply do not think that there is always a reason against sexual intercourse.[23]

As does Victor Tadros:

> there is no prima facie reason against having sexual intercourse. When one has consensual intercourse, it is not as though the prima facie reason against having intercourse has been balanced or outweighed by the fact that it was consensual. There is no prima facie reason at all.[24]

The explanation for why the *absence of consent* is an element of the offence in sexual offences (rather than being available as a justificatory defence) is premised upon the view that there are no general reasons not to engage in sexual intercourse. By inserting this 'orthodox view' into Campbell's conceptual distinction between offences and defences, Campbell, Gardner, Shute and Tadros argue that sexual intercourse itself cannot be an offence. Instead, the further condition — the absence of consent — is required to define the scope of a criminal wrong.

[22] Gardner (n 1) 820.

[23] Stephen Shute, 'Second Law Commission Consultation Paper on Consent: (1) Something Old, Something New, Something Borrowed: Three Aspects of the Project' (1996) Crim L R 684, 690.

[24] Victor Tadros, *Criminal Responsibility* (OUP 2005) 107.

5.3

In opposition to this prevailing view, others have argued that there are general reasons not to engage in sexual acts. George Fletcher, for instance, viewed a variety of touchings (touching, sexual contact, forcible sexual contact, and nonconsensual sexual contact) in 'ascending incrimination', and argued that 'sexual contact' itself satisfied the 'minimal set of elements necessary to incriminate the actor' since to 'initiate touching of the genitals is hardly routine, the touching requires a good reason'.[25]

Whereas Fletcher views the touching of the genitals to be 'hardly routine', Williams views consensual sexual intercourse to be 'such a normal and frequent activity'.[26] As Campbell explains, 'except insofar as it may point to more fundamental issues' the 'relative frequency or infrequency of occurrence' of the conduct cannot explain why the conduct is or ought to be permitted or prohibited.[27] Rather, 'the idea of normality and abnormality', if interpreted in a value-laden way, is 'getting closer to the truth'.[28] Hence, whether there are general reasons not to engage in penetrative sex or sexual touching will therefore depend on some kind of value-laden view or understanding of the act and not the frequency or infrequency of the act.

Michelle Madden Dempsey and Jonathan Herring have argued that sexual penetration is *morally* a 'prima facie wrong' that 'calls for justification'.[29] This 'alternative view' suggests that 'if a man penetrates the vagina or anus of a woman with his penis, he should do so for a good reason'.[30] They identify a culmination of factors that explain the 'prima facie wrongfulness' of sexual penetration. These factors include: (i) the risk of physical and psychological harm that stem from sexual penetration, (ii) the negative social meaning associated with sexual penetration, and (iii) the use of physical force on another person in sexual penetration. With respect to these three factors, I will contend here that: (i) the risk of harm does not provide *general* reasons not to engage in penetrative sex, (ii) in my previous work I dismissed too readily the saturation of negative social meaning associated with sexual penetration, and (iii) the use of force makes penetrative sex not only a *pro tanto* moral wrong, but a *pro tanto* legal wrong as well.

[25] George P Fletcher, *Rethinking Criminal Law* (Little Brown 1978) 707.

[26] Glanville Williams, 'Offences and Defences' (1982) 2 Leg Stud 233, 254.

[27] Campbell (n 11) 82.

[28] Campbell (n 11) 82.

[29] Michelle Madden Dempsey and Jonathan Herring, 'Why Sexual Penetration Requires Justification' (2007) 27 OJLS 467, 467.

[30] Dempsey and Herring (n 29) 469.

According to Dempsey and Herring, (i) sexual penetration carries the risk of physical harm. The potential physical harm is three-fold: the risk of sexually transmitted diseases, the risk of unwanted pregnancy, and the physical injuries (abrasions, lacerations, tearing or chafing of tissues) that are 'not uncommon' in consensual sexual intercourse.[31] Dempsey and Herring also suggest that penetrative sex 'poses a nontrivial risk of causing some significant psychological harm'.[32] These physical and psychological harms, when they materialise, are world-grounded reasons against penetrative sex. These reasons, however, are not general reasons and therefore unable to explain the 'prima facie wrongfulness' of penetrative sex (for the purposes of satisfying Campbell's conception of an offence).[33] To explain why, let us revisit how Shute and Gardner explain why 'harms' are unable to explain the wrongfulness of rape. We can then apply the same reasoning to account for why the 'nontrivial risks of harm' do not explain why sexual penetration calls for an explanation.

Sexual penetration in the absence of consent is wrongful. Sexual penetration in the absence of consent is also harmful. It is tempting to explain the wrongfulness of nonconsensual sexual intercourse with reference to the harmfulness of nonconsensual sexual intercourse. In addition to the physical and psychological injuries that a victim may suffer, the traumatic experience itself may generate a feeling of violation, a sense of insecurity and a loss of trust. Although the seriousness of these harms cannot be understated, Shute and Gardner contend that they do not explain the wrongfulness of rape.[34]

The difficulty is that we are attempting here to isolate the element that explains why *all instances* of nonconsensual penetrative sex are wrong. The variation in physical or psychological injuries that may or may not be inflicted during nonconsensual sexual penetration makes the harm (understood as the injury suffered) too specific to the particular instance of rape for it to explain the wrongfulness of all instances of rape. The same is true of the feelings that the experience of rape may generate. Since the reactions and attitudes of victims of rape will vary, understanding the harm (as the feelings of violation, insecurity or loss of trust) will depend on the evaluations of the particular victim.

[31] Dempsey and Herring (n 29) 477, citing Robert J Hoffman and Sandhya Ganti, 'Vaginal Lacerations and Perforation Resulting from First Coitus' (2001) 17 Pediatr Emerg Care 113 and Ejaz Ahmed, Shahab Ahmed Syed and Naz Parveen, 'Female Consensual Coital Injuries' (2006) 16 J Coll Physicians Surg Pak 333.

[32] Dempsey and Herring (n 29) 479.

[33] Dempsey and Herring were 'not directly concerned with questions of criminalisation'. Their aim was to 'simply map the moral landscape of sexual penetration'. See Dempsey and Herring (n 29) 467.

[34] Shute and Gardner (n 5) 5.

As discussed in essay one, rather than these harms constituting the wrongfulness of rape, these harms *aggravate* the wrongfulness of rape.[35] A victim may feel violated because a serious wrong has been committed to her, but her feeling of violation is not what makes the nonconsensual penetrative sex wrong; the wrongfulness of the act 'remains even in the absence of these harms'.[36] Recall how Shute and Gardner argued that the 'pure case' of rape, 'stripped of distracting epiphenomena' is where a 'victim may be forever oblivious to the fact she was raped'.[37] There remains a serious wrong committed against the victim even where the associated harms are not experienced by the victim.

Returning now to Dempsey and Herring's claim that the prima facie wrongfulness of sexual penetration stems from a 'nontrivial risk of significant harm'. These harms do not provide *general* reasons not to engage in sexual penetration. This is because, as Dempsey and Herring accept, there are exceptions to these reasons not to engage in penetrative sex, and view these exceptions as cumulative.[38] It is the existence of these exceptions that is problematic. In terms of physical harm, the fact that there are instances of penetrative sex where there is no risk of sexually transmitted disease or pregnancy suggests that the nontrivial risk of harm is not a *general* reason not to engage in penetrative sex. Rather, the risk of significant harm only generates particular and person- and context-specific reasons not to engage in penetrative sex. If there is a general (and defeasible) reason not to engage in sexual intercourse, then the reason will be generally applicable (i.e. apply to all instances of the act) and not dependent on person- and context-specific factors.

Dempsey and Herring also suggest that (ii) 'the prima facie wrongfulness of conduct can be grounded in the negative social meaning of the conduct', and identify a current social meaning of penile penetration of a woman's vagina or anus as 'an act through which she is rendered less powerful, less human, whilst the male is rendered more powerful and more human'.[39] It is tempting, for the same reasons as outlined above, to dismiss this as a *context-specific* concern for the social meaning that is associated with penetrative sex that will not provide *general* reasons not to engage in penetrative sex. I previously asserted that, given that there are social contexts in which penetrative sex is not associated with a negative social meaning, the negative social meaning of penetrative sex

35 Shute and Gardner (n 5) 7.
36 Shute and Gardner (n 5) 7.
37 Shute and Gardner (n 5) 7.
38 Dempsey and Herring (n 29) 473.
39 Dempsey and Herring (n 29) 481, 485.

does not provide *general* reasons not to engage in penetrative sex[40] This under-appreciated the critique.

Dempsey and Herring are right to be attentive towards the social context in which sexual penetration occurs. Recall Andrea Dworkin's claim (which we encountered in essay two) that '[t]here is a deep recognition in culture and experience that intercourse is both the normal use of a woman ... and a violative abuse' and that 'when he enters her, he confirms for himself and for her what she is: she is something, not someone; certainly not someone equal.'[41] Recall, too, Catherine Mackinnon's explanation that dominance is 'not an artificial overlay upon an underlying inalterable substratum of uncorrupted essential sexual being.'[42] Instead, '[i]t has no basis in anything other than the social reality its hegemony constructs.'[43] In this way, the universality of domination represents a *general* reason against intercourse that calls for an explanation. It is not that some sexual practices express these social structures but, rather, *all* sex lies in a state of shame in light of what sex-as-we-know-it is.

As Campbell explained in his account of the conceptual distinction between offences and defences, whether there are general reasons against an activity will depend on social 'circumstances' and underlying 'values.'[44] Shute has also remarked:

> reason-based approaches can provide a principled way of separating out the offence elements of a crime from the defence elements ... everything, in fact, depends on the underlying value judgments, which are themselves sensitive to the context in which the issues arise.[45]

Note that the above feminist critique would resist the implication that dominance is context-specific. As we know from before, for McKinnon, 'male supremacy is largely universal, if always in specific [cultural] forms.'[46] I return to this point momentarily. For now, we can appreciate the difficulty with assessing whether there are any general moral reasons not to engage in penetrative sex: what underlying value judgments can we make about penetrative sex *in general*? The difficulty stems from the variety of contexts and circumstances in which sexual penetration occurs. When we think about an act of penetrative

40 Jesse Wall, 'Sexual Offences and General Reasons Not to Have Sex' (2015) 35 OJLS 777, 785–86.
41 Andrea Dworkin, *Intercourse* (Free Press 1987) 140–41.
42 Catharine A MacKinnon, *Toward a Feminist Theory of the State* (Harvard UP 1989) 173.
43 MacKinnon (n 42) 173.
44 Campbell (n 11) 82.
45 Shute (n 23) 690.
46 MacKinnon (n 42) 151.

sex, we, perhaps unavoidably, place the act in a particular context. We then disagree about whether there are general reasons against sexual penetration because we have in mind a context and set of circumstances that may differ significantly from the contexts and circumstances that others have in mind. As Peter Westen vividly explains:

> Consider two hypothetical acts of sexual intercourse . . . a loving married couple, having always striven to be entirely honest with one another, celebrate a non-alcoholic 30th wedding anniversary by having sexual intercourse . . .
>
> In contrast, a girl, celebrating her 16th birthday in a bar, drinks enough to place her blood-alcohol limit at twice that allowed for driving but less than sufficient to render her incompetent to have sex . . .
>
> Duff may have something like the married couple in mind when he says that 'it makes no sense to citizens of contemporary liberal democracies [that] we should . . . have to answer to our fellow citizens . . . for every act of sexual penetration'. And he is right: the married couple has nothing to account for . . .
>
> Michelle Madden Dempsey and Jonathan Herring have something like the 16-year-old in mind when they say that sexual intercourse requires moral justification. And they are right too. The 31-year-old, married father of three is socially understood to have something to account for in having unprotected sexual intercourse with the heavily intoxicated 16-year-old.[47]

In trying to determine whether sexual penetration is, itself, a '*prima facie* moral wrong', Dempsey and Herring ultimately adopt the same methodology as Gardner, Shute, Tadros, and Duff. In resolving this disagreement, 'it might be thought that the solution depends on which side is correct about how sexual intercourse is socially understood'.[48] Yet, as Westen explains, it is a mistake 'to think that lawful sexual intercourse is socially understood to be either costly or costless under all the circumstances under which it occurs'.[49]

The implication from Westen is that there may be many instances where sexual penetration is undertaken in a context where the social meaning of penetration renders the woman 'less-powerful', 'violated', or 'less human',[50] but the existence (and frequency) of these instances do not produce general reasons not to engage in penetrative sex. Equally, it follows from Westen that

[47] Westen (n 12) 573.
[48] Westen (n 12) 571.
[49] Westen (n 12) 573.
[50] Dempsey and Herring (n 29) 485.

there may also be many instances where sexual penetration is undertaken in a loving and mutually respectful relationship, but the existence (and frequency) of these instances do not preclude there being general (defeasible) reasons not to engage in sexual intercourse. Unlike owning a radio without a licence, the social conditions and circumstances in which people engage in sexual acts are too diverse to generate a statement about 'whether or not sexual intercourse is socially understood to involve costs that agents ought morally to address'.[51] For Westen, both sides pose this question 'that cannot be answered'.[52]

More broadly, we encountered the same methodological *cul-de-sac* in Essay 2 (at 2.4). There, we encountered the question of whether we have the 'generative freedom' to transcend the social constructs that ingrain heterosexual sex in patriarchal meaning without just 'recapitulating identifications in experience that are already socially constructed under patriarchal terms'.[53] For the likes of Varden and de Beauvoir, the generative freedom is possible (and therefore the dominance critique is not universal). For McKinnon, all sex lies in the shadow of the patriarchy it affirms. Both threads follow the critical method and collate instances of a socially and culturally embedded phenomenon to develop a concept (sex *as-we-know-it*). To then ask the question of whether all sex involves 'costs that agents ought morally to address' implies that we can access a further concept (sex *as-it-should-be*) that is not a culturally embedded phenomenon. We could say, echoing Westen, that both sides pose a question 'that cannot be answered'. It cannot be answered because the method forecloses the answer.

Dempsey and Herring are nonetheless able to identify a *general* feature of sexual penetration that explains its '*prima facie* wrongfulness'. They contend that (iii)

> one reason why penile penetration of the vagina or anus is properly understood to require justification is due to the physiological fact that force is required to achieve such penetration . . . if a penis is to achieve penetration, it must push through muscled walls into the vagina or anus.[54]

In identifying this general feature of sexual penetration, Dempsey and Herring brush over a normative premise. That is, they do not explain *why* the application of force to another person's body is (*prima facie*) wrongful (or contrary to

[51] Westen (n 12) 572.
[52] Westen (n 12) 572.
[53] Valerie Giovanini, 'Alterity in Simone de Beauvoir and Emmanuel Levinas: From Ambiguity to Ambivalence' (2019) 34 Hypatia 39, 43.
[54] Dempsey and Herring (n 29) 473.

general (and defeasible) reasons). The application of force to another person may be harmful to the person, and the application of penetrative force may express a negative and subordinating social meaning, but for the reasons canvassed above, these harms or meanings do not provide general reasons not to apply penetrative force.

Beyond physical, psychological, or social harms, an activity may be wrongful if it infringes a person's rights or interests. Again, an analogy with the wrongfulness of nonconsensual sexual penetration is helpful here. Since we can explain (in the following section) the wrongfulness of nonconsensual sexual penetration in terms of the infringement of the person's rights or interests, we may be able to, by reduction, explain how the wrongfulness of the application of force lies in its interference with a right or *interest* of the person who is subject to the force. Note that we are now viewing sexual penetration as a physiological action. We are forced to do this for the reasons advanced by Westen: since sexual penetration occurs in a variety of different social contexts, we cannot view sexual intercourse with reference to a single 'underlying value judgment'.[55] We may, however, be able to generate an underlying value judgment about the application of penetrative force to another person's body.

5.4

As we have considered in Essay 1, Shute and Gardner locate the wrongfulness of rape in terms of 'the sheer use of the person', which is an infringement or denial of their personhood.[56] Shute and Gardner also contemplate, and then discard, an account of the wrongfulness of nonconsensual intercourse that explains the wrong in terms of an infringement of the proprietor's rights, citing GA Cohen's description of rape as the nonconsensual 'borrowing of sexual organs'.[57] This is an analogy that I have relied upon earlier and that I will defend here further. That claim has been that, like the rights of a property-rights holder, each person has exclusive use and control of their own body (as a self-owner). Rather than detailing the ways in which a self-owner can use their body, we carve out a sphere of 'indefinite and undefined' activity through the duties we perform in respect of the right of self-ownership. The further implication, which has more immediate relevance, is that the principle of

[55] Shute (n 23) 690.
[56] Shute and Gardner (n 5) 14–17.
[57] GA Cohen, *Self-Ownership, Freedom and Equality* (CUP 1995) 244; Shute and Gardner (n 5) 9.

self-ownership (and the 'non-use value' that it protects) can explain why the application of force to a person's body is a *pro tanto* wrong.

According to Shute and Gardner's characterisation of the right to 'self-ownership':

> The wrongness of rape . . . comes of the fact that the victim of rape has a proprietary interest in, and derived from that a proprietary right over, her own body. It is her body, she owns it, nobody else may use it without her say-so.[58]

Shute and Gardner identify a series of problems with this property rights-based account of the wrongfulness of nonconsensual sexual intercourse. In one sense, their critiques are apt: there are some key differences between an item of property and a person's body. The problem with Shute and Gardner's critique is that no one (least of all GA Cohen) relies on a full-blown analogy with *property* rights to explain the rights or interests that we have of our body. By extension, the right to self-ownership does not rely on a full-blown analogy with property rights to explain the wrongfulness of nonconsensual penetrative sex.

Instead, the wrongfulness of nonconsensual penetrative sex can be explained in terms of the infringement of the right to *self-ownership*, where the right to self-ownership is not synonymous with property rights. In responding to Shute and Gardner's critiques, I will substantiate what is meant by 'the infringement of the rights of self-ownership'. I will then attempt to explain why there are general reasons not to engage in penetrative sex that are based on the principle of self-ownership.

According to Shute and Gardner, we ought to reject the analogy between our property rights and our relationship with our body on the basis that

> one cannot . . . analogize what happens to oneself to what happens to what one owns, because oneself cannot be an addition to what one owns. This is the first and major flaw in all self-ownership doctrines, including but not restricted to those that focus on ownership of one's body.[59]

This criticism mischaracterises the principle of self-ownership. Let us start, therefore, by clarifying what is meant by 'self-ownership'. As Ngaire Naffine explains, the expression 'self-owners' has become 'a sort of legal shorthand,

[58] Shute and Gardner (n 5) 9.
[59] Shute and Gardner (n 5) 13.

a rhetorical device, which serves to accentuate the fullness of the rights enjoyed by persons in relation to themselves'.[60] We can therefore understand the basic notion of 'self-ownership' as Cohen's proposition: 'that each person enjoys, over herself and her powers, full and exclusive rights of control and use'.[61] This is the basis of the analogy between rights of self-ownership and property rights: both represent the power to exclude an open set of persons[62] and 'literally and figuratively provide the necessary walls to separate oneself from others'.[63]

'Self-ownership' describes a functional relationship of exclusive control by a person over their body. It confers, according to Cohen, 'the fullest right a person (logically) can have over herself provided that each other person also has just such a right'.[64] Importantly, Cohen explains further:

> The term 'self' in the name of the thesis of self-ownership has a purely reflexive significance. It signifies that what one owns and what is owned are one and the same, namely, the whole person.[65]

It is therefore not a contradiction to say that 'I' have 'full and exclusive rights of control and use' over 'my body'. Just as it is not a contradiction to describe someone as 'self-governing', 'self-legislative', or 'autonomous'. We can formulate these concepts without forcing a separation between the governor and the governed, the legislator and the legislated, or the *autos* (the 'self') and the *nomos* (the 'law'). Similarly, the right to self-ownership does not rely on the separation or alienation of the 'owned thing' from the 'owner'.

Shute and Gardner are correct in saying that 'oneself cannot be in addition to what one owns'.[66] Yet, since the right to self-ownership does not alienate the owner from the owned thing, the right to self-ownership does not position the body as an *additional* item of property. Insofar as 'ownership' represents 'full and exclusive rights of control and use', we can describe ourselves as self-owners, where oneself is *rudimentarily* what one owns.

[60] Ngaire Naffine, 'The Legal Structure of Self-Ownership: Or the Self-Possessed Man and the Woman Possessed' (1998) 25 J Law Soc 193, 194.

[61] Cohen (n 57) 12.

[62] JE Penner, *The Idea of Property in Law* (OUP 1997) 74: 'The contours of the legal right to exclude others from one's body are the product of legal and moral ingenuity in recognizing appropriate general duties *in rem*.'

[63] Jennifer Nedelsky, 'Law, Boundaries and the Bounded Self' (1990) 30 Representations 162, 168.

[64] Cohen (n 57) 213.

[65] Cohen (n 57) 69.

[66] Shute and Gardner (n 5) 13.

Shute and Gardner also criticise the right to self-ownership for viewing the relationship with oneself as a contingent relationship. Whilst it is true that the relationship between the property rights-holder and an item of property is a contingent relationship, the principle of self-ownership need not import this feature from the analogy with property. In fact, we ought to resist conflating notions of ownership with notions of property. I can exercise 'full and exclusive rights of control and use' over my body and 'full and exclusive rights of control and use' over the clothes in my wardrobe,[67] but my relationship with myself and my relationship with my clothes are ultimately different. As James Penner explains:

> Only those 'things' in the world which are contingently associated with a particular owner may be objects of property; as a function of the nature of this contingency, in theory nothing of normative consequences beyond the fact that the ownership has changed occurs when an object of property is alienated to another.[68]

It therefore follows:

> A necessary criterion for treating something as property . . . is that it is only contingently ours; we much show why it is ours because it might well not have been.[69]

Property rights represent a contingent relationship between the owner and the owned thing. A dimension of the contingency of the ownership relationship is that a subsequent owner is able to stand in the same position with regards to the owned thing as the original owner. In contrast, the relationship of exclusive use and control over our bodies (our self-ownership) is a non-contingent relationship; another person cannot stand in the same position as ourselves with regard to our body.

Shute and Gardner are therefore correct that the analogy between nonconsensual sexual intercourse and the infringement of *property rights* is a poor analogy and renders 'one's relationship to oneself contingent in such a way that there is no longer any self to any owning, of itself or of anything else'.[70]

[67] cf Shute and Gardner (n 5) 12.
[68] Penner (n 62) 111.
[69] Penner (n 62) 112.
[70] Shute and Gardner (n 5) 14.

But such a criticism cannot be levelled against an account of nonconsensual sexual activity as an infringement of the right of *self-ownership*.

Shute and Gardner's third criticism follows from the above two concerns. According to their interpretation, a 'consequence' of the self-ownership doctrine is the 'alienation of the body from the self'.[71] The value of the body, 'like other tools and receptacles and artefacts', therefore becomes the *use value*:[72] that is, 'the valuable things' that can be done with the body.[73] The principle of self-ownership is interpreted by Shute and Gardner as protecting only a 'use value', whereas Shute and Gardner want to locate the wrongfulness of nonconsensual sexual intercourse in the denial of someone's *non-use value*. The 'non-use value' is a further value that is denied when we 'use' or 'treat' people 'as something other than people'.[74]

The problem is that there is nothing in the right to self-ownership that implies that the 'full and exclusive rights of control and use' are premised solely on the use value of the body. Rather, the 'full and exclusive rights of control and use' are promoted as a means of protecting the non-use value of each person. By asserting exclusive rights of control, the self-owner prevents their body from being 'used' as only a functionally useful *thing*. According to Robert Nozick, for instance, rights of self-ownership 'reflect the underlying Kantian principle that individuals are ends and not merely means'.[75] As we shall see, this is the same *non-use value* that Shute and Gardner appear to premise their account of the wrongfulness of rape upon.[76] Therefore, the right to self-ownership is able to explain the wrongfulness of nonconsensual sexual penetration. Sexual offences infringe rights of exclusive control over the body, where such rights secure the 'non-use value' that persons may not be used for another's sexual ends without their consent.

Unsatisfied with explanations based on harms or the infringement of property rights, Shute and Gardner explain the wrongfulness of rape in terms of the 'objectification' or 'abuse' of another person. Proceeding from the premise that people, unlike things, have a value that is beyond their 'use value', the wrongfulness of nonconsensual sexual intercourse is explained by Shute and Gardner as the 'the sheer use of the person' where the sheer use of human

[71] Shute and Gardner (n 5) 14.
[72] Shute and Gardner (n 5) 14.
[73] Shute and Gardner (n 5) 9.
[74] Shute and Gardner (n 5) 14.
[75] Robert Nozick, *Anarchy, State, and Utopia* (Basic Books 1974) 31.
[76] Shute and Gardner (n 5) 14: 'to use people without at the same time respecting this further non-use value involves treating them as something other than people. It means treating them as things.'

beings is '*ab*use'.[77] According to Shute and Gardner, it is then possible to explain 'how consent comes to be pivotal' to the wrongfulness of nonconsensual sexual intercourse.[78] Since only the subject can consent, 'by being astute to another's consent, someone who has sexual intercourse with that other is not treating that other . . . merely as a means'.[79] In other words, a person's astuteness to another's consent is a recognition of the other person's non-use value.

As I have explained before, Shute and Gardner are ultimately correct in their explanation of the wrongfulness of nonconsensual penetrative sex. The wrongfulness of nonconsensual penetrative sex can be explained in terms of the denial of a person's 'non-use value'. Their mistake has been to dismiss the right to self-ownership as recognition of the non-use value of people. For Shute and Gardner:

> [T]he value of having a system of sexual relations in which people control by consent the treatment of their bodies secures optimal respect for the ultimate value of people.[80]

But having a system of sexual relations, alone, is not enough. We need an all-things-considered desirable one. As we encountered in the previous essay, 'a person's act is an exercise of a normative power' if it is 'all things considered, desirable that that person should be able to bring the change about or prevent it by performing that act'.[81] It is merely my suggestion here that such a 'system of sexual relations' (or a conventional practice) *ought to be* a system founded upon the right to self-ownership, where a person exercises a normative power to waive a pre-existing duty (not to apply force) on the basis that is 'all things considered, desirable that that person should be able to bring the change about'. When constructed properly, the principle of self-ownership provides a way of connecting 'the ultimate value of people' (their non-use value) with the wrongfulness of a particular act (nonconsensual penetrative sex). In other words, a practice that recognises the right to self-ownership, and the exclusionary boundary around the body that the right draws, is the best available practice to protect the ultimate value of people. If so, and if the recognition of rights of self-ownership is a social practice that promotes 'the ultimate value of

77 Shute and Gardner (n 5) 16.
78 Shute and Gardner (n 5) 17.
79 Shute and Gardner (n 5) 17.
80 Shute and Gardner (n 5) 19.
81 Joseph Raz, 'Normative Powers (revised)' (2019) Oxf J Leg Stud Research Paper 36/2019, 2 <https://ssrn.com/abstract=3379368> accessed 1 December 2024.

people', then there are general (and practice-grounded) reasons not to engage in penetrative sex.

So far, in addition to Campbell's conceptual distinction between offences and defences, we have identified and developed two important ideas. First, that the application of force (sufficient to penetrate muscled walls) is a general feature of sexual penetration that calls for an explanation. Recall that Dempsey and Herring presumed that the application of force calls for an explanation. The reason for this, I have suggested, is that the application of penetrative force is an infringement of the rights of self-ownership. It is this rights infringement that is able to explain why there are general reasons not to apply penetrative force to another person. Second, that *nonconsensual* sexual penetration is wrong because it is contrary to the principle that every person has exclusive rights of control and use over their own body. We are now at the stage where we can connect these two ideas and explain why there are general reasons not to engage in penetrative sex.

The claim here is that the application of force is use and control by the person other than the self-owner and, thereby, conduct that is *pro tanto* contrary to the right of self-ownership. The contradiction between self-ownership and the application of penetrative force is therefore as follows: given the principle that each person exercises 'full and exclusive rights of control and use' over their body, and given the 'physiological fact that force is required to achieve' penetration, the activity of forceful penetration—of pushing through the muscled walls of another person—renders the person other than the self-owner in control of the self-owner's body. If we were to cast the net wider and consider the penetration of the vagina or anus without the application of force,[82] the contact and physical invasion of the body would nonetheless be the use and control of the body by the other. Simply put, penetration of the vagina or anus, forceful or otherwise, is use and control by the other, rather than use and control by the self. This is the *pro tanto* legal wrong thesis.

5.5

Having articulated the claim, I can now respond to five (of six) objections to the *pro tanto* legal wrong thesis (leaving the sixth for the next essay). These objections are:

[82] Dempsey and Herring (n 29) 474.

1. wrongfulness can only supervene on the absence of consent,
2. sex cannot be *pro tanto* anything,
3. justified sex leaves no moral residue,
4. the *pro tanto* wrong is morally trivial, and
5. the *pro tanto* wrong is a not a culpable wrong.

And for the next chapter:

6. the *pro tanto* wrong is legally trivial.

We can easily anticipate the first objection. Proponents of the 'prevailing view' argue that penetrative sex will only be an infringement of a person's rights of self-ownership where the sex is inconsistent with the way in which the person exercises their rights of control and use. According to this objection, it will only be a wrong when the penetration is *contrary* to the person's exercise of their right of self-ownership. If a person consents to the penetrative sex, then the activity is consistent with the person's self-ownership. If a person does not consent to the sexual intercourse, then it is an infringement of a person's self-ownership and the denial of their 'non-use value'. Hence, the likes of Campbell, Gardner, Shute, Tadros, and Duff are likely to respond by suggesting that the activity is only contrary to the rights of *control* over the body when the activity is *nonconsensual.*

It may appear as if we have made no progress in combating the prevailing view. Except we can now identify the presumption that underlies the orthodox view. Proponents of the orthodox view presume that a person exercises their rights of control over their body in favour of sexual activity and intercourse. That unless we know that the sexual activity was nonconsensual, we presume that it is consistent with a person's self-ownership. I have suggested here that this underlying presumption may stem from the context in which these commentators place the activity of sexual intercourse. To that extent, the 'context' and 'circumstances' of sexual penetration are epiphenomenal and we should focus on the phenomenon of penetrative sex as a physiological action.

For Gardner, sexual intercourse 'is not *per se* an unwelcome turn of events'.[83] It is not clear what features the '*per se*' in this statement is keeping out of the equation (or is leaving in the equation). Sexual penetration '*per se*' must, for Gardner, have some kind of positive or welcoming feature that enables us to view it as a 'not unwelcome' turn of events. It is this feature that then enables

[83] Gardner (n 1) 820.

the presumption that a person would exercise their rights of control over their body in favour of sexual intercourse. However, there is no reason why the law should reflect this presumption that underlies the prevailing view.

This presumption, I suggest, follows from a viewpoint that is blinkered by two mistakes that we have already encountered in this discussion. The first is mistaking frequency for normativity. It may be that most instances of sexual penetration are instances where both participants in the sexual intercourse are exercising their rights of exclusive control over their bodies in favour of the intercourse. We then presume that a person would exercise their rights of exclusive control over their body in favour of penetrative sex because we perceive it as a 'normal and frequent activity'[84] (despite the alarming instances of unwanted sexual touching highlighted by Dempsey and Herring).[85] Yet recall Campbell's explanation, that the 'relative frequency or infrequency of occurrence' is only relevant insofar as 'it may point to more fundamental issues'.[86] To put it bluntly, the frequency or commonality of *pro tanto* wrongful conduct does not disqualify the conduct from being *pro tanto* wrongful.

The second mistake that blinkers our viewpoint is that we, following Campbell's direction,[87] search for a value-laden understanding of the conduct by looking at the context and social circumstances in which the conduct occurs. We view sexual penetration in a social context, and the context in which most theorists presume is context in which sexual intercourse *per se* is socially understood as *not* involving 'costs that agents ought to morally address'.[88] Given the positive, 'costless', or 'not unwelcoming' social context in which sexual penetration occurs, we then presume that a person exercises their rights of exclusive control over their body in favour of sexual penetration. Yet, as Westen makes clear,[89] this approach is not available to theorists given the variety of contexts in which sexual penetration occurs. We cannot make general statements about sexual penetration *per se* that draw upon fundamentally variable social contexts and circumstances.

The presumption therefore stems from our thinking about sexual penetration in terms of the frequency of (not wrongful) sexual penetration and in terms of the social context in which (not wrongful) sexual penetration occurs. The core of the problem is that we need to assess sexual penetration '*per se*',

[84] Williams, 'Offences and Defences' (n 26) 254.
[85] Dempsey and Herring (n 29) 481.
[86] Campbell (n 11) 82.
[87] Campbell (n 11) 82.
[88] Westen (n 12) 572.
[89] Westen (n 12) 572.

and sexual penetration '*per se*' is a physiological action. Once we strip away assumptions about generally 'normal activities' and general 'social understandings', there remains no basis for presuming that every person exercises their rights of self-ownership in favour of penetrative sex *per se*.

In other words, once we strip away the distracting assumptions, we are left with a choice, whether we

> should assume that an adult is willing to have sex, even with strangers and in unexpected encounters, until the individual specifically indicates the contrary. Or, should *un*willingness be assumed, even in the setting of parties and dates, until the person signals receptivity to intercourse?[90]

Leaving aside the type of parties that Stephen Schulhofer attends, the choice remains between two conventional practices: the 'no means no' convention (where an objection generates an obligation on another person not to do something) and the 'yes means yes' convention (where consent *waives* a primary obligation that is owed by another person not to do something). The 'no means no' convention represents a presumption that we exercise our rights of control over our bodies in favour of sexual activity. The 'yes means yes' convention is built on the opposing premise: when force is applied to another person in order to achieve sexual penetration, then we ought to presume—*as we do in all other instances of application of force*—that the penetration was an infringement of a person's self-ownership, and therefore contrary to general reasons.

The first objection to the *pro tanto* legal wrong thesis is often followed by a further objection: (2) sex is not *generally* anything. In response to both *pro tanto* wrong theses, Greasley notes:

> There is nothing particularly interesting or special about these kinds of reasons to avoid sex. They reflect the limitless context-specific reasons we may have against engaging in pretty well any activity.[91]

To defend the prevailing view, we might want to say that the morality of sex *per se* is 'neither here nor there'. To follow Greasley's thread, she is right, insofar as it is difficult to think of any human activity or interaction that is always worthwhile (or always harmful). The closest we can get is a general norm with some

[90] Stephen J Schulhofer, 'Consent: What It Means and Why It's Time to Require It' (2016) 47 U Pac L Rev 665, 666.

[91] Kate Greasley, 'Sex, Reasons, *Pro Tanto* Wronging, and the Structure of Rape Liability' (2021) 15 Crim Law Philos 159, 160.

exceptions. It is wrong to kill another person (except in self-defence or defence of another), it is wrong to stupefy or cut another person (except in surgery), it is wrong to punch or tackle another person (except in boxing or rugby), and so on. My claim here (the *pro tanto* legal wrong thesis) is that the common denominator in all of these activities is the application of force to the body of another person, and I then seek to add sex to the general norm. But, in doing so, I can concede that consent can and does perform the required justificatory or exculpatory work (addressed in the next essay).

Here, I suggest that the division of labour between practice-grounded, will-grounded, and world-grounded reasons (from Essay 4) can help. The all-things-considered morality of sex is informed by practice-grounded, will-grounded, and world-grounded reasons. As we have already seen, consensual sex can be harmful and denigrating, and consensual sex can be pleasurable and affirming. Sex can be wrongful to the extent that it can be contrary to worthwhile practice-grounded norms and still chosen and willed by both participants. The harmfulness of sex, like the worthwhileness of sex and the morality of sex, all things considered, engages considerations well beyond our present concern for the offence–defence distinction. Trying to understand sex (in general) in terms of all of the interests that sex (in general) can promote or harm is a tiresome, and perhaps fruitless, exercise.

However, the *pro tanto* legal wrong thesis need not be concerned with limitless context-specific reasons. The *pro tanto* legal wrong thesis is concerned with the *existence* of an obligation not to apply force (as opposed to the *generation* of the obligation). As such, it is concerned with the role that practice-grounded reasons can play in facilitating the expression of choice and, in doing so, opening up morally worthwhile options of social interaction (and closing off harmful ones). The contention here is merely that the 'yes means yes' convention (where sex is *pro tanto* wrong) is a better, self-ownership-respecting, convention than the 'no means no' convention (where the sex is *pro tanto* permissible). In terms of the all-things-considered morality of sex, it might be neither 'here nor there'. But if consent is a normative power, which exists because of the value of facilitating human interaction, then there is a choice to be made between the 'no means no' convention and the 'yes means yes' convention. The *pro tanto* wrong thesis is an argument in favour of the latter convention, in place of the former, without having to commit to a fundamental position on the morality of sex *per se*.

The third objection is the 'remainders objection', and it is an interesting one. The objection is that with all justified *pro tanto* wrongdoing, the justified person has reasons to regret that they committed the *pro tanto* wrong.

Campbell,[92] Gardner, Dempsey, and Herring all adopt a 'remainders thesis' that suggests that 'justified action still leaves a remainder of conflicting reasons that were, regrettably, not conformed to'.[93] It follows that 'justified prima facie wrongdoing leaves a moral residue of regret',[94] and the regret 'generates reasons to prefer less wrongful alternatives to securing the values that justify prima facie wrongful conduct'.[95] Greasley adds that a justified person also had reasons to avoid—and not seek out—the *pro tanto* wrong.[96] Our intuition is that there is no reason to regret, nor any reason to avoid, consensual sex. If we accept this intuition (and accept the remainders thesis), then sex (itself) cannot be a *pro tanto* wrong.

According to the remainders thesis, what is distinctive about justified wrongdoing is that 'its commission, albeit justified, remains regrettable'.[97] A justified wrong generates regret, or leaves a moral residue, because the value that the general prohibition protects remains to be counted in the overall moral calculus. For instance, there is an exception to the general prohibition not to intentionally cause another's death in circumstances of self-defence. But in such circumstances, the victim's right to life is a value that is not cancelled out.[98] The loss of life remains as something to regret, even when the act was justified. Similarly, there is an exception to the general prohibition not to drive dangerously or recklessly in circumstances where it is necessary to rush a person with life-threatening injuries to hospital. But in such circumstances, the value behind speeding limits, observing traffic signals, and so on is not cancelled out by those circumstances. The driver may be justified, but still has reasons to regret the endangerment of others through their justified actions.

In comparison, if we do want to 'cancel out' a value, and subtract it from the moral calculus, we cancel it out in constructing the elements of the wrong.[99] For example, the act of 'taking a book' is only wrong when that book belongs to another person. Theft, then, is the intentional taking of property that belongs to another person. Taking a book that belongs to you has no residual regret (such as that it used to belong to another person), rather the elements of the wrong simply have not been constructed. The prevailing view holds that consensual sex is akin to this third example (taking a book that belongs to you);

[92] Campbell (n 11) 83.
[93] Gardner (n 1) 820.
[94] Dempsey and Herring (n 29) 488.
[95] Dempsey and Herring (n 29) 488.
[96] Greasley (n 92) 162.
[97] Gardner (n 1) 820.
[98] Simester (n 8) 32–33.
[99] Simester (n 8) 437.

there is nothing to regret about consensual sex because the elements of the wrong simply have not been constructed.

Dempsey and Herring embrace the implications of the remainders thesis.[100] In earlier writing, I have sought to avoid the implications of the remainders thesis by upending Raz's claim that 'permission does not alter the reasons against the action. It will still harm the person's interests'.[101] I have argued that 'the provision of consent . . . *does alter* "the reasons against the action" or "the set of reasons a person otherwise has not to sexually penetrate another"' on the basis that 'consent can have a transformative effect'.[102] In hindsight, there is an impasse here, between my concern for normative powers and 'practice-grounded' reasons and (what I take to be) Raz's and Greasley's occupation with non-normative interests and 'world-grounded' reasons.

Let me explain this impasse. In my view, the reason why there is no residual regret from consensual activities is because consent is a normative power, and as a normative power, it acts on the normative phenomena of wrongs and obligations. In doing so, normative powers create a dynamic moral situation; they enable each person to change their moral circumstances. In comparison, acting in self-defence and acting in necessity are static moral situations; they are a response to the circumstances that we find ourselves in and cannot change.

When it comes to normative powers, we have the 'freedom to have an active role in determining the reasons we have'.[103] We have the freedom to waive obligations that are owed to us (forgiveness), we have the freedom to generate obligations that are owed to other people (promise-making), and we have the freedom to forbear an obligation that would otherwise be owed to us (consent). Normative powers are powerful enough to determine (to remove, to add, to suspend) moral reasons. By virtue of the normative power of the consenting person, a *pro tanto* wrongdoer has no reason to regret their justified wrongdoing, because they acted against reasons removed from the moral situation, without moral residue.

Does consensual sex then still 'harm the person's [non-normative] interests'? As we know, there are 'limitless context-specific reasons' to avoid sex, and to have sex, none of which are 'particularly interesting' to the general (im)permissibility of sex. As we have discussed, consensual sex can be worthwhile and affirming, or harmful and denigrating. The reason, you may recall, is that whilst consent can transform the normative situation (it can act on the phenomena

[100] Dempsey and Herring (n 29) 488.
[101] Joseph Raz, *Practical Reason and Norms* (2nd edn, OUP 1999) 96.
[102] Wall (n 40) 792.
[103] Ruth Chang, 'Do We Have Normative Powers?' (2020) 94 Proc Aristot Soc Suppl Vol 275, 298.

of wrongs and obligations), it cannot cure all the defects of the context-specific moral situation. In terms of regret, we might regret 'context-specific reasons' that undermine the value of consensual sex; Dempsey and Herring provide a compelling account for this regret.[104]

Otherwise, in terms of regret, we can also regret the circumstances we find ourselves in, and the agency we exercise in trading off competing values: the value of your own life versus the value of the life of an aggressor or the threat to life of an injured friend versus the risk of injury to another road user. There is moral residue because one value could not be upheld, instead one value was pursued at the expense of the other. When it comes to consent, however, there is no trade-off. A person's choices as to their body are respected by the general obligation (not to apply force), and when consent is communicated and the obligation is waived, a person's choices as to their body are respected.

The fourth objection contends, correctly, that there is nothing culpable about sex *per se*. The *pro tanto* wrong thesis is inevitably an argument about the structure of the criminal law. If we are considering which convention—'no means no' or 'yes means yes'—ought to be adopted by the criminal law, then we are triggering questions of criminalisation. Hence, it is easy to move from the wrongfulness of sex *per se* to the culpability of sex *per se*. But we ought not to move too quickly. Dempsey and Herring, for instance, merely 'map[ped] the moral landscape of sexual penetration' and were 'not directly concerned with questions of criminalisation'.[105]

Dempsey has subsequently argued against the *pro tanto* legal wrong thesis on the basis that

> the state's proper concern is to ensure that its subjects are able to live together in community as free and equal citizens. When it comes to crimes against the person, the state must grant each person the legally recognized and protected power of consent over how her body is treated, but it should neither criminalize nor require justification for sex *per se*.[106]

So far in this essay I have merely engaged a criterion (the Campbell–Gardner criterion) that proponents of the prevailing view themselves use to explain why, according to them, the question of consent ought to be on the offence side

[104] Dempsey and Herring (n 29) 488.
[105] Dempsey and Herring (n 29) 467.
[106] Michelle Madden Dempsey, 'The Normative Force of Consent in Moral, Political, and Legal Perspective' in Tatjana Hörnle (ed), *Sexual Assault: Law Reform in a Comparative Perspective* (OUP 2023) 25.

of the offence–defence distinction. It is, ultimately, my contention that the best way for the state to legally recognise the power of consent over how a person's body is treated is to require a justification for sex *per se*. But to contend this, I need to say something about justifications and excuses (in the next essay) and say something about the culpability of the wrongdoing *simpliciter* (the wrong without the excuse or justification). In any case, nothing has been said so far about the culpability of sex *per se*.

Nonetheless, I seem to be tarred with the implication that sex *per se* is culpable, even culpable in the way that rapists are culpable. Apparently:

> Wall thinks, because there are general reasons to avoid sexual penetration as such in 'all instances', it can be fittingly picked out as the offence-subset of rape—without reference to consent—as per Campbell's test.[107]

Formally, culpability attaches upon the finding of criminal liability, which requires not just the elements of the offence (here, penetrative sex coupled with intention) but also the absence of a justification or excuse (here, the provision of consent or a mistaken belief in consent). As I will explain in the next essay: If sex (itself) is a *pro tanto* wrong, where the justification of consent requires that the defendant acted on explanatory reasons (why he acted) that related to the guiding reasons (the permitted reasons for acting), then a person is only liable (and culpable) when that person cannot provide the justification. In light of this, it is at least tenable to say that a person who engages in penetrative sex and who cannot provide a consent-based justification or excuse (in the above sense) has committed a culpable wrong.

The fifth objection attempts to trivialise the *pro tanto* wrongfulness of sex. If consent can justify the *pro tanto* wrong, then, according to Greasley, the thesis that there are 'general reasons against consensual sex' is reduced to 'no more than that there are reasons for doing otherwise that *would* have applied were the circumstances different'.[108] In other words, the *ex ante* reasons (against sex) are trivial when compared to the *ex post* reasons (in favour of sex). Or, alternatively still, the practice-grounded reasons are trivial when will-grounded reasons seem to do all the moral work. These reformulations of the objection are correct, but do not trouble the *pro tanto* wrong thesis.

To understand why, recall how I introduced the offence–defence distinction (in *L'Hôtel de l'information imparfaite*). I suggested that the criminal law

[107] Greasley (n 92) 165.
[108] Greasley (n 92) 170.

should treat the events in Room 1 and the events in Room 2 the same. In both rooms, there was the application of force sufficient to cause bruising, and in both rooms, we have imperfect information about the circumstances under which the force was applied. The imperfect information limits our attention to the *ex ante* reasons that can inform the offence–defence distinction (and limits our attention to the practice-grounded reasons for the 'yes means yes' convention). No doubt, in employing the 'yes means yes' convention, we shift the legal work to the defence side of the offence–defence distinction (and shift the moral work into *ex post* and will-grounded moral reasons). The point is that this is where the legal and moral work ought to be performed.

To respond to the triviality objection, let me now conclude with a different allegory. According to Greasley's own allegory:

> It is a reason not to accelerate down a road if I might plough into a pedestrian crossing the street. I'm in the middle of nowhere and there is no pedestrian for miles. Is there a 'general reason' against accelerating down the road? If the putative general reasons against sexual penetration can be disappeared by dint of consent alone, we are ostensibly barred from holding that they apply as a matter of *generality*.[109]

I am not sure how strictly the analogy holds, but if it does, I admire the sexual confidence. The point here is helpful. There are many instances where the *ex ante* (or practice-grounded) reason 'disappears by dint of' an *ex post* (or will-grounded) reason of consent. The ease (and frequency) with which they vanish is not a reason to consider the *ex ante* (practice-grounded) reason to be trivial. My contention here is that there are nontrivial reasons (the right to self-ownership and the non-use value of the person) in favour of a practice where there is an obligation not to penetrate a person's body until they waive or suspend that obligation (the 'yes means yes' convention). Hence, my road-safety allegory would be different:

> It is a reason not to accelerate down a road if I might plough into a pedestrian crossing the street. I'm in the middle of nowhere and I cannot see a pedestrian, but there is a stop sign. The sign applies *generally* (even if there are no pedestrians). It does not prevent me from proceeding, but I am held to a particular standard for how I proceed through the intersection. Ultimately, it is not for an injured pedestrian themself to show that I proceeded through the

[109] Greasley (n 92) 171.

> intersection contrary to the standard, because I was the one driving and there was a stop sign.

Sometimes we have road signs (which generate rights and obligations). Their function is to coordinate an interaction (for practice-grounded reasons). At some intersections, we need a stop sign (the yes means yes convention) in place of a give way sign (the no means no convention). As we will eventually see, this reshapes how a person needs to account for how they proceeded through the stop sign. The stop sign (the yes means yes convention) is the so-called 'alternative and extreme view'.[110] The next essay starts to consider the implications of this view.

[110] John Child and David Ormerod, *Smith, Hogan, and Ormerod's Essentials of Criminal Law* (2nd edn, OUP 2017) 279.

6

Justifying and Excusing Sex

6.1

'[T]he offence/defence distinction', according to Michelle Madden Dempsey, 'marks no significant practical distinction because . . . the burden of persuasion remains on the prosecution as to both offence elements and (the absence of) affirmative defences'.[1] One reason to dismiss the *pro tanto* legal wrong thesis might be that the reallocation of consent from being, in its absence, an element of the offence to being a justificatory or exculpatory defence makes no practical difference. The main purpose of this essay is to identify how the legal standard for consent requires more from the defendant when consent represents a justificatory or exculpatory defence than when the absence of consent is an element of an offence. This account provides a response to the 'no practical difference' objection to the *pro tanto* legal wrong thesis.

This account also connects the (albeit unorthodox) *pro tanto* legal wrong thesis with another (albeit unorthodox) legal position: the expressive consent standard. In most jurisdictions,[2] and for most commentators,[3] consent is an internal phenomenon. Consent, according to the orthodox view, is an internal attitude of willingness, intention, waiver, or acquiescence ('attitudinal consent').[4]

[1] Michelle Madden Dempsey, 'The Normative Force of Consent in Moral, Political, and Legal Perspective' in Tatjana Hörnle (ed), *Sexual Assault: Law Reform in a Comparative Perspective* (OUP 2023) 24.

[2] See *R v JA* [2011] SCC 28, [2011] 2 SCR 440, [23]: 'Consent for this purpose is actual subjective consent in the mind of the complainant at the time of the sexual activity in question'; *R v Olugboja* [1982] QB 320 (CA), 321: '"consent" . . . covers a wide range of states of mind in the context of intercourse between a man and a woman, ranging from actual desire on the one hand to reluctant acquiescence on the other'; *R v Millar* [1998] QCA 276, [2000] 1 Qd R 437, [7]: 'It is in the nature of things rare for consensual conduct involving intimacy of this kind to be preceded by formal offer and acceptance. In some instances, consent is capable of being inferred from acquiescence in the continuation of the activity.'

[3] See Heidi M Hurd, 'The Moral Magic of Consent' (1996) 2 Leg Theory 121, 124; Larry Alexander, 'The Moral Magic of Consent (II)' (1996) 2 Leg Theory 165, 166; Seana Valentine Shiffrin, 'Promising, Intimate Relationships, and Conventionalism' (2008) 117 Philos Rev 481; Joshua Dressler, 'Where We Have Been, and Where We Might Be Going: Some Cautionary Reflections on Rape Law Reform' (1998) 46(3) Clev St L Rev 409.

[4] Peter Westen, *The Logic of Consent: The Diversity and Deceptiveness of Consent as a Defense to Criminal Conduct* (Routledge 2016) 4–5, 4.

Sex and Self-Ownership. Jesse Wall, Oxford University Press. © Jesse Wall 2025.
DOI: 10.1093/9780191987809.003.0006

For a few commentators,[5] and a few jurisdictions,[6] consent is both an external and an internal phenomenon. Consent, according to this unorthodox view, amounts to words and overt conduct that manifest or express the attitude of willingness, intention, waiver, or acquiescence ('expressive consent').[7] I will contend here that the 'practical difference' of viewing sex as a *pro tanto* wrong is that the consent standard is required to obey the logic of justifications and excuses, and that only the expressive consent standard can satisfy that logic.

In this essay, I will defend two main claims. The first claim is:

1. Justifications and excuses for wrongdoing must 'rely on reason',[8] whereas the negation of the elements of wrongdoing need not be reason-based.

As I will explain (at 6.2), justifications and excuses are predicated upon 'explanatory' reasons (that the defendant did act on) and guiding reasons (that the defendant ought to have acted on).[9] Justifications require the defendant to have acted on both guiding and explanatory reasons, and excuses require the defendant to be 'justified' in acting on their explanatory reasons.[10] To fortify the suggestion that 'the negation of the elements of wrongdoing need not be reason-based', I will demonstrate (at 6.3) how defendants acting upon incomplete guiding and explanatory reasons can succeed in negating an element of wrongdoing, whereas they would fail at establishing (the evidence for) a justificatory or exculpatory defence.

[5] See Nathan Brett, 'Sexual Offenses and Consent' (1998) 11 CJLJ 69; Stephen J Schulhofer, 'Rape in the Twilight Zone: When Sex is Unwanted But Not Illegal' (2005) 38 Suffolk UL Rev 415, 422; David P Bryden, 'Redefining Rape' (2000) 3 Buff Crim L Rev 317, 426; Lois Pineau, 'Date Rape: A Feminist Analysis' (1989) 8 L & Phil 217, 238–39; Tom Dougherty, '*Yes Means Yes*: Consent as Communication' (2015) 43 Philos Public Aff 224, 234.

[6] See DC Code, s 22–3001(4) (2018) ('words or overt actions indicating a freely given agreement'); Minn Stat, s 609.341(4) (2017) ('words or overt actions by a person indicating a freely given present agreement'); 13 VSA, s 3251(3) (2017) ('words or actions by a person indicating a voluntary agreement'); Rev Code Wash (ARCW), s 9A.44.010(7) (2017) ('actual words or conduct indicating freely given agreement'); 940 Wis Stat Ann, s 940.225(4) (2018) ('words or overt actions . . . indicating a freely given agreement'). See also Stephen J Schulhofer, 'Consent: What It Means and Why It's Time to Require It' (2016) 47 U Pac L Rev 665, 669.

[7] Westen (n 4) 5: 'Factual Expressive Consent'.

[8] John Gardner, 'Justifications and Reasons' in AP Simester and ATH Smith (eds), *Harm and Culpability* (Clarendon Press 1996) 121.

[9] Joseph Raz, *Practical Reason and Norms* (2nd edn, OUP 1999) 16–20, 18: 'We should admit that we use reasons in both ways. We could even distinguish between two notions of reason. . . . Only reasons understood as facts are normatively significant; only they determine what ought to be done. . . . The other notion of reasons is relevant exclusively for explanatory purposes and not at all for guiding purposes'; Gardner, 'Justifications and Reasons' (n 8) 103.

[10] See Gardner, 'Justifications and Reasons' (n 8) 122: 'For by their nature excuses take the world as the defendant justifiably sees it rather than as it is. They look to what the defendant believes to be applicable reasons for action, so as long as she does so on the basis of genuinely applicable reasons for belief.'

I then consider (6.4) these incomplete justifications with reference to consent and sexual penetration. This enables the second main claim about the legal definition of consent:

> 2. Only a definition of consent that includes both objective elements ('overt words and actions') and subjective elements ('an attitude of acceptance, willingness, or acquiescence') requires the defendant to have acted on both guiding and explanatory reasons or otherwise be 'justified' in acting on his explanatory reasons.

The practical difference, therefore, between the orthodox approach and the *pro tanto* legal wrong thesis is that the latter requires a more demanding standard of expressive consent.

It follows, therefore, that if sexual penetration is a *pro tanto* wrong, which requires a justification, then the inquiry into the complainant's consent is concerned with the reasons that governed (or 'guided') and informed (or 'explained') the defendant's action. These sets of reasons require both the complainant's attitudinal (subjective) and expressive (objective) consent. Here, expressive consent permits another person to act on a set of reasons in favour of the action, rendering an actor culpable for engaging in penetrative sex in the absence of that permission. Moreover, I will argue here that it is only possible to capture these instances of culpability when we treat sexual penetration as a *pro tanto* wrong and apply a standard of expressive consent.

To animate this argument, consider the following scenario:

> Two teenagers, A and B, attend a summer camp. During a week of fishing, canoeing, and campfires, A and B have also been flirting, hand-holding, and occasionally kissing behind the boat shed. Late, on the last night of camp, A enters B's tent. A proceeds to kiss and embrace B whilst B remains still. A then undresses B and proceeds to engage in penetrative sexual intercourse. B remains silent and still throughout.

Now split this scenario into two alternative versions of events:

> At Summer Camp (1), B(1) *objected to* the sexual intercourse. However, B(1) was panic-stricken; B(1) was fearful that A(1) might become aggressive and was also concerned about awakening the other campers, causing a scene, and having others find out about the intercourse. So B(1) remained silent and still.

> At Summer Camp (2), B(2) *willed* the sexual intercourse. However, as a shy, naive, and nervous teen, B(2) was uncertain as to how to react and wanted to avoid any embarrassment from saying or doing 'the wrong thing'. So B(2) remained silent and still.

As a first and rough cut, I will contend here that the sexual penetration at Summer Camp (1) was a *culpable*, and *wrong*, act. The absence of B(1)'s attitudinal consent means that the sexual penetration at Summer Camp (1) was a wrong committed against B(1). A(1) might have had a mistaken belief that B(1) attitudinally consented to the sexual penetration. However, for A(1) to be excused for the wrong act, it ought to be necessary that A(1) had a mistaken belief in B(1)'s attitudinal consent that was nonetheless a 'justified' or 'reason-based' belief. Absent B(1)'s expressive consent, A(1) is culpable insofar as A(1) is unable to show that the mistaken belief was a reason-based belief.

I will also contend here that the sexual penetration at Summer Camp (2) was a *culpable* but *permissible* act. The penetrative sex between A(2) and B(2) was a *pro tanto* wrong that was rendered permissible by virtue of B(2) internally consenting to the intercourse. However, for A(2) to be justified in performing a *pro tanto* wrong, it is necessary that B(2) internally consented *and* that A(2) responded to reasons in favour of B(2)'s consent. Absent B(2)'s expressive consent—absent words and overt conduct that expressed B(2)'s attitude of willingness to engage in the specific sex act—A(2) will be unable to identify such reasons.

6.2

To respond to the 'no practical difference' objection, I need to show that the criminal law demands more of a defendant when an inquiry is governed by the defence side of the offence–defence distinction. To do so, I will explain how when the criminal law views conduct through the lens of a justification or excuse, the criminal law inquires into a defendant's reasons for action. When considering justificatory and exculpatory defences, the defendant's reasons for action are directly relevant to the task of showing that the defendant is justified in, or excused for, the performance of a wrong act. In comparison, when the criminal law considers inculpatory elements, it is only interested in the defendant's reasons for action indirectly, as a means to evidence a particular state of mind.

Since we are concerned with how the law inquires into a defendant's 'reasons for action', allow me to make two brief preliminary points about 'reasons for action'. First, when we inquire into a person's reasons for action, we are investigating the 'facts' that entered into the defendant's deliberation about what they ought to do and 'that constitute[d] a case for (or against) the performance of an action'.[11] When we say 'that facts are reasons', we are 'using the term "fact" . . . to designate that in virtue of which true or justified statements are true or justified'.[12] For example, a person may take an umbrella when leaving home on the basis that it is raining (coupled with the intention or desire to stay dry). Alternatively, a person may take an umbrella on the basis that there is a high chance of rain in the forecast (again, coupled with the intention or desire to stay dry). The rain or the forecast of rain are reasons in favour of taking an umbrella when leaving home. However, if a person was to 'misread[] a weather report in the newspaper' as forecasting a very high chance of rain when it actually forecasts no chance of rain,[13] then there would be 'in fact no reason for which' they acted.[14]

Second, when we inquire into a person's practical reasoning about what they ought to do, we expect that they will act on an 'undefeated' reason.[15] That is, whilst there may be reasons for and against the performance of an action and such reasons may defeat one another, we expect that a person will act on the reasons that remain after the practical conflict of reasons.[16] For example, the likelihood of rain in the forecast may be high (and the need to stay dry may be great), meaning that the forecast may defeat or outweigh the inconvenience of carrying the umbrella. In which case, there is an undefeated reason in favour of taking the umbrella, and we would expect a person to act for that undefeated reason. For an act to be 'reason-based', it needs to be performed for an undefeated reason. That being so, we have reason to be concerned with the practical unreasonableness of another person not taking their umbrella. With these preliminaries in mind, let us turn to consider when we are interested in another person's practical reasoning.

[11] Joseph Raz, *From Normativity to Responsibility* (OUP 2011) 36.

[12] Raz, *Practical Reason and Norms* (n 9) 17.

[13] Gerald Beaulieu, 'Can Explanatory Reasons Be Good Reasons for Action?' (2013) 44 Metaphilosophy 440, 448.

[14] Beaulieu (n 13) 448.

[15] Gardner, 'Justifications and Reasons' (n 8) 111. See also John Gardner, 'The Mysterious Case of the Reasonable Person' (2001) 51 UTLJ 273, 275–76.

[16] Gardner, 'Justifications and Reasons' (n 8) 111: 'it is a basic principle of practical rationality . . . that one should always act for *some* undefeated reason, i.e., that at least one of the (guiding) reasons in favour of doing as one did should have been one's (explanatory) reason for doing it.'

If an act is morally neutral, a person's 'reasons for action' are normatively immaterial. For instance, if there is no general norm against sexual penetration, then sexual penetration is normatively inert. Instead, the prohibitory norm requires the further inculpatory element of the absence of consent. Where there is no prohibitory norm against the action, 'the actor's motives for acting in this non-wrongful and non-regrettable fashion are largely irrelevant'.[17] Since the actor is engaged in a presumptively permissive activity, they have no need to seek permission to act, nor any need to act for any particular set of reasons. It therefore 'does not matter why the defendant acted as he did, so long as that is how he acted'.[18] In other words, if sexual penetration is morally neutral, the defendant's 'motivation' and reasons for acting are 'beside the point'.[19] Rather, the focus is on the further inculpatory element of the absence of the complainant's 'consent' (or the defendant's knowledge of the absence of the complainant's consent) that is necessary for the activity to fall under the prohibitory norm.

In comparison, if sexual penetration is a *pro tanto* wrong, then the task of justifying the wrong is concerned with both the complainant's consent and the defendant's reasons for acting. This implication of viewing penetrative sex as a *pro tanto* wrong requires some explanation. To start, if sexual penetration is taken to be a *pro tanto* wrong, then there is a prohibitory norm against it. Put more simply, if sexual penetration was itself wrong, then there would be 'a rule against it'. A prohibitory norm represents a reason against an activity *that also* governs the relationship between that reason and other considerations for and against the activity. Whilst we may ordinarily be permitted to engage in a weighing up or trading off of reasons for and against an action, when the law generates a prohibitory norm, it provides a *protected reason* not to do something.[20] The protected reason is insulated from the conflict of reasons for (and against) the action, since any 'countervailing considerations are defeated in advance of any practical conflict'.[21]

As we have encountered in the previous essay, there may be a general reason not to engage in sexual penetration on the basis of the right of self-ownership. If this general reason was to be treated as a protected reason, then the presumptive impermissibility of sexual penetration would preclude 'all reasons

[17] Vera Bergelson, 'The Meaning of Consent' (2014) 12 Ohio St J Crim L 171, 177. See also Gardner, 'Justifications and Reasons' (n 8) 107: 'justification is called for only when one also has some reason *not* to act, believe, etc. as one does. The unobjectionable, in other words, is in no need of justification.'
[18] Gardner, 'Justifications and Reasons' (n 8) 117.
[19] Gardner, 'Justifications and Reasons' (n 8) 117.
[20] Joseph Raz, *The Authority of Law: Essays on Law and Morality* (Clarendon Press 1979) 17–19.
[21] Gardner, 'Justifications and Reasons' (n 8) 115.

in favour of sexual penetration'.[22] In other words, the 'rule against it' would circumvent the weighing up of reasons for and against the activity. For example, whilst the likelihood of rain in the forecast may be high (and the need to stay dry may be great), if the umbrella was the property of another person, then there would be a prohibitory norm against taking it. We would therefore expect that a person's deliberation on the reasons in favour of and against taking the umbrella would be precluded by the prohibitory norm.

Under the *pro tanto* legal wrong thesis, sex can nonetheless be justified through the provision of consent. Not that consent provides a 'reason in favour of penetration'. Rather, the provision of consent by one person grants permission to another person to act for a set of reasons that would otherwise be pre-emptively excluded from consideration.[23] When a person consents, they 'exercise a normative power to permit (or empower) another to do something that the other has, or would otherwise have, a duty not to do',[24] and the reason not to do an activity is no longer protected.

Consent, as a justification, therefore represents a '*cancelling permission*[] to perform, under certain specified conditions, the actions which [the law] criminalizes'.[25] Such justifications do not defeat the reason against the activity but instead act to remove the 'secondary layer of protection' that the reason (against the activity) had by virtue of being a *protected* reason.[26] Consent and justifications, in general, represent exceptions to the pre-emptive exclusion from considering countervailing reasons for action. Whilst the law may prohibit an activity, and pre-emptively exclude countervailing reasons for action from the equation, the law may also provide justificatory defences, which permit a certain set of countervailing reasons for action to re-enter the equation.

In particular, there are two important ways that this 'certain set of countervailing reasons' may re-enter a defendant's practical reasoning about whether they should perform an action. As Gardner explains:

[22] Gardner, 'Justifications and Reasons' (n 8) 116: 'So far as the criminal law is concerned *all* reasons in favour of performing the criminalized action are defeated by virtue of the law's . . . authority.'

[23] John Gardner, 'Justification under Authority' (2010) 23 CJLJ 71, 78–80

[24] Gardner, 'Justification under Authority' (n 23) 75: 'To consent is to exercise a normative power to permit (or empower) another to do something that the other has, or would otherwise have, a duty not to do (or no power to do).'

[25] Gardner, 'Justifications and Reasons' (n 8) 117: 'What the law does, which nevertheless creates a role for some justificatory defences, is to provide us with *cancelling permissions* to perform, under certain specified conditions, the actions which it criminalizes. . . . The same is not true in a case to which the definition of the crime does not extend, i.e., in which "an element of the offence is negated".'

[26] See Gardner, 'Justifications and Reasons' (n 8) 117; John Gardner, 'Fletcher on Offences and Defences' (2003) 39 Tulsa L Rev 817, 823; John Gardner, 'In Defence of Offences and Defences' (2012) 4 Jerusalem Rev Leg Stud 110, 118–21.

> [T]he law not only regulates the actions which one may perform, but also regulates the reasons for which one may perform those actions. It regulates the actions which one may perform by making some of them into criminal offences, which are prima facie wrongs. *It regulates the reasons for which one may perform those actions by picking out certain reasons in favour of their performance as legally acceptable reasons.*[27]

Justificatory defences require an examination of two aspects of the defendant's reasons for action. The first concerns the reasons that are acceptable or permitted reasons for action by virtue of the justification. The second concerns the reasons that a defendant acted on. These are 'guiding reasons' and 'explanatory reasons'[28] respectively. Guiding reasons 'bear on what one ought to do or believe',[29] whereas explanatory reasons are 'the reasons that the agent or believer had for acting or believing as she did'.[30]

There is a logical relationship between these two sets of reasons insofar as a defendant's explanatory reasons will also be understood—*by the defendant*—to be the applicable guiding reasons.[31] However, the defendant may be acting under a mistaken belief that the explanatory reasons are also the applicable guiding reasons. In which case, the action will not be justified, since, according to Gardner, 'to claim a justificatory defence, one must not only have, but act for, one of those permitted reasons'.[32] As will be discussed further below, where a defendant mistakenly believes that his or her explanatory reasons are also guiding reasons *and* that mistaken belief is a 'justified' or a 'reason-based' belief, the defendant will be excused for (but not justified in) his or her wrongdoing.[33]

Hence, to argue that an action is justified is to make two related claims. It is to claim that the act was, all things considered, the right thing to do—that whilst the act may be contrary to a prohibitory norm, certain countervailing considerations rendered it a justified contravention. To claim a justification is to also claim that the act was performed *because* it was the right thing to do—because the countervailing considerations justified contravening the norm.

The key point is that guiding and explanatory reasons are required when the defendant is seeking to justify a wrong. Yet where the same factor forms an

[27] Gardner, 'Justifications and Reasons' (n 8) 117 (emphasis added).
[28] Raz, *Practical Reason and Norms* (n 9) 16–20.
[29] Gardner, 'Justifications and Reasons' (n 8) 103.
[30] Gardner, 'Justifications and Reasons' (n 8) 109–10.
[31] Gardner, 'Justifications and Reasons' (n 8) 103.
[32] Gardner, 'Justifications and Reasons' (n 8) 117.
[33] Gardner, 'Justifications and Reasons' (n 8) 119 (footnote omitted): 'To excuse an action is not, of course, to justify that action. Rather, one justifies one's belief that the action is justified.'

inculpatory element (rather than a justificatory or exculpatory defence), there is no need to inquire into the defendant's reasons for action. Herein lies the fundamental point of contrast between the *pro tanto* legal wrong thesis and the orthodox approach. Bergelson explains the contrast in the following way:

> Committing a prima facie wrongful act requires an explanation, and the explanation brings in the perpetrator's reason for acting. . . . Thus, wrongfulness of an act is not reducible to a breach of the victim's rights; it also includes a poor reason for action.
>
> . . . when the act is prima facie morally neutral, we do not need to question the actor's reasons for action.[34]

If sexual penetration is normatively inert and neutral, and it is the absence of consent that is necessary to generate the prohibitory norm, then the relevant question concerns whether the sexual penetration was performed in the absence of consent. However, if sexual penetration is a *pro tanto* wrong, then it calls for a justification. Such a justification must represent a set of reasons for action that are recognised as acceptable reasons in favour of an otherwise prohibited activity (guiding reasons), *and* the defendant must have acted on those reasons (explanatory reasons). As we may be able to anticipate, viewing sexual penetration as a *pro tanto* wrong—as calling for a justification—broadens the inquiry into the defendant's reasons for action. It becomes necessary to consider both the complainant's consent (in order to identify a guiding reason) and the defendant's responsiveness to this (in order to identify an explanatory reason).

6.3

I have so far shown that once a prohibitory norm is in place, justifying or excusing a departure from that norm requires explanatory and guiding reasons. The contrast so far has been between an inquiry into an inculpatory element, which is indifferent to the defendant's reasons for action, and an inquiry as to a justificatory or exculpatory defence, which examines these reasons. However, it remains to be demonstrated how this requirement of explanatory and guiding reasons makes a practical difference. To demonstrate the difference, I will start by exploring here two instances where the defendant

[34] Bergelson (n 17) 179.

has an incomplete set of reasons for action. As we shall see, the incompleteness of the defendant's reasons for action matter when they are used to ground a justification or an excuse. In contrast, the quality of the defendant's reasons for action are immaterial to negating an element of the offence.

The first instance of when a defendant has an incomplete set of reasons for action arises where the defendant acts on 'a mistaken claim about the factual preconditions' of a justificatory defence.[35] That is, when the defendant mistakenly believes that there are sufficiently good reasons to justify a wrong act. For example, consider a defendant who murders a victim mistakenly believing them to be an aggressor. The defendant may seek to justify his or her actions by claiming self-defence. Similarly, another defendant may burn a field of corn acting on a mistaken belief that it would serve as a firebreak and prevent a forest fire from engulfing a nearby town. The defendant may seek to justify his or her actions by claiming necessity on the basis that they would result in the lesser of two harmful outcomes. A third defendant may drive with excess blood alcohol in order to rush a friend to hospital under the mistaken belief that a minor injury was a life-threatening one. The defendant may seek to justify his or her actions by claiming duress of circumstances. In all these examples, the defendant has an explanatory reason to perform a wrong act but is not acting according to a guiding reason in favour of the action.

Let us focus on the self-defence claim. Consider further if this defendant was subject to a criminal code that defined the elements of culpable homicide to include the absence of self-defence. A defendant who acted on a mistaken belief in self-defence would not satisfy the elements of this culpable homicide definition. This is because 'one of the necessary elements of the offence[]—a negative element—[would] remain[] unsatisfied'.[36] The defendant would not have the requisite intent to cause the death of a *non-aggressor*. As Fletcher argues, '[i]f the absence of self-defence is an element of homicide, then no one can be guilty of intentional homicide who mistakenly thinks that he or she is being attacked'.[37] If the elements of culpable homicide require intentionally causing the death of a non-aggressor, then the defendant's belief that the victim was an aggressor will be sufficient to negate the elements of the offence. There may be no reasonable basis for the defendant's mistaken belief that the victim was an aggressor. However, the absence of any reasons for the mistaken belief is only relevant to the element of intent in that it may make the mistaken

[35] George P Fletcher, 'The Nature of Justification' in Stephen Shute, John Gardner, and Jeremy Horder (eds), *Action and Value in Criminal Law* (Clarendon Press 1993) 178.
[36] Fletcher (n 35) 177.
[37] Fletcher (n 35) 178.

belief difficult to evidence. If the defendant acted on the mistaken belief that the victim was an aggressor, then the defendant's actions would not satisfy the elements of the prohibitory norm, and there would be no wrong calling for an inquiry into the defendant's reasons for action.

In comparison, if the defendant was subject to a legal system where self-defence was available as a justification, we would expect the defendant to provide reasons for his or her belief that the victim was an aggressor (explanatory reasons). We would also expect the defendant to provide evidence that the victim was in fact an aggressor (guiding reasons). Absent a guiding reason, it cannot be said that the action was justified in the sense that it was the right thing to do. There was no (guiding) reason to act contrary to a prohibitory norm in order to render the action the right thing to do, *all things considered*. Nonetheless, the defendant may be subject to a criminal code that (technically) 'justifies', or (more accurately) excuses, a wrong act where there is a mistaken belief as to the justifying circumstances *and* where that mistaken belief is a justified belief. That is, the defendant's actions would be justified if his or her mistaken practical reasoning contained an undefeated *reason* for his or her belief that the victim was an aggressor (a justified mistake).[38]

This requirement of a 'justified' or reason-based mistake isolates instances where the defendant's *belief* that his or her actions were justified was a 'justified belief'. In such instances, the defendant's unjustified actions (coupled with a justified belief) may be *excused*.[39] A defendant may therefore be *excused* from liability for intentionally killing another (or burning a field of corn or drink-driving) if two conditions are met. First, the defendant would need to *explain* his or her reasons for acting in terms of justifying circumstances, such as self-defence (or necessity or duress of circumstances). Second, the defendant would need to show that his or her mistake as to the applicable guiding reasons was justified or reason-based. Hence, the wrong act is not justified, but it may be excused if the defendant's *mistaken* practical reasoning contained an undefeated reason in favour of performing it.

A justified mistake as to a justifying factor therefore renders it a 'non-culpable wrong act'.[40] For Heidi M Hurd, a non-culpable wrong act is nonetheless wrong, as it 'violates the maxims of our best moral theory'.[41] However, it is non-culpable in the sense that it was done without:

[38] Gardner, 'Justifications and Reasons' (n 8) 120–22.
[39] Gardner, 'Justifications and Reasons' (n 8) 120.
[40] Heidi M Hurd, 'Justification and Excuse, Wrongdoing and Culpability' (1999) 74 Notre Dame L Rev 1551, 1558.
[41] Hurd, 'Justification and Excuse, Wrongdoing and Culpability' (n 40) 1558.

> intending to do an action that is wrongful, knowing that one [would] do an action that is wrongful, or failing to infer from available evidence that one [would] do an action that is wrongful.[42]

It follows that the actor is 'nonculpable if she does an action justifiably believing it to be right' and, alternatively, that the actor is 'culpable if she does an action believing it to be wrong or unjustifiably believing it to be right'.[43] Each defendant intended to do the right (ie justified) thing in attempting to defend themselves, halt a forest fire, or take a seriously injured person to hospital. A justified mistake[44] as to a justifying factor precludes culpability in this way, without affecting the moral status or permissibility of the act.

The key contrast here is between the indifference that inculpatory elements have towards a defendant's reasons for action and the examination that justificatory and exculpatory defences undertake on a defendant's reasons for action. Where there is a mistake as to a justifying factor, and the factor is located as an inculpatory element, the mistake may negate a requisite element of the offence. In comparison, where the factor is located as a justification or excuse, the defendant may be excused for the wrong act only if his or her mistaken belief is justified or reason-based.

The second instance of where the incompleteness of the defendant's reasons for action is relevant to justifications and excuses, and is irrelevant to inculpatory elements, is 'the problem of objective justification'.[45] This problem arises where the defendant acts contrary to a prohibitory norm whilst being ignorant of the justifying circumstances. A defendant may set out to kill the victim and do so whilst being unaware that the victim himself was moments away from killing the defendant. In addition, a defendant may maliciously burn a field of corn whilst being unaware that the burnt field would serve as a firebreak and save a nearby town from being engulfed by a forest fire. Further, a defendant with excessive blood alcohol may set out to drive a friend to hospital unaware that his or her friend's injury is a life-threatening one. Each defendant would be doing the right (ie justified) thing whilst being ignorant of the circumstances that justify an action.

42 Hurd, 'Justification and Excuse, Wrongdoing and Culpability' (n 40) 1558.

43 Heidi M Hurd, 'Justifiably Punishing the Justified' (1992) 90 Mich L Rev 2203, 2207.

44 See Hurd, 'Justifiably Punishing the Justified' (n 43) 2207: 'An actor is epistemically justified in believing an action to be right if, under the circumstances, she has invested a reasonable amount of time, talent, diligence, and resources to acquire information about her circumstances and to determine the demands of morality in such circumstances'; cf Gardner, 'Justifications and Reasons' (n 8) 120: 'It is not enough that one made a mistake as to justification.... There must have been an undefeated reason for one's belief, emotion, etc.'

45 Fletcher (n 35) 179.

Let us again start with the circumstances of self-defence. If 'murder' was defined to include the absence of self-defence as an element, 'one would be inclined to think that the objective presence of [the intended victim's] aggression would be sufficient to prevent realization of the offence'.[46] It is akin, according to Fletcher, to the defendant attempting to kill a scarecrow:

> If the objective fact that the intended victim is in fact a scarecrow precludes liability for homicide, then, by extension, the objective fact that the intended victim is an aggressor should have the same effect.[47]

It would therefore be possible for a defendant to act objectively in self-defence without being aware that their victim was an aggressor. Where the prohibitory norm (the elements of culpable homicide) includes the element of the absence of self-defence, there is no need to inquire into the reasons that govern the defendant's action. The objective fact of the victim's aggression negates the element of the offence.

In comparison, if the claim of self-defence is available to the defendant as a justificatory or exculpatory defence, then the law inquires into the defendant's explanatory and guiding reasons for acting. As a result:

> [O]nly those who have acted with knowledge of the justifying circumstances . . . should be able to claim a good reason for infringing a protected interest and rely upon a claim of justification.[48]

Hence, 'objective justifications' are problematic, since they represent only guiding reasons—and not explanatory reasons—for action. If claims of self-defence (or necessity or duress of circumstances) are available as defences rather than as negating an element of the offence, 'objective justifications' fail to justify performing actions that are contrary to a prohibitory norm.

The absence of explanatory reasons prevents a defendant from being exculpable. The act may not have been wrong in the sense that—all things considered—it was right act to perform. The defendant nonetheless remains culpable; he or she acted intentionally to infringe a protected interest, or acted intentionally contrary to a prohibitory norm, without having any justifying reason. These are instances of 'culpable right actions'.[49] They are actions 'that

46 Fletcher (n 35) 179.
47 Fletcher (n 35) 179.
48 Fletcher (n 35) 179.
49 Hurd, 'Justification and Excuse, Wrongdoing and Culpability' (n 40) 1565.

one has a right to do' by virtue of the objective justification (or guiding reason) 'but that one does with bad intentions or for bad reasons'[50] or, by extension, inadequate reasons in favour of the *pro tanto* wrong. We can nonetheless attach moral blame to culpable right actions on the basis that 'they *tried* to do unjustified actions, even though they did not, in fact, succeed'.[51]

The problem of objective justification only applies where the defendant's justificatory factor is located on the defence side of the offence–defence distinction. In which case, the defendant is unable to justify his or her wrong act, since the defendant cannot identify an explanatory reason in favour of the act. In comparison, if the justificatory factor is located on the offence side of the offence–defence distinction, the fact that the action was the right thing to do will negate an element of the offence, regardless of the absence of an explanatory reason in favour of the act.

6.4

It is now possible to return our attention to consent in the context of sexual offences. In this section, we will consider the problem of mistaken justification and the problem of objective justification where the justificatory factor is 'consent'. In doing so, the two elements of the legal definition of consent emerge. The contention here is that where the question of consent is located on the offence side of the offence–defence distinction, *what counts as consent* is only a consenting attitude (the subjective element). In comparison, where the question of consent is located on the defence side of the offence–defence distinction, what counts as consent is the combination of observable behaviour (the objective elements) and internal attitude (the subjective element).

Consider a case where a defendant claims that he had a mistaken belief that a complainant consented to the penetrative sexual activity. It follows from the above discussion that if a sexual offence (such as rape) is defined as sexual penetration in *the absence of consent*, a defendant may seek to raise reasonable doubt as to the inculpatory elements. The defendant may claim that his actions were not accompanied by knowledge of the absence of consent. This situation is similar to a defendant charged with murder negating the inculpatory element of 'the absence of self-defence' by claiming that they mistook the victim for an aggressor. Because 'non-consent is an element of rape . . . the

[50] Hurd, 'Justification and Excuse, Wrongdoing and Culpability' (n 40) 1565.
[51] Hurd, 'Justification and Excuse, Wrongdoing and Culpability' (n 40) 1566.

required intent is the intent to have intercourse without consent'[52] or the intent to have intercourse whilst knowing that the intercourse is non-consensual. Hence, where the absence of consent is an inculpatory element, there is no need to examine the reasons for the defendant's actions. It is enough for the defendant to raise reasonable doubt as to *mens rea* element of the offence.

Moreover, it ought to also follow from the above discussion that if the absence of consent is an inculpatory element, 'the reasonableness of the mistake' as to the complainant's consent 'is neither here nor there'.[53] Yet most legal systems will not tolerate unreasonable beliefs in the complainant's consent being used to negate an inculpatory element. Rather, most criminal codes modify the inculpatory element and require that the mistaken belief be based upon reasonable, or non-reckless, grounds.[54] We will return to explain this 'excuse-style modification' below, once we get a sense of how a reason-based mistake as to the complainant's consent can be exculpatory.

But first, note how the inculpatory element (the absence of consent) is concerned with either the complainant's state of mind or the defendant's knowledge of this. The complainant's behaviour and external expression of her internal attitude through words and conduct provide only an evidential basis from which we can draw inferences about the complainant's state of mind or the defendant's knowledge of this. At first blush, that may make sense. It makes sense *to the extent that* it is the complainant's internal attitude towards the action that is relevant to the task of determining the *permissibility* of the action.[55] It is the complainant's subjective or internal attitude of intention, will, or acquiescence—her 'attitudinal consent'—that is doing the work of 'transforming' the moral status of the act.[56]

On Hurd's account, to 'consent' to an action is to form the 'intention' that another person cross what would otherwise be (in the absence of consent) a 'moral boundary'.[57] On Larry Alexander's account, to consent is 'to forgo valid

[52] Fletcher (n 35) 178.

[53] Gardner, 'Justifications and Reasons' (n 8) 121 (footnote omitted).

[54] See, for instance, Sexual Offences Act 2003 (UK), ss 1(1)(c), 2(1)(d), 3(1)(d), and 4(1)(d); Criminal Code RSC 1985 c C–46, ss 153.1(5), 153.1(6), 265(4), and 273.2; Crimes Act 1900 (NSW), ss 61HA(3)(b) and 61HA(3)(c); Criminal Code Act 1899 (Qld), s 24; Criminal Law Consolidation Act 1935 (SA), ss 47, 48, and 48A; Criminal Code Act 1924 (Tas), s 14A; Crimes Act 1958 (Vic), ss 36A, 36B, 38(1)(c), 39(1)(c), 40(1)(d), 41(1)(d), 42(1)(d), and 47(1)(c)(ii); Criminal Code Act Compilation Act 1913 (WA), s 24; Crimes Act 1961 (NZ), ss 128(2)(b) and 128(3)(b).

[55] Kimberly Kessler Ferzan, 'Consent, Culpability, and the Law of Rape' (2016) 13 Ohio St J Crim L 397, 400: 'permissibility should track wrongdoing; that is, permissibility should depend on the underlying act's nature and quality and not the defendant's culpability'.

[56] Heidi M Hurd, 'The Normative Force of Consent', in Peter Schaber and Andreas Müller (eds), *Routledge Handbook of the Ethics of Consent* (Routledge 2018) 44, as cited in Ferzan (n 55) 405. See also Larry Alexander, 'The Ontology of Consent' (2014) 55 Anal Philos 102.

[57] Hurd, 'The Moral Magic of Consent' (n 3) 124, cited by Bergelson (n 17) 172.

rights-based moral objections to the act'.[58] In either case, the action becomes *permissible* by virtue of one person's internal attitude towards another person's actions. According to this orthodox view (of what consent requires), where the complainant's consent is contested, we may inquire into her externalised behaviour. However, we may only do so 'to seek evidence of that person's state of mind in the same way that we seek evidence of other morally and legally relevant subjective states'.[59] Hence, being grounded in respect for the autonomous agent, the requirement of consent, which determines whether an act is permissible or impermissible, concerns the complainant's internal attitude towards the act—her attitudinal consent.[60]

It may also make sense, at first blush, that the defendant's state of mind should be relevant to the task of determining the *culpability* of his actions. If the act is 'prima facie' morally neutral, the defendant will only be culpable if he intends to perform an action that is wrongful or knows that he is performing a wrongful action.[61] Again, the complainant's externalised behaviour is therefore only relevant to determining whether the defendant knew that the complainant did not attitudinally consent to the penetrative sex.

It follows that where the absence of consent is an inculpatory element, the complainant's attitudinal consent will render or 'transform' the morally neutral act into a permissible act. In the absence of the complainant's attitudinal consent, the defendant's own mistaken belief that the complainant attitudinally consented renders a wrongful act non-culpable. Therefore, where the question of consent is located on the offence side of the offence–defence distinction, *what counts as consent* is attitudinal consent (and only attitudinal consent).

In contrast, where the question of consent is located on the defence side of the offence–defence distinction, there are roles for both objective and subjective elements of consent. If consent is available as a defence, then a defendant's mistaken belief in the consent of the complainant may also provide an excuse for the wrongful act. However, in order to excuse the wrong act, the defendant needs to have acted on the basis of a justified or reason-based belief in a justifying factor. Recall that reasons for action are 'facts' that 'constitute a

[58] Alexander, 'The Moral Magic of Consent (II)' (n 3) 166.

[59] Hurd, 'The Moral Magic of Consent' (n 3) 125.

[60] Shiffrin (n 3) 500: 'The idea that an agent can intentionally form an obligation through the exercise and expression of her will alone (and not by first transforming the state of affairs around her) comes part and parcel with any plausible conception of an autonomous agent'; Hurd, 'The Normative Force of Consent' (n 56) 44, as cited in Ferzan (n 55) 405: 'To respect persons as autonomous is thus to recognize them as the givers and takers of permissions and obligations. . . . One very powerful means by which persons will their own moral laws—by which they alter the moral landscape for themselves and for others—is by granting or withholding consent to other's actions.'

[61] Hurd, 'Justification and Excuse, Wrongdoing and Culpability' (n 40) 1558.

case for (or against) the performance of an action'.[62] A *justified but mistaken belief* in the complainant's consent has two important tasks. First, it shows that there was a fact (in the defendant's mistaken deliberation) that constituted the case for the belief in the complainant's consent. Second, it shows that the belief was justified in the sense that it was based on an undefeated reason (in the defendant's mistaken deliberation) for that belief. It follows that the defendant's excuse requires justified explanatory reasons, not merely an explanatory belief.

We can now return to explain the excuse-style modification of the absence of consent. Most criminal codes modify this inculpatory element to include a mistaken belief that consent existed as long as this was based upon reasonable, or non-reckless, grounds. Whilst inculpatory elements are not beholden to the logic of excuses, this may nonetheless represent a concession that a mistaken belief in the consent of the complainant, even where the absence of consent is an inculpatory element, *should* obey some of the logic of excuses.[63] According to this logic, a defendant should only avoid blame and criminal liability for sexual penetration in the absence of the complainant's attitudinal consent where it was 'reasonable' to believe that this consent existed. Alternatively, the excuse-style modification may 'go beyond what the logic of excuses requires'.[64] It may 'serve to orientate the law towards general application to people living many different forms of life', rather than individualising the law towards particular defendants and their particular individualised mistaken beliefs.[65] Nonetheless, despite the excuse-style modification, the inculpatory element still concerns whether the defendant has the required state of mind but constricts the grounds upon which this can be formed. The focus remains on the defendant's state of mind about that of the complainant.

In comparison to these modified inculpatory elements, the requirement of explanatory *reasons* (where consent is exculpatory) introduces two different accounts of *what consent is*. We have already encountered the orthodox view (of what consent is), which explains consent as attitudinal—as concerning the internal will, intention, or acquiescence of the complainant. If consent is only attitudinal, then it follows that determining whether the defendant had a mistaken belief that the complainant consented is also an internal, subjective inquiry. However, if a mistaken belief as to the complainant's consent needs to be a *justified* or *reason-based belief*, then an additional element of consent is required—the externalised behaviour of the complainant becomes *necessary*

[62] Raz, *From Normativity to Responsibility* (n 11) 36. See also Beaulieu (n 13) 440.
[63] Gardner, 'Justifications and Reasons' (n 8) 120.
[64] Gardner, 'Justifications and Reasons' (n 8) 121.
[65] Gardner, 'Justifications and Reasons' (n 8) 121.

to the defendant's explanatory reasons. There must have been behaviour 'that communicate[d] the person's willingness to engage in a specific act of sexual penetration or sexual contact'.[66] Note that *what counts* as externalised behaviour that communicates a person's willingness, in the context of the relationship (if one pre-exists) and in the broader social context, may raise challenging questions of interpretation and application of the standard of consent (I take this up in the next essay). Nonetheless, the standard of consent requires externalised words and conduct. Absent such words and conduct, the defendant cannot show that his mistaken belief in the complainant's consent was based on a fact that he considered. Further, the defendant cannot show that this belief was justified in the sense that it was based on what he saw as an undefeated reason. In the absence of expressive consent, the defendant is unable to suggest that his mistaken belief was justified or reason-based.

Herein lies the first connection between the *pro tanto* wrong thesis and the expressive consent legal standard. If sexual penetration is a *pro tanto* wrong, a *justified mistaken belief* in consent may excuse the wrong. In order to have a *mistaken* belief, the defendant needs to have acted on explanatory reasons in favour of the complainant's attitudinal consent. And, in order for the mistaken belief to be a *justified* mistaken belief, the defendant's explanatory reasons must represent an undefeated reason, in favour of the complainant's attitudinal consent, in the defendant's (mistaken) deliberation. Any such *reasons* in favour of the complainant's attitudinal consent must be grounded in observable behaviour that communicates her willingness to engage in the specific act. For the defendant to have a justified mistaken belief in the complainant's 'consent', the mistaken belief must therefore be grounded in the complainant's *expressive* consent: her 'words or overt actions'.

Let us now forge the second connection between the *pro tanto* wrong thesis and the requirement of expressive consent. Recall the problem of objective justification: where the defendant does a justified act whilst being ignorant of the justifying circumstances. If sexual penetration is morally neutral, and the absence of consent is inculpatory, a defendant's ignorance of the complainant's attitudinal consent is immaterial. Sexual penetration is only wrongful, and the applicable prohibitory norm is only engaged, when the penetration is coupled with the absence of the complainant's attitudinal consent. After all, it is the complainant's internal attitude that renders the act permissible or impermissible. It therefore follows that a defendant will not be criminally liable provided

[66] American Law Institute, 'Model Penal Code: Sexual Assault and Related Offenses, Tentative Draft No. 2' (15 April 2016) s 213.0(3). See also Schulhofer, 'Consent' (n 6); Ferzan (n 55) 414.

that the complainant internally willed or acquiesced. The defendant would not be liable even if he acted without a belief in, or awareness of, the complainant's attitudinal consent.

However, if sexual penetration is a *pro tanto* wrong, and calls for justification, then a defendant's ignorance of the complainant's attitudinal consent is problematic. In order for the defendant to be justified in performing a wrong act, he needs to have acted on guiding and explanatory reasons in favour of the action. The complainant's *attitudinal* consent represents a guiding reason in favour of the action (or, more accurately, a guiding *permission* to act on reasons in favour of the action that is recognised as a cancelling permission).[67] However, in order to be justified in performing the wrong act, the defendant needs to be also acting on explanatory reasons. The defendant needs to have acted on an undefeated reason in favour of the permission. Only the complainant's *expressive* consent—her words or conduct that 'communicate[] . . . willingness to engage in a specific act of sexual penetration or sexual contact'—can qualify as such explanatory reasons.[68] The fact of the complainant's internal attitude cannot be an explanatory reason, since it is not—by itself—a fact that can enter the defendant's deliberation. As we have seen, even if the defendant had a belief in the complainant's attitudinal consent, such a belief needs to be founded upon explanatory *reasons* for action. Unless the defendant acted on the basis of the complainant's expressive consent, the defendant would not have acted on explanatory reasons, and therefore cannot justify his wrongdoing.

Hence, the second connection between the *pro tanto* wrong thesis and the requirement of expressive consent emerges. If sexual penetration is a *pro tanto* wrong, then the task of justifying it requires guiding and explanatory reasons. Such reasons can be located in the 'consent' of the complainant. Whilst the attitudinal consent of the complainant can provide an applicable guiding reason, a defendant must explain his actions with reference to the complainant's 'consent' in order to identify an explanatory reason. Only the complainant's expressive consent—her externalised behaviour—can feature in the defendant's deliberation on what he ought to do. Hence, expressive consent, which encapsulates the subjective and objective elements of consent, is necessary to justify the *pro tanto* wrong of sexual penetration.

[67] Gardner, 'Justifications and Reasons' (n 8) 117; Gardner, 'Justification under Authority' (n 23) 78–80.

[68] American Law Institute (n 66) s 213.0(3).

6.5

Let us now return to A and B at summer camp. Here, we will consider the roles that attitudinal and expressive consent play in capturing the moral quality of the act and the moral culpability of the actors in the alternative scenarios of Summer Camp(1) and Summer Camp(2). In doing so, I will contend that the sexual penetration at Summer Camp(1) was a culpable wrong act and that the sexual penetration at Summer Camp(2) was a culpable right act. I will also contend that we can only identify such instances of culpability when we treat sexual penetration as a *pro tanto* wrong and apply a standard of expressive consent.

As I have explained, if sexual penetration is a morally neutral act, and the absence of consent is an inculpatory element, the criminal law would apply an *attitudinal* standard of consent to this scenario. In which case, whether B(1) 'consented' to the sexual intercourse depends solely on B(1)'s internal or subjective attitude of willingness, intention, or acquiescence towards the specific act. Recall that B(1) objected to the sexual intercourse at Summer Camp(1) but remained silent and still throughout. Since it is B(1)'s attitude towards the act that determines its permissibility, the absence of B(1)'s attitudinal consent means that the sexual intercourse at Summer Camp (1) was a wrong act.

However, A(1) may claim a mistaken belief in B(1)'s 'consent'. We therefore encounter the problem of a mistaken justificatory factor. If we apply a standard of attitudinal consent, then we invite an inquiry into A(1)'s state of mind; we need to determine whether A(1) was (subjectively or internally) aware of B(1)'s (subjective or internal) objection or non-consent. The broader context and B(1)'s externalised behaviour contribute to an evidential basis from which we are required to make inferences about A(1)'s (internal) awareness of B(1)'s (internal) objection or non-consent. If A(1) had a mistaken belief in B(1)'s consent (or a mistaken belief on reasonable or non-reckless grounds), then the inculpatory elements of the offence would not be satisfied, and no sexual offence would have been committed. According to the orthodox account, a wrong had been committed, but A may be non-culpable, despite the absence of a reason-based excuse for the wrong. The implication here is that whilst attitudinal consent may determine the permissibility of the act, it does not always capture the culpability of the actor.

In comparison, if sexual penetration is a *pro tanto* wrong, then we would expect A(1) to justify the wrong by identifying guiding and explanatory reasons for action. The absence of B(1)'s attitudinal consent means that A(1) was not acting for guiding reasons and would be unable to show that the wrong was justified. If A(1) claims a mistaken belief in B(1)'s attitudinal consent, A(1) would need to show that the act was performed with a justified (or reason-based) mistaken belief in B(1)'s attitudinal consent. The problem for A(1) is that there cannot have been an undefeated reason (in A(1)'s mistaken deliberation) in favour of the belief that B(1) willed, intended, or acquiesced to the specific act. B(1)'s behaviour did not communicate or express an attitude of willingness and acquiescence. A(1) might have acted on an explanatory belief without acting on a justified explanatory *reason*, and A(1)'s mere explanatory *belief* will be unable to excuse the wrong.

If sexual penetration is a *pro tanto* wrong, then the sexual intercourse at Summer Camp(1) represents a culpable wrong. A(1) might not have intended to have penetrative sex in the absence of (attitudinal) consent, and A(1) might not have known that the penetrative sex was in the absence of (attitudinal) consent; nonetheless, A(1) intentionally performed a *pro tanto* wrong (penetrative sex) in the absence of B(1)'s expressive consent, thereby being unable to garner the guiding and explanatory reasons to justify the wrong or the reasons to justify the mistake. The exact degree of culpability will vary significantly and depend on the circumstances. At one end of the spectrum, A(1) may have failed 'to infer from available evidence' that there was no attitudinal consent.[69] At the other end, A(1) may have intended to have penetrative sex with the further intention or knowledge that it was in the absence of attitudinal consent. Whilst we do not yet have a means of calibrating these degrees of culpability,[70] the key point is that in the absence of B(1)'s *expressive* consent, A(1) is (to some degree) culpable for the wrong.

At Summer Camp(2), B(2) willed the sexual penetration but remained still and silent throughout the intercourse. As I have explained, there is no 'problem of objective justification' if penetrative sex is a morally neutral act. If the absence of attitudinal consent is an inculpatory element of the wrong, then B(2)'s internal attitude negated an element of the prohibitory norm. Moreover, if it is B(2)'s internal attitude that ultimately determines the permissibility of the act, then B(2)'s internal wilfulness towards the act 'transformed' a *pro tanto* neutral act into a permissible one.

However, if penetrative sex is a *pro tanto* wrong, then an objective justification is problematically incomplete. Whilst A(2) is able to identify a *guiding* reason in favour of the *pro tanto* wrongful act (B(2)'s attitudinal consent), A(2) is unable to identify an *explanatory* reason in favour of the act. There were no

69 Hurd, 'Justification and Excuse, Wrongdoing and Culpability' (n 40) 1558.
70 Ferzan (n 55) 433–35.

words or conduct that communicated B(2)'s 'willingness to engage in a specific act of sexual penetration'.[71] A(2) therefore cannot identify a 'fact', which entered into his practical reasoning, that provides an undefeated reason in favour of the performance of the action.

Since A(2) cannot justify the *pro tanto* wrong—cannot identify both guiding and explanatory reasons in favour of the wrong—A(2) acted culpably (without performing a wrong act). Since it was B(2)'s attitudinal consent that determined the permissibility of the act, the sexual intercourse was permissible. Yet A(2) intentionally performed a *pro tanto* wrong without a *reason-based* belief that B(2)'s attitudinal consent justified the wrong. As with A(1), the degree of A(2)'s culpability will vary. A(2) may have proceeded with the sexual intercourse regardless of B(2)'s lack of expressive consent. A(2) may have proceeded with the sexual intercourse whilst being entirely inattentive towards, or unconcerned with, B(2)'s lack of expressive consent. A(2) may have proceeded with the sexual intercourse with some presumed licence to do so that had no basis in fact. At best, A(2) may have acted on a lucky guess about B(2)'s attitudinal consent that was entirely uninformed by B(2)'s behaviour. B(2)'s externalised behaviour provided no *reason* to believe that B(2) willed the sexual intercourse. If sexual penetration is a *pro tanto* wrong, then A(2)'s disregard for, or inattention towards, B(2)'s lack of expressive consent amounted to a 'culpable right action'.[72] To be clear, the degree of culpability in these possible scenarios is unlikely to be equivalent to the culpability of A 'raping' B (within the archetypical understanding of rape: sexual penetration in the absence of B's attitudinal consent and the absence of A having a 'reasonable belief' in B's attitudinal consent). A(2) may have committed a very distinct kind of culpable act. The key point is that a *pro tanto* wrong, the application of force sufficient to achieve penetration, cannot be justified in the absence of the applier of force acting on guiding reasons in favour of the *pro tanto* wrong. Similar to the defendants who were unaware of their justifying circumstances (of self-defence, necessity, or duress of circumstances), A(2) *acted without sufficient regard for* B(2)'s attitudinal consent and therefore performed a *pro tanto* wrong on the basis of inadequate reasons.

If we consider sexual penetration to be a *pro tanto* wrong, we can appreciate the inadequacy of only applying an attitudinal standard of consent. Whilst attitudinal consent determines the permissibility of the act, it does not always capture the culpability of the actor performing the act. The problems of mistaken

[71] American Law Institute (n 66) s 213.0(3).
[72] Hurd, 'Justification and Excuse, Wrongdoing and Culpability' (n 40) 1565.

justification and objective justification highlight this failure. Where a complainant did not attitudinally consent to penetrative sex, and the defendant had a belief in the complainant's consent *that was not based on the complainant's expressive consent*, the defendant is culpable in performing a *pro tanto* wrong without excuse or justification. Moreover, even where a complainant did attitudinally consent to penetrative sex, but the defendant engaged in penetrative sex in the absence of *the complainant's expressive consent*, the defendant is also culpable in performing a *pro tanto* wrong without excuse or justification.

The *pro tanto* legal wrong thesis, therefore, has at least one doctrinal implication: if consent is to operate as a justification, and a belief in consent as an excuse, then consent itself must consist of objective and subjective components. Only expressive consent can provide the explanatory and guiding reasons required for a justification, or the justified explanatory reasons required for an excuse. This is the practical significance of the *pro tanto* legal wrong thesis. However, as we can now turn to consider, the application of a definition of consent that consists of objective and subjective components risks either collapsing into attitudinal consent (where a belief about a belief is exculpatory) or criminalising non-culpable conduct (where the objective component of consent is context-insensitive). This is the 'expressive consent dilemma' that we will encounter in the next essay, and eventually solve in Essay 8.

7
The Expressive Consent Dilemma

7.1

'A private intention is insufficient for morally valid consent', according to Tom Dougherty.[1] Instead, 'morally valid consent always requires public behavior, and this behavior must take the form of communication in the case of high-stakes consent'.[2] By requiring 'words or overt actions by a person indicating a freely given present agreement',[3] the expressive consent standard seeks to capture the 'public behaviour' that Dougherty considers necessary for morally valid consent. In a similar way, the expressive consent standard may be able to capture the 'objective', 'justified', or 'reasonable' basis for a belief in consent that the criminal law might require for a mistaken belief to be an exculpatory belief.

I have only just endorsed the expressive standard of consent in the previous essay as a welcome implication of the *pro tanto* legal wrong thesis. I now turn to problematise it. The problem that we will encounter in this essay is that the expressive standard of consent either collapses back into the attitudinal standard or carves out a culpability gap. Regardless of how we try to delineate the expressive consent standard—as being 'public', 'objective', or 'reasonable'—we confront the choice of either following social practices or prescribing them. This creates a dilemma for the expressive consent standard. At one horn, if the expressive standard of consent follows social practices, then it amounts to little more than attitudinal consent. At the other horn, if the expressive consent standard instead prescribes a practice, then it convicts defendants whose blameworthiness stems merely from their ignorance of the prescribed practice.

To formulate this dilemma, I will defend the following four claims:

[1] Tom Dougherty, '*Yes Means Yes*: Consent as Communication' (2015) 43 Philos Public Aff 224, 227.

[2] Dougherty (n 1) 227.

[3] See DC Code, s 22–3001(4) (2018) ('words or overt actions indicating a freely given agreement'); Minn Stat, s 609.341(4) (2017) ('words or overt actions by a person indicating a freely given present agreement'); 13 VSA, s 3251(3) (2017) ('words or actions by a person indicating a voluntary agreement'); Rev Code Wash (ARCW), s 9A.44.010(7) (2017) ('actual words or conduct indicating freely given agreement'); 940 Wis Stat Ann, s 940.225(4) (2018) ('words or overt actions ... indicating a freely given agreement').

Sex and Self-Ownership. Jesse Wall, Oxford University Press. © Jesse Wall 2025.
DOI: 10.1093/9780191987809.003.0007

1. Both legal standards (expressive and attitudinal consent) require the finder of fact to evaluate the inference that a person (A) makes from another person's (B's) external behaviour to that other person's (B's) internal attitude.
2. The standard that the finder of fact uses to evaluate the inference can either incorporate social practices or prescribe the social practices to be followed.

3(a). A standard of inference (under the expressive consent standard) that *incorporates* social practices accommodates all possible inferences from B's behaviour to B's attitude (in the same way that the attitudinal consent standard does).

3(b). A standard of inference (under the expressive consent standard) that *prescribes* social practices identifies A's lesser culpability in terms of A's ignorance of the social practice (which does not sustain culpability for any wrongdoing).

The expressive consent dilemma (between collapse and culpability gap) is predicated upon a dichotomy between 3(a) the standard of inference being descriptive of social practices and 3(b) being prescriptive of them. We should be suspicious of dichotomies and excluded middles, but in order to appreciate the need for a third standard of inference (developed in the next essay), we need to discount these two.

This essay starts (at 7.2) with an initial collapse between the attitudinal and expressive consent standards: since both standards are concerned with inferences from external behaviour to internal attitudes, the legal standards direct the finder of fact to undertake the same inquiry. At 7.3, I then attempt to reconstruct the distinction by considering the further gloss on the expressive consent standard that permits only 'reasonable' inferences from external behaviour to internal attitudes. Here, we encounter the dilemma between a collapse back into the attitudinal standard (where 'reasonable' means 'ordinary') or a legal standard that does not identify sufficiently culpable conduct (where 'reasonable' means 'justified'). We encounter the same collapse at 7.4 when we consider an alternative gloss on the expressive standard that requires the communicative words or actions to be 'public' communications. Finally, at 7.5, I explain how the contention from the previous essay—that expressive consent provides an 'objective' basis to a belief in consent—is (by itself) also caught by the expressive consent dilemma. I am then able to gesture towards the solution to the expressive consent dilemma by appreciating the agenda for the next essay.

7.2

Throughout this essay we will see the distinction between attitudinal and expressive consent standard collapse, be reconstructed, and then collapse again. We can start with an initial distinction between

> *attitudinal standard*, where consent is an internal attitude of willingness, acceptance, or acquiescence and

> *expressive standard*, where consent is the words or overt actions of a person that indicate an internal attitude of willingness, acceptance, or acquiescence.

These standards appear to differ by locating consent either in the 'private' or 'internal' attitude of the consenting person or the 'public' or 'external' space that both the consenting person and the person who relies on the consent occupy.

Under the expressive consent standard, we would encounter some easy cases. One easy case is a scenario where:

> 1. *No communication:* A wakes B, and then proceeds to have sex with B, where B indicates neither her acceptance or willingness nor her objection or refusal (where A and B had no prior sexual interaction).

In (1) *No communication*, B *did not* consent to sex with A, on the basis that B did not express her willingness or acceptance through words or overt actions. Applying the same standard, B *did* consent to sex with A in a scenario where:

> 2. *Verbal acceptance:* A has sex with B after A propositions B by suggesting 'Let's fuck', and B replies, 'Okay'.

In (2) *Verbal acceptance*, B did express her attitude of acceptance through express words. And in (3) *Verbal rejection*, B expressed her objection, where:

> 3. *Verbal rejection:* A has sex with B after B verbally objects to the sex: 'No, don't'.

Under the expressive standard, hard cases will remain. Consider, for instance, a situation where:

> 4. *Enthusiastic undressing:* A has sex with B after A and B both kiss and then enthusiastically undress themselves at different ends of a hotel bed.

It is not obvious whether B's own 'enthusiastic undressing' in (4) *Enthusiastic undressing* is overt enough to be an action that indicates the willingness to have sex with A. The uncertainty is more profound in a similar scenario, where:

5. *Enthusiastic kissing:* A has sex with B after A and B both enthusiastically kiss, and A undresses B, in the bedroom at a house party.

It is not clear whether B's enthusiastic kissing in (5) *Enthusiastic kissing* is, itself, sufficient to express or communicate a willingness to have sex with A at a house party. Our intuition is most likely that *it doesn't.* Or, at least, *it shouldn't.* But therein lies an important but subtle distinction.

Under the attitudinal standard, we would encounter the same or similar pattern. We encounter the same easy cases, such as (1) *No communication*, (2) *Verbal acceptance*, and (3) *Verbal rejection.* Applying the attitudinal standard to (1) *No communication*, A can be convicted of a sexual offence when the passive behaviour of B provided no basis, or an insufficient basis, upon which A could have inferred an internal attitude of willingness;[4] applying the attitudinal standard to (2) *Verbal acceptance*, B's active communicative behaviour can provide an sufficient basis for A to infer that B had an attitude of acceptance; applying the attitudinal standard to (3) *Verbal rejection*, B's express verbal rejection removed any basis upon which A could infer a consenting attitude. In all these easy cases, it is A's inference from B's behaviour to B's attitude that is doing the work.

There will also be hard cases under the attitudinal standard. Whether A could infer an attitude of willingness or acceptance from (5) B's enthusiastic kissing (alone), or (4) B's kissing and enthusiastic and unaided undressing, is open-ended in the same way that it was under the expressive standard. Under either standard, the finder of fact can rely on the assumption that

> it is in the nature of things rare for consensual conduct involving intimacy of this kind to be preceded by formal offer and acceptance. In some instances, consent is capable of being inferred from acquiescence in the continuation of the activity.[5]

[4] Jonathan Witmer-Rich, 'Unpacking Affirmative Consent: Not as Great as You Hope, Not as Bad as You Fear' (2016) 49 Tex Tech L Rev 57, 77–78.

[5] *R v Millar* [1998] QCA 276, [2000] 1 Qd R 437, [7].

The distinction between the attitudinal and expressive standards appears to have vanished already. Whilst the attitudinal standard is concerned with the 'actual subjective consent in the mind of the complainant at the time of the sexual activity in question',[6] the externalised behaviour of the complainant forms the evidential grounds from which a person may infer as to their subjective state of mind. Since the only way to access a person's 'internal attitude' is through their externalised behaviour, the question of the complainant's attitudinal consent is always answered via the defendant's understanding of the externalised behaviour of the complainant.

Whilst the attitudinal definition of consent might direct our focus on to the private attitude of the consenting person, the focal point of the inquiry is inevitably the inference from behaviour to the attitude of the consenting person. The problem is that the expressive standard has the same focal point. It is defined in terms of the externalised and public behaviour (the 'words or overt actions by a person indicating a freely given present agreement'). And yet, the words and overt actions that are required to 'show' or 'manifest' must show or manifest *something*. That is, they must express or communicate some kind of attitude of willingness, intention, or waiver. Since any communication has some expressive content, under the expressive standard, the question becomes whether the behaviour of the complainant is behaviour that expresses an attitude of acceptance, or willingness, towards a specific act.

There is, nonetheless, one point of difference. The application of attitudinal consent to (1) *No communication* has traditionally 'accommodated the possibility that an instigator can legitimately *assume or infer* internal willingness, even where there is no external communication of that assumed internal state'.[7] It is the defendant's inference from behaviour to the attitude that is doing damage here, assuming a willingness in the absence of any expressive behaviour, and the standard of consent then accommodates this assumption.

Under the expressive standard, in comparison, B's passive behaviour cannot amount to consent. The difference in adopting the expressive standard is that it blocks an inference that the law traditionally accommodated; under the expressive standard, a defendant can no longer legitimately infer internal willingness from passive behaviour alone. Once the legal (ir)relevance of passivity is transformed,[8] then it will become a legal requirement that 'a person should

[6] *R v JA* [2011] SCC 28, [2011] 2 SCR 440, [23]: 'Consent for this purpose is actual subjective consent in the mind of the complainant at the time of the sexual activity in question.'

[7] Anna High, 'Comparing Affirmative Consent Models: Confusion, Substance, and Symbolism' (2023) 45 Syd LR 467, 473.

[8] Deborah Tuerkheimer, 'Affirmative Consent' (2016) 13 Ohio St J Crim L 441, 448.

have to communicate positive, verbal or nonverbal agreement to engage in penetration before someone else should be allowed to penetrate them'.[9] The shift from the attitudinal standard to the expressive standard therefore prevents a defendant (A) from relying on B's passivity as representing consenting behaviour.

Yet we can arrive at the same solution without the expressive standard. Under the traditional, attitudinal standard, it is possible to engraft inference-negating rules. Where a person is 'asleep, unconscious, or substantially intoxicated', it is not possible to infer an attitude of willingness or acceptance, and hence, under the criminal law, 'non-consent is established regardless of whether non-consent was actively communicated by resistance'.[10] We could add that 'it is not possible to infer consent from passive behaviour alone' as another inference-negating rule. A lot will then turn on how we understand 'passive behaviour *alone*' and whether prior sexual encounters, social and cultural practices, and relationship expectations displace the inference-negating rule (or are themselves displaced by the rule).

For now, it is enough to note that under both standards, we infer from behaviour to an attitude. The difference between *where* we locate the definition of consent—on the behaviour or on the attitude—seems to be immaterial to the practice of assessing a defendant's inference from a person's behaviour to that person's attitude. Immaterial, except for a prescribed rule that *negates* the inference from passive behaviour alone to an attitude of willingness. Either the move to expressive consent makes no difference or it amounts to the prescription of a rule about how we should communicate consent and understand the consenting or non-consenting behaviour of others.

7.3

The 'inference-negating rule' (that passive behaviour alone does not express consent) does not capture the spirit of the expressive standard. Proponents of the expressive standard are not merely motivated by the (1) *No communication* scenario. We ought to also be concerned with (5) *Enthusiastic kissing*, where a defendant can be acquitted of a sexual offence because an attitude of willingness *could* have been—but *should not* have been—inferred from the external

[9] Michelle J Anderson, 'Campus Sexual Assault Adjudication and Resistance to Reform' (2016) 125 Yale LJ 1940, 1978.

[10] High (n 7) 473–74.

behaviour of the complainant. The problem with the attitudinal standard is that when it comes to (5) *Enthusiastic kissing*, any given ambiguity in the external behaviour of the complainant enables the acquittal.

Yet if consent alters the normative relationship between two people, then Dougherty argues that 'people must have a common belief concerning which rights are created or eliminated'.[11] Especially in cases of 'high-stakes consent'—such as sex—where 'public behaviour . . . must take the form of unambiguous communication'.[12] In this way, Dougherty explains, 'consent . . . must operate publicly in order to generate the common belief'.[13] The permission that is required to touch, apply force, or penetrate a person must be a normative phenomenon that exists unambiguously in the public space, between the person granting permission and the person relying on the permission. The expressive consent standard can then require this unambiguous, and public, permission.

Similarly, Schulhofer is concerned with the sexual encounters that 'commonly occur' in situations that 'readily lend[ ] [themselves] to miscommunication, impaired capacity to express and/or interpret social signals, and inability to physically or verbally resist unwanted advances'.[14] The expressive standard, according to Schulhofer, 'prohibits penetration until a person communicates consent to a sexual act with words or conduct' and thereby mitigates the dangers of sexual abuse through coercion, incapacity, and miscommunication.[15] The implication here is that the risks associated with any impairment, ambiguity, misinterpretation, or miscommunication are borne by the complainant under the attitudinal standard, and ought to be reallocated to the defendant under the expressive standard. '[A] standard that prohibits penetration until a person communicates consent to a sexual act with words or conduct mitigates those dangers', according to Schulhofer, 'at no significant social cost'.[16]

Even my own account of the expressive consent standard, from the previous essay, relied upon the claim that only the complainant's *expressive* consent, which provides an objective component, can qualify as the 'explanatory reason' that any justification or excuse necessitates. The fact of the complainant's internal, subjective attitude cannot be an explanatory reason, since it is not—by itself—a fact that can enter the defendant's deliberation. Only expressive consent, I have argued, can justify sex, or ground a justified belief in consent in order to excuse sex.

[11] Dougherty (n 1) 250.
[12] Dougherty (n 1) 227.
[13] Dougherty (n 1) 251.
[14] Stephen J Schulhofer, 'Consent: What It Means and Why It's Time to Require It' (2016) 47 U Pac L Rev 665, 670.
[15] Schulhofer (n 14) 670.
[16] Schulhofer (n 14) 670.

The shared concern here is that the attitudinal standard affords the defendant the benefit of ambiguity and miscommunication, by allowing the inference to be the defendant's own inference (in his internal, private mind). The attitudinal standard, in effect, retreats into the attitudes and outlook of the defendant or instigator of sex. The common contention is that the expressive standard can resist this retreat back into the attitudinal. It does so by requiring more than a mere inference; it requires the instigator to act on an *unambiguous, unimpaired, uncoerced, objective*—or, at least, *reasonable*—expression of consent. On the expressive standard, (5) *Enthusiastic kissing* is much less likely to amount to consent, since an attitude of willingness to have sex with A is much less likely to be 'unambiguously' or 'reasonably' inferred from the 'public' and external behaviour of the complainant.

We can now reconstruct the distinction between the attitudinal standard and the expressive standard. In this section, we will build the distinction around 'reasonable' inferences from expressive behaviour (and move on to 'public' and 'objective' standards later). The contrast for this section is the second distinction between

> *attitudinal standard*: where consent is an internal attitude of willingness or acceptance and
>
> *expressive (reasonableness) standard*: where consent is the words or overt actions of a person that *reasonably* indicate an internal attitude of willingness or acceptance.

The distinction between the two standards is now no longer concerned with locating consent in private minds (attitude) or public spaces (behaviour), but with the standard of inference, from behaviour to attitude, that is available to the defendant or instigator of sex. One way to prevent the inference from merely taking place in the mind of the defendant or instigator of sex is to require that the inference, on the expressive standard, needs to be a 'reasonable' one. If our principal concern is with inferences (from behaviour to attitude) that could—but should not—be drawn, such as the inference in (5) *Enthusiastic kissing*, then one way of addressing our anxieties around (5) *Enthusiastic kissing* is to permit only reasonable inferences (and convict on unreasonable ones).

However, what amounts to a 'reasonable' inference can be understood in one of two ways. A reasonable inference can be one that is 'responsive to reasons'. More specifically, to be responsive to reasons is to act, hold a belief, make a decision, or draw an inference for 'undefeated reasons', 'reasons that are neither outweighed nor excluded from consideration by countervailing reasons'.[17] In this way, a reasonable inference is a justified one. An alternative formulation of a 'reasonable inference' allows for some latitude for the reasonable person who is inferring from another's behaviour to their state of mind. Rather than having to be justified in their inference, a person may draw a reasonable inference if it is an inference that an ordinary person would also draw. On this formulation, it becomes a question of how ordinary people (hopefully not on the Clapham omnibus) engage in consensual sexual encounters.

The reasonable inference from expressive behaviour standard creates a choice for the finder of fact, since the reasonable (justified) person is not the same as the reasonable (ordinary) person; a commonly held belief is not a belief held for undefeated reasons.

As John Gardner explains, in employing the first formulation of reasonableness (as justification), the finder of fact will 'assess whether the defendant's belief was justified, using whatever she [the finder of fact] regards as the proper standard for justified belief'.[18] In doing so, she needs to 'just think for herself about how to behave in sexual matters'.[19] In thinking for herself, she might adopt a 'formality rule' for reasonable inferences (from behaviour to attitudes).[20] According to the formality rule:

> (FR) an immediate interest in having sex with someone has to be communicated in words.[21]

In applying the formality rule, the finder of fact would only encounter easy cases. She would find that no reasonable inference was available to the defendant (A) in (1) *No communication* or in (3) *Verbal rejection.* It would be 'reasonable' to infer consent in (2) *Verbal acceptance.* For both (4) *Enthusiastic undressing* and (5) *Enthusiastic kissing*, since the immediate interest in having sex was not communicated in words, there would be no reasonable basis upon which for A to infer B was consenting.

Alternatively, in employing the second formulation, the finder of fact will understand her role to be to 'masquerade as what she imagines to be the person on the street'.[22] In doing so, she just needs to consider the belief that 'would be

[17] John Gardner, 'The Many Faces of the Reasonable Person' (2015) 131 LQR 563, 565.
[18] Gardner, 'The Many Faces of the Reasonable Person' (n 17) 572–73.
[19] Gardner, 'The Many Faces of the Reasonable Person' (n 17) 584.
[20] Gardner, 'The Many Faces of the Reasonable Person' (n 17) 573.
[21] Gardner, 'The Many Faces of the Reasonable Person' (n 17) 573.
[22] Gardner, 'The Many Faces of the Reasonable Person' (n 17) 574.

held by an average person in the defendant's position'.[23] In masquerading as an ordinary person, she might adopt a 'spontaneity rule', which sets out that

> (SR) immediate sexual interest is aptly communicated in non-verbal ways . . . so long as it is not verbally countermanded.[24]

If we adopt the second understanding of reasonable inferences, then reasonable inferences become the inferences that an ordinary person would draw from another person's behaviour to their attitude. On this understanding, what counts as a reasonable inference is informed by the fact that ordinary or commonplace sexual encounters are 'often non-verbal' with

> many men and women passively indicat[ing] their consent to sexual intercourse by not resisting, such as allowing themselves to be undressed by their partner, not saying no, or not stopping their partner's advances.[25]

This absence of 'direct expression of sexual desire' is often motivated by a desire 'to avoid awkwardness and embarrassment' in case of rejection.[26] In addition, a 'traditional sexual script' relies on the man initiating intimacy and sexual intercourse; the women (again, traditionally) acts as a 'gate keeper[]'[27] and is 'keenly aware of the social costs of breaking from the traditional script and engaging in the "wrong" kind of sexual communication'.[28] Here, the 'spontaneity rule' is well grounded in how a reasonable (ordinary) person would hold a belief in the consenting attitude of another person.

In applying the 'spontaneity rule' (under the second iteration of reasonableness), (2) *Verbal acceptance* and (3) *Verbal rejection* continue to be easy cases. Scenario (1) *No communication* continues to be ruled out by the expressive standard itself (the inference-negating rule from the requirement of 'words or overt actions'). The remainder of the scenarios are reopened: a reasonable (ordinary) inference may have been available in (4) *Enthusiastic undressing* since

[23] Gardner, 'The Many Faces of the Reasonable Person' (n 17) 573.

[24] Gardner, 'The Many Faces of the Reasonable Person' (n 17) 573.

[25] Terry P Humphreys and Mélanie M Brousseau, 'The Sexual Consent Scale—Revised: Development, Reliability, and Preliminary Validity' (2010) 47 J Sex Res 420, 421.

[26] Aya Gruber, 'Consent Confusion' (2016) 38 Cardozo L Rev 415, 448. See also Humphreys and Brousseau (n 25) 422.

[27] Susan E Hickman and Charlene L Muehlenhard, '"By the Semi-Mystical Appearance of a Condom": How Young Women and Men Communicate Sexual Consent in Heterosexual Situations' (1999) 36 J Sex Res 258, 259.

[28] Gruber, 'Consent Confusion' (n 26) 443, citing Michael W Wiederman, 'The Gendered Nature of Sexual Scripts' (2005) 13 Fam J 496.

unassisted undressing after kissing in a private setting may be considered an apt way to communicate, non-verbally, immediate sexual interest. Potentially, in (5) *Enthusiastic kissing*, a reasonable (ordinary) inference from enthusiastic kissing, followed by B allowing A to undress her, to a consenting attitude might, too, be available.

Hence, by employing the second iteration of reasonableness (the reasonable person as the ordinary person), the distinction between the attitudinal and expressive standard once again collapses. Under the attitudinal standard, it is an open-ended question for the finder of fact whether a person could have inferred from the behaviour of another person to a consenting attitude. Recall that on the expressive (reasonableness) standard, consent is defined in terms of the words or overt actions of a person that reasonably indicate an internal attitude of willingness or acceptance. If a 'reasonable indication' dissolves into what an ordinary person would take to be indicative of consent, then—*as per* the 'spontaneity rule'—an attitude of willingness or acceptance can be 'aptly communicated in non-verbal ways'. It then becomes a question of whether an inference—from (non-verbal) behaviour to a consenting attitude—was available to the defendant. This is the same question that is asked of the finder of fact under the attitudinal standard.

Perhaps, then, the first iteration of the reasonable inference standard can maintain the distinction. Recall that one way that an inference can be a reasonable one is if it is an inference that is justified or 'responsive to reasons'. If the expressive standard were to require a reasonable (justified) inference from behaviour to attitude, then it would resist the collapse into the attitudinal standard.

Rather than masquerading as the ordinary person in the defendant's position, a finder of fact can instead 'think for herself' as to how a person in the defendant's position ought to infer from the complainant's behaviour to the complainant's attitude. In doing so, the finder of fact can reasonably (ie with justification) prescribe some rules about how a person ought to infer consent. For instance, the finder of fact would suggest—and we would most likely agree—that (i) lack of protest or resistance does not mean consent, (ii) silence does not mean consent, (iii) prior consent is not present consent, (iv) coerced consent is not consent, (v) consent is only verbalised consent, and so on. If we are concerned with 'how can I be *justified* in believing that another person has a consenting attitude?', then rules (i) to (v) enable me to be justified, to be responsive to undefeated reasons. If we require the defendant's belief (in the consenting attitude of another person) to be responsive to reasons, then we need to *prescribe* how and when a belief in another's consent can be responsive to reasons. Regardless of how reasonable/ordinary people communicate their consent, this is how reasonable/justified people do it.

There is a practical concern with an expressive standard that prescribes reasonable (ie justified) conduct that is not reasonable (ie ordinary) conduct. Sherry Colb worries that

> we might, paradoxically, make it more difficult than it already is to get a conviction for acquaintance rape if the standard we present to the jury appears to condemn conduct of which jurors not only approve but in which they have likely engaged themselves.[29]

The concern here is that the finder of fact will not apply the prescriptive standard of expressive consent where it cuts across their own understanding of what amounts to the communication of consent.

There are broader concerns. The prescriptions (i) to (v) are not merely requiring that participants in sexual acts communicate; they are prescribing *how they ought* to communicate. The expressive (reasonable as justified) standard is prescribing a basic sexual script. Those who fail to follow the script—for instance, for those who fail to verbally communicate consent—may be acting carelessly or heedlessly, whilst engaging in a morally risky (and high-stakes) activity. We can be critical of people who engage in careless or heedless sex. The question is, however, whether the failure to adhere to the prescribed script is a culpable or blameworthy failure so as to engage the criminal law.

For Kimberly Kessler Ferzan, careless or heedless sex is not a sufficiently culpable failure to engage the criminal law.[30] She is concerned that the expressive standard replaces the *mens rea* requirement of knowledge or recklessness (under traditional legal standards) with either strict liability or a negligence standard (under the expressive consent standard). The archetypal defendant is culpable when they 'knowingly or recklessly impose[] sex on a person who has not willingly acquiesced'.[31] The expressive standard replaces the requirement of knowledge or recklessness with a negligence standard, since either the absence of verbal communication is reflective of unreasonableness or—more strictly—acting in the absence of verbal consent *is* unreasonable. Under the expressive

[29] Sherry F Colb, 'Conversation Before Penetration?', comment accompanying Michelle J Anderson, 'Rape Law Reform Based on Negotiation: Beyond the No and Yes Models' in Paul H Robinson, Stephen Garvey and Kimberly Kessler Ferzan (eds), *Criminal Law Conversations* (OUP 2011) 313.

[30] Kimberly Kessler Ferzan, 'Consent, Culpability, and the Law of Rape' (2016) 13 Ohio St J Crim L 397.

[31] Aya Gruber, 'Rape Law Revisited' (2016) 13 Ohio St J Crim L 279, 292.

standard, the defendant is criminally liable for unreasonable conduct (without engaging the *mens rea* of knowledge or recklessness). For Ferzan, heedless sex ought not to concern the criminal law since '[t]he criminal law has and should continue to take seriously that only those with a guilty mind should be subject to criminal sanction'.[32] In this way, Ferzan doubts whether expressive consent 'can be squared with retributive morality'.[33]

To understand why the expressive consent (as prescribed reasonableness) standard cannot be squared with retributive morality, we need to return to questions of criminal responsibility. The main reason why the expressive (prescribed reasonableness) standard cannot be squared with retributive morality is because, as a general principle of moral responsibility, 'no rational person can be faulted for failing to respond to a reason he is unaware applies to his conduct'.[34] We therefore reserve moral responsibility for those who act contrary to reasons that they knew applied to their situation. If the defendant ought to have but did not follow prescription (v) *consent is only verbalised consent* (in other words, the formality rule), then the defendant cannot be held responsible for instigating sex without a belief that the other person was consenting. More specifically, A's claim to be unaware of a will-grounded reason (that B did not consent) relies upon a practice-based reason that A can take silence and the absence of objection as an expression of B's consent. The effect of (v) *consent is only verbalised consent* is to remove from the moral equation the practice-based reasons that A should not have but did rely on. A may be negligent with regard to, but nevertheless ignorant of, B's lack of consent. If the general principle of responsibility holds, then it is not possible to attribute moral or criminal responsibility to A for being negligent.

Now, we can still allocate blame (resentment and regret) as appropriate reactive attitudes (see Essay 3 at 3.5).[35] In part, because A was ignorant of rule (v) *consent is only verbalised consent*, and in this sense, A is blameworthy *for his ignorance* of (practice-based) moral reasons (see Essay 4 at 4.4). But 'blameworthy' only in the much lesser sense (of a failure to attend to normative practices and the moral reasons that they augment). We cannot, in comparison, blame A, and hold A accountable, for failing to respond to the moral reasons that applied to his situation, such as the absence of B's consent to A's treatment of her. Hence, to the extent that A is blameworthy, he is only blameworthy for

[32] Ferzan (n 30) 439.
[33] Gruber, 'Rape Law Revisited' (n 31) 292.
[34] Douglas Husak, *Ignorance of Law: A Philosophical Inquiry* (OUP 2016) 152.
[35] Peter Strawson, 'Freedom and Resentment' in Gary Watson (ed), *Free Will* (2nd edn, OUP 2003).

his ignorance of the formality rule (or any other rule or norm that the expressive consent standard might prescribe).

We can therefore identify a significant culpability gap between the blameworthiness of the ignorant defendant, who is unaware of the relevant inference-forming rules (the formality rule), and Ferzan's archetypal defendant, who knowingly or recklessly imposes sex. The culpability gap suggests that the culpably ignorant defendant and the archetypal defendant do not belong in the same category. The further question of criminal responsibility is whether the culpability gap means that (a) the culpably ignorant defendant and the archetypal defendant belong in different criminal law categories or (b) the culpably ignorant defendant does not belong in any criminal law category.

To answer this further question of criminal responsibility we need to return to some of the conditions of criminalisation: in particular, the wrongfulness and antithesis conditions (see Essay 3 at 3.5). Recall that these require that

> *wrongfulness condition*: 'any prohibition of ϕ-ing can be justified only when ϕ-ing is a morally wrongful action'.[36]

> *antithesis condition*: the state can only punish ϕ-ing where ϕ-ing is antithetical to a value that the state is responsible for promoting (where 'antithetical conduct' is a conduct that 'manifests a disrespect for the interest or value that has been violated'[37] by demonstrating an unwillingness to be guided by the interest or value).

When it comes to heedless or careless sex, the wrongfulness hurdle can be cleared. That is, we can understand A's careless reliance on silence and the lack of objection as morally wrongful in the following way: A was under (and breached) an obligation to obtain consent from B, where the requirements of the obligation are specified by (inter alia) *the formality rule*. The wrong is *malum prohibitum*, and to that end, 'the wrongfulness of a rule-violation depends on the moral force of the rule'.[38] The *formality rule*, here, derives its moral force from the instrumental task of delineating the content of the obligation to obtain consent (where a failure to obtain consent is *malum in se*).

The second hurdle—the antithesis condition—cannot be cleared. This provides the second reason why the expressive (prescribed reasonableness)

[36] AP Simester and Andreas von Hirsch, *Crimes, Harms, and Wrongs: On the Principles of Criminalisation* (Hart Publishing 2011) 22.
[37] Grant Lamond, 'What is a Crime?' (2007) 27 OJLS 609, 621.
[38] Simester and von Hirsch (n 36) 37.

consent standard cannot be squared with retributive morality. The problem here is that *the formality rule* (or any other prescribed rules under consideration here) does *not* protect a value that the state is responsible for promoting. There are good reasons why, in intimate and morally high-stakes interactions, where consent represents a waiver or suspension of rights of self-ownership, consent ought to be verbal and unambiguous.[39] The harm involved in getting it wrong prompts the need for clarity and caution, without any significant social cost in requiring clarity.[40] The formality rule—or any other rule or prescription that the expressive consent standard can Trojan horse into the law—might work to reduce the risk of these harms. Whilst these risk-reducing measures are valuable, it is not a value that the coercive limb of the state—the criminal law—is responsible for promoting. Moreover, by prescribing sexual scripts, the expressive (prescribed reasonableness) standard is inconsistent with the sexual freedom to engage in, for instance, non-verbal consensual sex.

Alternatively, in an attempt to clear the second hurdle, we might focus on the obligation on A to obtain consent from B (the *malum in se*), and say in retort that the state *is* responsible for enforcing the requirements of consent-astuteness and promoting the right of self-ownership. However, we return to the earlier point. A person does not manifest an unwillingness to be guided by a value that the person is unaware applies to their moral situation. For example, in cases where 'the formality rule' is not followed (such as in (4) *Enthusiastic undressing* and (5) *Enthusiastic kissing*), A had reasons for believing that B willed, accepted, or agreed to the sex. A's reasons for this belief are discounted through the application of the formality rule. Yet, in (4) *Enthusiastic undressing* and (5) *Enthusiastic kissing*, A did not 'manifest a disrespect' for B's self-ownership; A only acted in ignorance of the formality rule. And again, A is blameworthy for being ignorant, but not accountable for the wrongdoing.

Here we encounter the expressive consent dilemma. If consent is understood in terms of the 'words or overt actions by a person indicating a freely given present agreement', then what counts as the 'words or overt actions' that indicate present agreement can be either a descriptive or a prescriptive question. If it is a descriptive question, then expressive consent collapses into attitudinal consent; the finder of fact (whilst masquerading as an ordinary person in the defendant's position) will infer consent (or the absence thereof) in the same manner as if she were applying the attitudinal consent standard. If it is a prescriptive question, then expressive consent embodies a state-sponsored

[39] Dougherty (n 1) 227.
[40] Schulhofer (n 14) 670.

sexual script, deviations from which would be punished by criminal sanction. This over-criminalises sex in the name of risk reduction. At the very least, there is a significant culpability gap between ignorance of the prescribed script that would be criminalised and the archetypal sexual offences that are currently criminalised.

Finally, before we move on from 'a reasonable indication of willingness or acceptance', a proponent of expressive consent could pivot the standard towards the following procedural requirement:

> *Expressive (procedural reasonableness) standard*: where consent is the words or overt actions of a person that, *after reasonable efforts to ascertain*, indicate an internal attitude of willingness or acceptance.

Under this 'failure to ascertain' standard, culpability 'is established whenever an accused fails to use some form of words or some type of conduct to ascertain consent'.[41] As Anna High explains, '[t]his requires, in order for an exculpatory state of mind to exist, that a sexual agent "stop and ask", by way of words or gestures'.[42] In other words, culpability attaches to the failure to complete a procedural checklist for ascertaining consent, and more broadly represents 'an obligation to *take steps* to ensure that when the time comes to act, one will know what one ought to know'.[43]

As we have seen (in Essay 4 at 4.4), a failure to perform certain procedural epistemic obligations is a plausible way to ground culpability for acting wrongfully even when the actor was unaware of the moral reasons they were acting against. I nonetheless explained how procedural failures are symptomatic of the source of culpability, but are not themselves a way of sustaining or deriving responsibility for the wrongdoing. The problem with grounding moral responsibility in procedural epistemic obligations alone is that moral responsibility becomes 'strict'. A person is culpable for their (two-fold) conduct—the initial conduct plus the procedural failing—without having a blameworthy attitude or morally problematic orientation towards the world (what the requirement of *mens rea* in the criminal law seeks to capture). The 'failure to ascertain' nonetheless points in the right direction, but we need some kind of mismanaged moral outlook to properly ground culpability (and I will pick up on this point in Essay 8).

[41] High (n 7) 489.
[42] High (n 7) 489.
[43] Gideon Rosen, 'Skepticism about Moral Responsibility' (2004) 18 Philos Perspect 295, 301.

For now, it is enough to note how the 'failure to ascertain standard' (alone) encounters the same dilemma. If 'reasonable efforts to ascertain' are understood in terms of the extent to which an 'ordinary person' would 'stop and ask', then, again, the expressive standard collapses into the attitudinal standard. Alternatively, if 'reasonable efforts' represent a required set of steps that a person ought to complete, the standard then becomes 'an overly prescriptive and inappropriate expansion of the *mens rea* of rape to require active ascertainment in all cases'.[44] Echoing Ferzan,[45] the concern here is that the 'failure to ascertain' standard replaces the *mens rea* requirement of knowledge or recklessness with a negligence-style standard of failure to take reasonable care and attention. Again, any such deviations from the state-sponsored procedural checklist 'cannot be squared with [the] retributive morality'[46] of the criminal law for the same reasons just canvassed: we reserve moral responsibility for those who act contrary to reasons that they knew applied to their situation, and we punish those who manifest a disrespect for values the state is responsible for promoting by demonstrating an unwillingness to be guided by those values.

7.4

You might think that the ambiguity in 'reasonableness'—between 'ordinary' and 'justified'—is a latent defect that we ought not to import into this discussion. It is, after all, a lawyer's gambit used to complicate a philosophical argument. The thread to pull on, nonetheless, is that however we construct the expressive consent standard, a choice needs to be made between *relying on* inferential rules and *prescribing* them. With that in mind, we can now reconstruct (for a fourth time) the distinction between the expressive and attitudinal consent standards, and anticipate the collapse. Recall the central tenet of Dougherty's contention, that 'what you do in the privacy of your own mind is not enough to waive your rights in the public sphere'.[47] If consent must operate in a public space to assert normative power—to be rights-waiving or permission-granting—then the expressive consent standard is best understood as an attempt to locate the normative power of consent in that public space. The third distinction is therefore between

[44] High (n 7) 489.
[45] Ferzan (n 30).
[46] Gruber, 'Rape Law Revisited' (n 31) 292.
[47] Dougherty (n 1) 251, where the 'slogan' is attributed to Laura Schroeter.

attitudinal (private) standard: where consent is *the private* attitude of willingness, acceptance, or acquiescence and

expressive (public) standard: where consent is *the public* words or overt actions of a person that indicate an attitude of willingness, acceptance, or acquiescence.

Words and overt actions are 'public' in a trivial sense; they are uttered or acted in an observable, objective, or 'public' space. The expressive (public) standard requires the words or overt actions to be public in the sense that the *meaning* that the words or actions convey is a shared or public phenomenon. Hence, when we try to 'locate consent' we are trying to locate meaning, in either the speaker's private intention, the hearer's private understanding, or the 'public' space that exists between the speaker and the hearer. If a shared understanding is necessary for the normative act of rights-waiver, then it would seem to follow that consent must be a form of communication that takes place in this public space.

In (2) *Verbal acceptance*, A's proposition to B—'Let's fuck'—would appear to be 'public' communication. As is B's reply, 'Okay'. It is easy to presume that A and B have a shared understanding of what the communication means. B is not attempting the mind-reading needed to unlock 'the moral magic' of A's attitude; A's attitude of willingness is out in the open, and B openly shares the reciprocal attitude. Even then, the meaning of the proposition 'Let's fuck' relies upon 'a network of intentions and recognition of intentions'.[48] For A to communicate to B, A needs to *intend* the propositional content ((p) I want to have sex with you)) through the utterance ((u) 'Let's fuck') and needs B to *recognise* that A is intending the propositional content, 'and further recognise that [B] is intended [by A] to recognise' the intentional propositional content.[49] The same is true for B's reply; the utterance ((u) 'Okay') needs to intend p (I also want to have sex with you) and for A to recognise that A intends p. For an utterance (u) to have illocutionary force (F) with a (p) propositional content, then

> [t]he speaker must create . . . this structure F(p), and then communicate that structure to the hearer by getting the hearer both to recognise this structure and to recognise that he is intended to recognise the structure.[50]

[48] Louise Anthony, 'Is There a "Feminist" Philosophy of Language?' in Louise Anthony (ed), *Only Natural: Gender, Knowledge, and Humankind* (OUP 2022) 120, discussing HP Grice, 'Meaning' (1957) 66 Philos Rev 377.

[49] John Searle, 'Grice on Meaning: 50 Years Later' (2007) 26(2) Teorema 9, 16.

[50] Searle (n 49) 16.

Note that we have reverted back into the language of intention and recognition. Hence, at first blush, we might think that our understanding of communication is still stuck in the private headspace of B inferring about the private headspace of A. Except what links an utterance (u) with propositional content (p)—what gives it illocutionary force (F)—are shared *conventions* (c). These shared conventions are public in the sense that 'once a semantic convention has arisen' the conventions are 'facts about the content of [a] convention can float free of the particular communicative intentions of any individual speaker on any individual occasion'.[51] In this way, communicative conventions are public conventions, ungoverned by the private headspace of A or of B.

Communicative conventions—by pulling propositional content into speech acts, utterance, and even body language—enable the familiar phenomenon of 'implicature', where there is a message that 'a speaker intends to convey but which is not part of, nor is strictly entailed by, the meaning of the sentence the speaker chooses to utter in order to convey that message'.[52] The propositional content is not necessarily entailed by the features of the utterance or speech act, but the proposition is nonetheless intended by the speaker, and that intention is recognised by the hearer.[53] For example, a (now dated) cliché for proposing sex is (u) 'come around to Netflix and chill'. Alternatively, the (outdated) cliché: 'come upstairs for coffee'. Note that there is nothing about the speech act itself that communicates a willingness or desire to have sex. What was *said* differs from what was *intended* by the speaker and what can be *recognised* by the hearer (namely, the speaker's proposal of sexual intercourse). The intention, and the recognition of this intention, is made possible through 'conventional connections between sentence-types and meanings'.[54] Shared meaning and communication is therefore made possible through intentional engagement with, and intended recognition of, public conventions.

So far, so good, for our distinction between the *private* attitude of willingness (the attitudinal standard of consent) and the *public* words or overt actions (the expressive standard of consent). In order for consent to be a performance of a normative power, the communication or representation of an attitude of willingness needs to be made through engagement with public communicative conventions. Both propositions—'Let's fuck' and 'Netflix and chill'—are public expressions of a willing attitude because the intended and recognised

[51] Anthony (n 48) 123.
[52] Anthony (n 48) 123; HP Grice, 'Logic and Conversation' in Donald Davidson and Gilbert Harman (eds), *The Logic of Grammar* (Dickenson 1975).
[53] Anthony (n 48) 124.
[54] Anthony (n 48) 123.

propositional content has illocutionary force by virtue of communicative conventions that both the speaker and the hearer are familiar with. The propositional content (the willingness to have sex with the other person) that has illocutionary force is a waiver of rights, *in a shared, or public*, space.

The conventional aspect of communicative conventions should, however, make us nervous. Recall the dilemma behind the ambiguity in 'reasonableness'; the standard of consent is either descriptive of a conventional rule (such as the spontaneity rule) or prescriptive of one (such as the formality rule). Being descriptive collapses the distinction (between expressive and attitudinal consent) and being prescriptive creates a culpability gap (and a criminalisation problem). I suggest that the same dilemma arises when expressive consent is 'public' by virtue of communicative conventions.

To illustrate, let us return to (4) *Verbal rejection*. Throughout the discussion so far, it has been treated as an easy, straightforward case. We might ask, as Husak and Thomas have, 'How can it be possible for [A] to make a . . . mistake about [B's] consent when [B] says 'no' or actively resists?'[55] To answer their question, Husak and Thomas considered a social context where a woman displaying an interest in sex gives the appearance of being promiscuous, and the appearance of being promiscuous comes at a social cost to the woman. Husak and Thomas cite a 1988 study where: '39% of Texas female college undergraduates reported they had said "no" when they wanted to have sex', '60.8% of the sexually experienced women in this study stated that they had said "no" when they intended to have sex', 'Ninety percent of the women in the Texas study who fit this category said that the fear of appearing promiscuous was at least somewhat important in explaining their behavior', and 'Forty-nine percent said fear of appearing promiscuous was moderately to very important'.[56]

Their empirical claim—or, for our purposes, a hypothetical one—is that B's verbal rejection of A's sexual advances might be intended to give the appearance of non-promiscuity whilst still intending the sex that ensues. In such a context, A may also be aware of this social convention, and A might recognise (or mistakenly recognise) B's intention to engage the social convention. To put it more formally: the (u) utterance or speech act 'no' can have the (p) propositional content that is consistent with consent to the sex because of a

[55] Douglas Husak and George C Thomas III, 'Date Rape, Social Convention, and Reasonable Mistakes' (1992) 11 L & Phil 95, 122.

[56] Husak and Thomas III (n 55) 122, citing Charlene L Muehlenhard and Lisa C Hollabaugh, 'Do Women Sometimes Say No When They Mean Yes? The Prevalence and Correlates of Women's Token Resistance to Sex' (1988) 54 J Pers Soc Psychol 872, 874.

(c) communicative convention where *A intends (p)* and B can *recognise* that *A intends (p)*. It is possible, therefore, for B to have understood (u) the speech act ('no') to have been intending (p) consent because of a particular (c) communicative convention. The speech act itself and the communicative convention are 'public' features of communication, and yet an acquittal in (4) *Verbal rejection* cases seems nothing short of outrageous, especially to expressive consent proponents.

There is, nonetheless, a way out of the verbal rejection problem. We can apply a 'general set of communicative conventions' according to which (c)* 'no (still) means no'. Under this approach, in (3) *Verbal rejection* B made the wrong implicature. B ought to have followed (c)* the general convention and not (c) the particular convention (c). In other words, even though an ordinary Texan in 1998 in B's position may have followed (c) the particular convention, B nonetheless followed the wrong sexual script, since B ought to have followed the (c)* general convention.

We can now see the same dilemma re-emerge. There are public elements to communication. Utterances, speech acts, and overt body language take place in the space observable by two people. The conventional practices that secure the meaning (or force) of a speech act also 'float free of the particular' speaker's intention or hearer's recognition. They are practices created and sustained by a community of language users. As 'public' as communication might be, we nonetheless arrive at the same choice as before; the public elements of the consent standard can either describe the communicative conventions that are practised (however morally risky and problematic) or prescribe the communicative conventions that ought to be practised.

The dilemma, once again, is between a collapse or a culpability gap. On the one hand, if 'public' expressive consent relies upon the communicative conventions that are practised, then nothing separates the expressive and attitudinal consent standards; under both standards, the finder of fact assesses whether it was possible to infer from B's words and actions to B's attitude of willingness or acceptance, by employing the particular and practised communicative conventions that give words and actions propositional content. If, on the other hand, the 'public' expressive consent standard prescribes the communicative conventions that ought to be followed, then A is merely culpable for being ignorant of the prescribed communicative convention. This culpable ignorance falls short of criminalisable conduct. Whilst the prescribed communicative convention may promote a value, it is not a value that the state is responsible for promoting, and whilst the state is responsible for promoting rights of self-ownership/duties of consent-astuteness, following a practised (albeit high-risk) communicative convention is not antithetical to the value of self-ownership.

7.5

It may be unclear, at this point, whether I have come to praise expressive consent or to bury it. In the previous essay, I praised the expressive consent standard for providing the 'explanatory reasons' required to justify a *pro tanto* wrong. I suggested that only the overt words and actions of another person—their objective and externalised behaviour—can be an explanatory reason because only their externalised behaviour can feature in the defendant's deliberation as to the reasons he should act on. Yet, given the discussion here, we can anticipate the collapse of the fifth distinction, between

> *attitudinal (subjective) standard*: where consent is *the subjective* attitude of willingness, acceptance, or acquiescence and
>
> *expressive (objective) standard*: where consent is *the objective* words or overt actions of a person that indicate an attitude of willingness, acceptance, or acquiescence.

First of all, if the objective words and overt actions are to have relevant propositional content, then they must be words or actions that express or communicate a subjective attitude of willingness or acceptance. As we know, the focal point of both standards is the inference from the objective to the subjective, from the words or actions to the attitude. Second, we then have a choice as to how we assess the inference. The standard of inference can describe practices (in terms of social rules or semantic conventions) or it can prescribe practices. The former, descriptive-and-objective, standard collapses the distinction, and the latter, prescriptive-and-objective, standard confronts problems in terms of culpability and criminalisation.

To briefly follow the first horn of the dilemma: the expressive consent standard that gives way to existing social practices prompts the same findings of fact as the attitudinal consent standard accommodates. Under both standards, it is an open-ended question of fact whether

> the complete absence of externalised behaviour in (1) *No communication*,
> the conventional language of 'Let's fuck'/'Okay' in (2) *Verbal acceptance*,

> the conventional language of 'No, don't' in (3) *Verbal rejection*,
> the overt actions in (4) *Enthusiastic undressing*, and
> the less overt actions in (5) *Enthusiastic kissing*

can form a basis upon which A could infer from 'objective words or overt actions of B' to a belief that B had 'an attitude of willingness, acceptance, or acquiescence' towards A's treatment of B.

Alternatively, to follow the second horn: if the expressive consent standard, instead, prescribes social and semantic rules, then the findings of fact are context-insensitive. If, for instance, the finder of fact prescribes the formality rule ('consent is only verbalised consent'), then there are no circumstances where B consented in (1) *No communication*, (3) *Verbal rejection*, (4) *Enthusiastic undressing*, or (5) *Enthusiastic kissing*, nor any circumstances where A could have a mistaken belief in consent. The dilemma, again, is between a collapse or a culpability gap.

However, dilemmas are built on dichotomies, and some dichotomies are false. The mistake we have so far been labouring under is holding the inference (from behaviour to attitude) to either a descriptive or a prescriptive standard. The standard of inference could, however, be held to a different standard: an epistemic standard. The excluded middle—between the finder of fact 'masquerading as an ordinary person' and the finder of fact 'thinking how another ought to behave'—is for the finder of fact to require that another person act on 'undefeated reasons' in their (albeit mistaken) judgement.[57] If '[i]t is not enough that one made a mistake as to justification, but rather, [t]here must have been an undefeated reason for one's belief',[58] a mistaken belief can be exculpatory when one is 'epistemically justified in believing an action to be right'.[59]

Avoiding the expressive consent dilemma then turns on understanding how a person might be epistemically justified in their mistaken belief. For Hurd, an actor can be epistemically justified in a belief if

> under the circumstances, she has invested a reasonable amount of time, talent, diligence, and resources to acquire information about her circumstances and to determine the demands of morality in such circumstances.[60]

[57] Gardner, 'The Many Faces of the Reasonable Person' (n 17) 565.
[58] John Gardner, 'Justifications and Reasons' in AP Simester and ATH Smith (eds), *Harm and Culpability* (Clarendon Press 1996) 120.
[59] Heidi M Hurd, 'Justifiably Punishing the Justified' (1992) 90 Mich L Rev 2203, 2207.
[60] Hurd (n 59) 2207.

Hurd offers a proceduralist understanding of an epistemic justification. Her account affords some philosophical foundations to the 'reasonable efforts to ascertain' standard (considered above at 7.3). As I explained, 'the reasonable efforts to ascertain' standard points in the right direction, but does not evade the horns of the expressive consent dilemma: reasonable efforts can also be ordinary efforts (the collapse) or prescribed efforts (the culpability gap).

To evade the expressive consent dilemma, we need to pivot slightly. In order to understand the process that an epistemically justified person needs to engage in (the time, talent, diligence, and resources that need to be expended), we need to consider types of reasons that we expect the epistemically justified person to determine and act on (the demands of morality in their circumstances). We know that the demands of morality include the requirement to have reasons to believe that the other person would agree to the treatment of them (the principle of consent-astuteness). Note that this demand is also an epistemic demand: it requires a justified belief in the mental state (agreement, willingness, or acceptance) of another person. To understand how a person can have a mistaken but epistemically justified belief in the mental state of other person, we need to understand how a justified belief in another's mental state is possible. Hence, to praise expressive consent, and not bury it, we need to pivot to consider the problem of other minds, in the next essay.

8
I Don't Know About You

8.1

'The sorts of things that I can find out about myself are the same as the sorts of things that I can find out about other people', explains Ryle, 'and the methods of finding them out are much the same'.[1] If so, then how I know that I want to have sex with another person is 'much the same' as how I know that the other person wants have sex with me. Yet, these are different phenomena. In this essay, I will isolate how my knowledge of my own mental states ('self-knowledge') differs from a justified belief in the mental states of another person ('a justified belief'). I do so with a background agenda already in place: I need to provide a way out of the expressive consent dilemma by identifying a standard of inference (from behaviour to attitude) that is neither descriptive of sexual scripts nor prescriptive of them. I will develop in this essay an 'epistemological' standard of inference that avoids the expressive consent dilemma, and revives the endorsement of the expressive consent legal standard.

The first task of this essay is to resolve an apparent tension between two intuitions about the mental states of other people. One intuition is that the mental state of another person remains beyond my full comprehension ('the alterity intuition'), and the other is that we are nonetheless capable of having an epistemically justified belief in the mental state of another person ('the knowledge intuition'). I will resolve this tension by explaining how self-knowledge is 'asymmetrical' with a justified belief in the mental states of another person. Explaining the asymmetry then enables me to defend the following three main claims about a justified belief in the mental state of another person. These claims are:

1. 'Self-knowledge' and 'justified beliefs' are both inferential; we infer from (p) promptings to a (P) proposition through (l) 'linking assumptions'.

[1] Gilbert Ryle, *The Concept of Mind* (Hutchinson's University Library 1949) 155.

Sex and Self-Ownership. Jesse Wall, Oxford University Press. © Jesse Wall 2025.
DOI: 10.1093/9780191987809.003.0008

2. The (1) linking assumptions required for a justified belief (in the mental state of another person (B)) are grounded in B-specific reasons that B is expressing a mental state.
3. It therefore follows that the epistemic standard of inference (for a justified belief in another's consenting attitude) requires B-specific reasons that B is expressing a consenting attitude.

If the third claim is sound, then we have a way of interpreting and applying the expressive consent legal standard, by importing this epistemic standard of inference, that avoids the expressive consent dilemma. I will suggest here that the expressive consent standard (that embodies the epistemic standard of inference) can both resist the collapse into the attitudinal standard and capture culpable mistaken beliefs in the consent of another.

This essay begins (at 8.2) by foregrounding two intuitions (the 'alterity intuition' and the 'knowledge intuition') whilst canvassing three problems associated with 'other minds' (the conceptual problem, the epistemic problem, and the empirical problem). The essay then takes up the task (at 8.3) of resolving the apparent tension between the 'alterity intuition' and the 'knowledge intuition', which then enables me (at 8.4) to formulate an epistemic standard of inference as distinct from a descriptive or prescriptive standard of inference. Finally (at 8.5), the challenge that remains is to demonstrate how the epistemic standard of inference avoids the expressive consent dilemma.

8.2

The existence of minds other than your own raises a host of philosophical questions. Let us start by isolating three distinct problems (that each have two variants, one general and one specific). The first problem is conceptual. How, we might ask, is it possible that I can *conceive* of a mind other than my own? If our minds are *that with which we conceive of other things*, how can we conceive of—or think about—the *mind* of another person? As Merleau-Ponty asked, 'How can the word "I" be made plural? How can we form a general idea of the I? How can I speak of another I than my own?'[2] This problem, as just stated, is the general formulation of the conceptual problem, since it concerns the mind in general. We could formulate a *specific* variant of the conceptual problem. How, we might ask, is it possible that I can conceive of a particular

[2] Maurice Merleau-Ponty, *Phenomenology of Perception* (Donald A Landes tr, Routledge 2012) 364.

mental state—such as anger, pain, desire, or willingness—of another person? More precisely, the specific-conceptual problem concerns not just the problem of how we can understand that another person has particular mental states but 'the problem of extending the very same concept to others that I apply in my own case'.[3] How is it possible, the specific formulation of the conceptual problem asks, that I can extend *my own concept* of anger, pain, or desire so that the same concept applies to another mind?

I highlight the conceptual problem to introduce the first of two intuitions about other minds that I seek to affirm throughout this discussion. That is, the suggestion that even if we can somehow overcome the conceptual problem of other minds, and accept that we can conceive of the mind or mental states of another, there nonetheless remains a 'dimension of the other person that essentially escapes my comprehension'.[4] The implication is that we are never able to understand or conceive of other minds *in the same way* that we conceive of our own minds or comprehend any other things that we encounter in the world. In this way, we can only ever dissolve the problem of other minds (remove the opacity of the other) but not solve the problem (comprehend the other).[5] This invokes a philosophical method that foregrounds the 'alterity' ('otherness') of the other person and recognises the existence of a perspective that is not one's own. On Emmanuel Levinas' account, the alterity of the other 'transcends' our comprehension of the other, and 'it has been a tendency of the mainstream of Western philosophy' to

> emphasize comprehension of alterity (and especially that of the other person) at the expense of what he calls the 'transcendence' of the other. . . . To put it differently, philosophers have generally failed to appreciate the fact that there is, and must be, a dimension of the other person that essentially escapes my comprehension.[6]

In recognising the transcendence of the other, Ngaire Naffine explains how it entails

> respect for the unknowable otherness of the other, that part of the other which cannot be swept up in my understanding of him or her. Always, the other

[3] Søren Overgaard, 'Other Minds Embodied' (2017) 50 Cont Philos Rev 65, 68.
[4] Søren Overgaard, 'Rethinking Other Minds: Wittgenstein and Levinas on Expression' (2005) 48 Inquiry 249, 261.
[5] Taylor Carman, *Merleau-Ponty* (Routledge 2008) 135.
[6] Overgaard, 'Rethinking Other Minds' (n 4) 261.

> remains someone beyond my full comprehension and beyond my ability to make of that other simply what they are to me. The other escapes my attempt to pin her down, to sum her up.[7]

How we understand the other informs our respect for the other. Specifically, respect for the alterity of the other informs the principle of consent-astuteness. To address or ameliorate our concerns with instrumentalising another person (using another person's body as a means to an end), we must have

> *principle of consent-astuteness*: reasons to believe that the person would agree to our treatment of them.

As the discussion here unfolds, the principle will become more burdensome. It will require us to have

> *principle of consent-astuteness (alterity)*: person-specific reasons to believe that the person would agree to our treatment of them.

To understand the need for the additional burden, we need to start by considering a further aspect of the problem of other minds: namely, the epistemological problem of other minds. Even if we can think about or conceive of the mental states of others (the conceptual problem), we still need to consider how we can be *justified in thinking* that another person (generally) has a mind or that another person has a (specific) mental state. For instance, even if other minds are conceivable, how do I know that there are other minds in a lecture theatre, not mindless zombies[8] or (just as absent-minded) hungover undergraduate students? In terms of the specific variant of the epistemological problem, even if I can extend my concept of pain, anger, or willingness to another person's mental life, how can I *be justified* in believing that the other person is in pain, angry, or willing to do something?

These epistemological problems might not seem insurmountable, and the second intuition that I seek to affirm throughout this discussion is that we can, on occasion, form such a justified belief. We often *know* that another person is in pain, is angry, or is willing, and hence 'very often we do have reliable knowledge about the feelings and thoughts of other persons'.[9] The

[7] Ngaire Naffine, 'Possession: Erotic Love in the Law of Rape' (1994) 57 MLR 10, 31–32.
[8] Thomas Nagel, *The View from Nowhere* (OUP 1986) 19.
[9] Overgaard, 'Rethinking Other Minds' (n 4) 250.

specific-epistemological problem of other minds is, in some circumstances, easily dissolvable.

As you can anticipate, it is the specific formulation of the epistemological problem that is most pertinent to our understanding of another person's consent to sex. If the duty of consent-astuteness requires that A has reasons to believe that B is willing to have sex with A, then we need to understand how A *can have reasons* for their belief that B has a consenting attitude. To require a belief in the consent of another person requires us to address the specific-epistemological problem of other minds. In doing so, note how we are holding a person's belief in the consenting attitude of another person to an epistemic standard. It is the use of an epistemic standard that will help us avoid the expressive consent dilemma.

The problem of other minds also represents an empirical problem. Even if we can form justified beliefs about the mental states of others, then we need to ask: How do we find out about these things? What methods or techniques can and do we use to perform 'the task of forming beliefs or judgments about others' mental states'?[10] What, in the ordinary course of life, do we look for when we are assessing the mental states of others in general? And how, in the ordinary course of law, do we look for particular states of mind, such as acceptance or willingness? Separating the epistemic from the empirical highlights the real possibility that we gather 'evidence' of another person's state of mind that falls short of epistemological standards of justified beliefs in another's state of mind.[11] In the ordinary course of life, we might have beliefs in the states of mind of others that are honest but not justified, and any other person in our circumstances might also form these same unjustified beliefs.

Here we encounter the first horn of the expressive consent dilemma in the context of the problem of other minds: when the state of mind of another person is an open-ended question of fact, the question of fact can accommodate any inference from behaviour to attitude. The second horn of the dilemma arises where we prescribe methods or techniques for how to perform 'the task of forming beliefs or judgments about others' mental states'. As we can now anticipate, the eventual way out of the expressive consent dilemma involves a pivot from the empirical problem of other minds to confronting the epistemic problem.

[10] Alvin I Goldman, 'Theory of Mind' in Eric Margolis, Richard Samuels and Stephen P Stich (eds), *The Oxford Handbook of Philosophy of Cognitive Science* (OUP 2012) 402; Overgaard, 'Other Minds Embodied' (n 3) 69.

[11] Andrew Melnyk, 'Inference to Best Explanation and Other Minds' (1994) 72 Australas J Philos 482, 483.

For now, we can note an apparent tension between the intuitions I have asserted here. The first is the intuition that we can never resolve the transcendence of other minds. It follows that we cannot understand or comprehend the mental states of another person, not in the same way that we can understand our own mental states. This creates an asymmetry between a justified belief in our own mental states (self-knowledge) and a justified belief in the mental states of another person. The second is the intuition that we can, on occasion, overcome the specific-epistemological problem of other minds, insofar as it is possible to have a justified belief in the mental state of another person that is just as reliable as our own self-knowledge.

8.3

I have so far set up an apparent tension between two intuitions. In this section, I aim to resolve the tension by delineating how 'self-knowledge' is asymmetrical with a 'justified belief'. We can start by accepting that there is a 'profound asymmetry' between a justified belief in our own mental states and a justified belief in the mental states of another person.[12] Consider, for instance, four propositions:

P1: I want to have another child
P2: I want to have sex with her.
P3: She wants to have another child.
P4: She wants to have sex with me.

The way in which we can justify our beliefs in the first two propositions is not the same as our justified beliefs in the second two. There is an intuitive sense in which we experience our own thoughts and mental states 'directly' and the thoughts and mental states of others 'indirectly'. When it comes to sex and physical intimacy, for instance, we can understand our own attitudes towards an intimate act when it applies to us. We are familiar with our own attitudes of desire, willingness, acquiescence, reluctance, and objection. Like lightning striking us, our own thoughts and attitudes can present themselves as being direct thoughts and attitudes. We can say, at least, that *we experience them* directly. The consent of another—another person's attitude of acceptance,

[12] Paul A Boghossian, 'Content and Self-knowledge' in Peter Ludlow and Norah Martin (eds), *Externalism and Self-knowledge* (CSLI Publications 1998) 151.

willingness, or acquiescence—is different. We experience another person's attitude through their expression or manifestation of that attitude, through their 'externalised behaviour'. We also know that our own mental states tend to correlate with certain behavioural patterns. This sets up an intuitive inference about the mental states of others. An inference that we ought to treat with caution.

The inference works in the following way. When we experience a range of mental states, from pain and anger to embarrassment and hope, we also observe that a range of external states are associated with these mental states: the hot coffee and the wincing of my mouth is associated with my pain, the half-assembled IKEA furniture and staring into middle-distance is associated with my frustration, the criticism of an error and the flushness of my face is associated with my embarrassment, and so on. We can make generalisations about the correlative relationship between our own external behavioural states and our own mental states. Based upon these generalisations that hold true for our own mental states, we can then analogise from our own mental states to the mental states of others. We may then infer that others, who are in similar circumstances and who exhibit the same behaviour, have the same mental state that we do. When someone drinks hot coffee and winces and contorts their mouth, we can reason by analogy that since *we would be in pain* in the same circumstances and behave in the same way, we might be justified in believing *that they are in pain*. However, consider how reasoning by analogy works to justify a belief that another has an attitude of willingness or acquiescence towards a sexual act or activity. We may observe, from our own experience of attitudes of willingness, acquiescence, or objection, that our mental state of consent or refusal is associated with certain behavioural states. We may reason that: *when I desire* sexual intercourse, *I am physically amorous* in a particular way; *if I were to object* to sexual intercourse, *I would protest* in a particular way.

We can already anticipate why the analogical inference is epistemically weak. The analogy proceeds from the assumption that 'one learns from one's own case what thinking, feeling, sensation are'.[13] This assumption, Malcolm explains, 'leads first to solipsism and then to nonsense'.[14] The external behavioural state itself cannot be the 'criterion of the psychological phenomena' (otherwise we are abandoning the analogical inference in favour of direct perception).[15] Rather, we 'note[] something in [ourselves] that [we] call "thinking"

[13] Norman Malcolm, 'Knowledge of Other Minds' (1958) 55 J Philos 969, 974.
[14] Malcolm (n 13) 974.
[15] Malcolm (n 13) 975.

or "fear" or "pain"', and we try to 'infer the presence of the same in others'.[16] We then need some criterion for what is 'the *same* in others',[17] but the only criterion is our own experience of the psychological phenomena. The analogy invites us to consider our own experiences, and then justify a belief in the mental state of another person based upon our own experiences. It is solipsistic insofar as any such analogy denies the possibility that another mind might represent a different point of view of the world than one's own. The analogy presumes, in other words, that by reasoning from our own case, we can understand and comprehend the other by reference to our own experiences. 'Consent', under the analogical inference, becomes self-centred. Under the analogical inference, what another person's consent amounts to is determined by our own experience with the mental state of willingness or acquiescence with regard to sexual activity.

Hence, the analogical inference provides a weak solution to the specific-epistemological problem of other minds. It is nonetheless introduced here for two reasons. The first is to revisit the dangers of open-ended questions of fact under the attitudinal standard of consent. If the finder of fact is to assess a person's assessment of another person's state of mind, and if the assessment is an open-ended question of fact, then there is nothing to prevent the use of analogical inferences. A person's amorous activity, their body language, dancing, and clothing, as well as the absence of a vocalised or forthright protest, provide a set of circumstances and behaviour by that person that may be analogous to the circumstances and behaviour that manifest the finder of fact's consent (in their own experience). The second idea concerns the inconsistency between the analogical inference and the respect of alterity. The mental state of another person is a point of view of the world that we cannot convert into our own point of view. And yet we do just that when we assume that the correlation between external behaviour and internal mental states that we experience is a correlation that occurs in other people in the same way. The analogical inference therefore cannot be a solution to the epistemological problem of other minds that is also consistent with the required respect for alterity.

You may feel, at this point, that I am setting the bar too high by discrediting analogical reasoning from our own set of experiences of mental states. After all—one might object—our own experience of our mental states and associated behavioural states are all that we have to reason from. And the objection is right; self-knowledge is a helpful reference point. If our own experience of

[16] Malcolm (n 13) 975.
[17] Malcolm (n 13) 975.

our own mental states is our reference point, then let us consider how self-knowledge is possible.

Self-knowledge may seem to be an odd phenomenon to call into question. After all, we tend to experience our own mental states with an unquestionable degree of certainty and reliability. Self-knowledge is concerned with whether we believe in a certain proposition concerning our own mental states, and whether we are justified in such a belief. It is true that we tend to know, with sufficient certainty and reliability, when we are angry, anxious, or fearful. Hence, a belief in some propositions seem easy to justify. We are then tempted to say that '[k]nowledge of one's own thoughts is normally direct'.[18] That is, we directly perceive propositions; we directly perceive that *P5: I am angry* in the same way that we directly perceive that *P6: It is raining*. As I will explain here, whilst we may experience our own mental states as being directly perceived, any justified belief in our own mental states is inferential.

To begin to understand why self-knowledge is inferential, let us first consider some less obvious propositions. For instance, we may ask ourselves: *Q1: Do I want another child?*, *Q2: Do I want to have sex with her?*, or *Q7: Do I like this new job?* In these instances, we might experience much less certain and reliable instances of 'self-knowledge'. If anything, we might become inert in self-doubt and uncertainty. Lawlor has explained how we might justify our belief that *P1: I want another child*.[19] We might start noticing a series of experiences, thoughts, and recollections; we might find ourselves (p(i)) 'lingering over the memory of how a newborn feels in one's arms' or observe in ourselves (p(ii)) 'an emotion that could be envy when an acquaintance reveals her pregnancy'.[20] Our mind may also return to (p(iii)) anxiety about home finance, (p(iv)) concern for career sacrifices, or (p(v)) a sense of 'completeness' with the current constitution of the family unit. These 'internal promptings' (p(i)–(v)) provide the evidence for or against a justified belief in a proposition (P), and such promptings might be enough to 'make a self-attribution that sticks',[21] enabling us to say that we (P1) *want another child* with a sense of 'ease or settledness'.[22]

Note that the internal promptings—the memories, emotions, and anxieties—do not amount to the proposition *P1: I want another child*. Rather, we make an inference from these internal promptings to a belief in the proposition. The

[18] Quassim Cassam, 'What Asymmetry? Knowledge of Self, Knowledge of Others, and the Inferentialist Challenge' (2017) 194 Synthese 723, 724.
[19] Krista Lawlor, 'Knowing What One Wants' (2009) 79 Philos Phenomenol Res 47, 57.
[20] Lawlor (n 19) 57.
[21] Lawlor (n 19) 57.
[22] Lawlor (n 19) 57.

best explanation of these internal promptings, (p(i)) nostalgia and (p(ii)) envy, is that *P1: I want another child.* To have a justified belief in such a mental state therefore requires first-order mental states (p(i), p(ii), p(iii), etc) that prompt a second-order, propositional mental state (P). The best explanation of the first-order promptings is the second-order mental state. We do not directly perceive the proposition (P), rather we arrive at a proposition (P) indirectly, by virtue of a deductive inference about our mental states.[23] Consent—or attitudes of willingness, acceptance, or acquiescence—works the same way. We may notice promptings (p) of sexual desire or disinterest, states of anxiety or ease, closeness or alienation, from which we infer that *P2: I want to have sex with this person* or *~P2: I do not want to have sex with this person.*

Even for more obvious knowledge, such as *P5: I am angry* or *P6: It is raining*, our knowledge is indirect in the same way.[24] Take the proposition *P6: It is raining.* Despite the immediacy with which we may affirm this belief, we nonetheless indirectly form a justified belief in P6. Let us say that I formed P6 by looking out the window and (p(i)) *observing rain.* We might say, with Moran, that I 'have a right to assume that my reflection on the reasons in favor of rain provided an answer to the question of what my belief about the rain is' provided that we can 'assume that *what* my belief here is was something determined by the conclusion of my reflection on those reasons'.[25] This assumption provides 'the right sort of link between' asking 'Do I believe that it is raining?' and 'Is it raining?'.[26]

To have a justified belief in *P6: It is raining,* I must infer something from my 'reasons in favour of rain'. That is, I must infer my observation p(i): *I can observe rain* is good enough to generate *P6: It is raining.* Ordinarily, p(i) is good enough to generate P, because of the 'linking assumption' between what I am observing and what I am justified in believing.[27] To demonstrate, let us tease the example out a little further, and replace p(i): *I can observe rain* with p(i)*: *There are drops of water on my window* and p(ii): *There are dark grey clouds in the sky.* Here, we can see the linking assumption is doing more work. If I have a justified belief in P6: *It is raining,* it is because I am justified in making the link between p(i)*: *There are drops of water on my window*, p(ii): *There are dark grey clouds in the sky*, and P6: *It is raining.* If I also knew that p(iii): *My windows are being washed today*, then I still might believe P6, but it may not be

[23] Cassam (n 18) 730.
[24] Cassam (n 18) 731.
[25] Richard Moran, 'Responses to O'Brien and Shoemaker' 11 (2003) Eur J Philos 402, 405.
[26] Moran (n 25) 405.
[27] Cassam (n 18) 735.

a justified belief. As Cassam argues, it then follows that: 'my belief that I believe it's raining wouldn't be justified . . . unless I am *justified* in making or believing the linking assumption'.[28] The same with *P5: I am angry*: we need linking assumptions to connect the promptings p(i): *I am speaking rapidly*, p(ii): I *cannot maintain eye contact with B*, and p(iii): *my pulse is racing* with the proposition *P5: I am angry* with B. These linking assumptions may be easy to establish, and hence make self-knowledge stable and reliable, but these linking assumptions also render even trivial self-knowledge to be inferential knowledge.

We can begin to appreciate the way in which self-knowledge is indirect knowledge. We infer from a range of evidence, data, or promptings ('there are drops of water on my window', 'newborn memories linger') to an explanation ('it is raining', 'I want another child') *and* we make a second-order assessment about that inference, to make sure that the explanation is the *best available explanation* and to 'make a self-attribution that sticks'.[29] Our justified belief in our own mental states is, in this way, indirect.

We are now able to return to our justified beliefs in the mental states of others. And here is the pay-off: if self-knowledge is epistemologically indirect (even when we directly experience the mental states that prompt the inference), then it is now much easier to appreciate how our justified beliefs in the mental states of others are also epistemologically indirect. The difference being that rather than making inferences from internal prompts or our own observations (in the case of self-knowledge), we are making inferences about the externalised behaviour of others. Here the evidence from which we infer is another's behaviour in context; the best explanation of someone wincing from drinking hot coffee is *that they are in pain*, the best explanation of someone being flushed in the face whilst an error of theirs is being publicly highlighted is *that they are embarrassed*, and so on.

Nonetheless, the intuition that we can, on occasion, *perceive* another's mental state still lingers. For some, such as McDowell:

> one can literally perceive, in another person's facial expression or his behaviour, that he is in pain, and not just infer that he is in pain from what one perceives.[30]

[28] Cassam (n 18) 733.
[29] Lawlor (n 19) 57.
[30] John McDowell, 'On the Reality of the Past' in John McDowell (ed)), *Meaning, Knowledge and Reality* (Harvard UP 1998) 305.

Here we need to untangle perceptual knowledge from non-inferential knowledge.[31] In the case of 'another is in pain', we can form a justified belief in *P8: She is in pain* by perceiving (p) her facial expression. The basis of our justified belief—the promptings that we draw upon—is perceptual. The perceptual prompting (p) is direct. We nonetheless arrive at a justified belief in *P8: She is in pain* indirectly. We infer that P is the best explanation of p, *and* we draw the inference with ease and immediacy. It may not be an inference that we consciously consider, but to have a justified belief, the justification relies upon the strength of that inference. For instance, I might perceive that a *banana is ripe.*[32] The yellowness of the banana is *perceived*, and, therefore, it is tempting (but mistaken) to say that my knowledge of its ripeness is *direct.* In fact, my justified belief in the ripeness of the banana is indirect; the basis of my inference is a direct experience of the banana's colour.

Our epistemological response to both self-knowledge and a justified belief in another's mental state is therefore inferential. To have a justified belief in another's mental state or our own, we make an inference to the best explanation of what we perceive. In some cases, an inference about the mental state of another may even be easier to draw than an inference about our own mental state. We might, for instance, have more certainty in a belief that *my friend wants another child* than a belief that *I want another child.*

At this point, the asymmetry between self-knowledge and a justified belief in the mental state of others begins to disappear. We can nonetheless revive the asymmetry in terms of how we encounter the promptings that we link to propositions. For self-knowledge, the objects of our inquiries—whether they be the emotion of envy, frustration, or the raindrops on a window—are illuminated by a particular means of inquiry. We experience certain promptings (envy, frustration, or drops of water) and we infer from them to propositions (I want another child, I am angry, or it is raining outside). When it comes to raindrops, Levinas explains, these 'objects have no light of their own; they receive borrowed light'.[33] It is through our own *reflection* of our own mental states, or through our own *comprehension* of external objects, that we can infer from promptings to propositions. It follows for Levinas that when we perceive other things, they have a 'plastic manifestation or disclosure'.[34] 'Plastic', like

[31] Cassam (n 18) 737.

[32] Fred I Dretske, *Seeing and Knowing* (Routledge & Kegan Paul 1969) 159; Søren Overgaard, 'Other People' in Dan Zahavi (ed), *The Oxford Handbook of Contemporary Phenomenology* (OUP 2012) 470–71.

[33] Emmanuel Levinas, *Totality and Infinity: An Essay on Exteriority* (Alphonso Lingis tr, Duquesne UP 1969) 74.

[34] Levinas, *Totality and Infinity* (n 33) 296.

clay, is mouldable and malleable—*able to have a form impressed upon it.* The disclosure of other things 'renounces . . . its hither unpublished existence'.[35] It unfolds, or is formed, under the weight of my deduction, into something that I can comprehend.

For Levinas, this is not how we encounter and come to understand another person. The presentation and expression of another person 'does not disclose an inward world previously closed, adding thus a new region to comprehend'.[36] The mental states of another person are not our own reflection or 'external objects lying open to view',[37] but nor are they entirely closed off from us. Another person's mental life 'is something that, unlike *any* object, presents *itself*, expresses *itself*, as an independent and inalienable source of meaning'.[38] Here we encounter the first intuition again. The transcendence of another person is 'not due to the fact that she has perceptual access to private entities that I cannot perceive'.[39] 'Rather', Overgaard interprets, 'her inaccessibility has to do with the circumstances that she is the one expressing herself'.[40] Hence, for Levinas, when another person expresses herself,

> the manifestation and the manifested coincide; the manifested attends its own manifestation . . . in the sense that we say of someone that he presents himself by stating his name . . . he remains always the source of his own presence.[41]

Consider, by way of example, two ways of learning about the name of a co-participant at a seminar or conference. You may learn her name from the handout, timetable, flier, etc, or she may introduce herself during the morning tea break. When she states her own name, she is attending to her own presentation. Whilst her name may not have been hidden from me, her expression of herself is different from if I had learnt it from some other source. It is *her* presentation of *herself*: the 'manifestation and the manifested coincide'.[42] In the same way, when we encounter another,

[35] Levinas, *Totality and Infinity* (n 33) 296.
[36] Levinas, *Totality and Infinity* (n 33) 212.
[37] Overgaard, 'Rethinking Other Minds' (n 4) 262.
[38] Overgaard, 'Rethinking Other Minds' (n 4) 262–63; Levinas, *Totality and Infinity* (n 33) 51.
[39] Overgaard, 'Rethinking Other Minds' (n 4) 263.
[40] Overgaard, 'Rethinking Other Minds' (n 4) 263.
[41] Levinas, *Totality and Infinity* (n 33) 296.
[42] Levinas, *Totality and Infinity* (n 33) 296.

> [i]t is not that her mental life is hidden from me, but precisely the fact that she expresses it to me that reveals both her inner life and the fact that it escapes my grasp in an important sense. For as expressed to me, it is precisely her life, and not mine.[43]

The expressive behaviour of another person ('the Other') reveals a point of view on the world (their mental state), which is a point of view that I cannot adopt (*their* mental state). It is in this way that the Other's expression 'at once gives and conceals the Other'.[44] It reveals a present mental state whilst being the source of his or her presence.

We can therefore understand the asymmetry of knowledge of mental states in terms of the *same* inferential belief about fundamentally *different* perceptions of a mental state. The asymmetry between self-knowledge and a justified belief is not an epistemic asymmetry; the justified belief in a proposition derives inferentially, in both cases, from the best explanation of promptings. Rather, the asymmetry is concerned with how those promptings are available for inference. For self-knowledge, the promptings are *perceived by their source* (the self), and for a justified belief, the promptings are *presented by their source* (the other). As Wittgenstein put it, '[m]y thoughts are not hidden from [the other], but are just open to him in a different way than they are to me'.[45] Contrary to Ryle, the methods of finding 'the sorts of things that I can find out about myself' very much differ from the methods for 'the sorts of things that I can find out about other people'.[46] It follows that the mental states of others are not hidden from me; they are directly expressed or presented to me, but since they are presented *to* me, they are open to me in a different way than my own mental states, which are presented *by* me. *Crucially*, what makes a justified belief epistemically burdensome is that for a state of mind to be presented (or manifest), we need reasons to take the presentation to be a person attending to their own presentation.

We can now resolve the apparent tension between our two intuitions about other minds. We 'very often . . . do have reliable knowledge about the feelings and thoughts of other persons'[47] (the second intuition) because we can make inferences from what we directly perceive about them, and those inferences

[43] Overgaard, 'Rethinking Other Minds' (n 4) 268.

[44] Emmanuel Levinas, *Time and the Other* (Richard A Cohen tr, Duquesne UP 1987) 78–79.

[45] Ludwig Wittgenstein, *Last Writings on the Philosophy of Psychology: The Inner and the Outer, 1949–1951, Vol 2* (GH von Wright and Heikki Nyman eds, CG Luckhardt and Maximilian AE Aue trs, Blackwell 1992) 34–35.

[46] Ryle (n 1) 155.

[47] Overgaard, 'Rethinking Other Minds' (n 4) 250.

can be supported by the reasons we have to perceive them as attending to their own presentation. It nonetheless remains the case that there is a 'dimension of the other person that essentially escapes my comprehension'[48] (the first intuition), since our perceptions of the other person are presented to us from an independent and inalienable source—their point of view—that we can have no point of view on.

8.4

Enough continental hand-waving. We now need to identify a standard for when we can have a justified belief in a mental state. An epistemic standard, that is, that can inform how we ought to understand and interpret the expressive consent legal standard, and structure the legal standard in a way that avoids the expressive consent dilemma.

Let us start with the stable ground of self-knowledge. Even our own understanding of our attitude of willingness or acceptance towards a sexual act is indirect. We make an inference about our internal promptings (p(i), p(ii), etc)—of desire or sexual indifference, closeness or alienation, ease or insecurity, nonchalance or anxiety—to attribute to ourselves a belief that *P: I do/ ~P: I do not want to have sex with this person.* Our justified belief in P (or ~P), which derives from our best explanation of p(i), p(ii), etc, may be immediate or may require deliberation, but it is inferential nonetheless.

Beyond self-knowledge, we encounter the readily available, but epistemically weak, analogical inferences about the mental states of others. I have already explained the problem with analogising from one's own experience with attitudes of consent. The weakness is that it presupposes that there is behaviour that one can observe in one's own case that can be taken as correlating with consent in all cases. The analogical reasoning projects one's own experience with attitudes of willingness or acquiescence on to other people's experiences. This self-centred, solipsistic consent is inconsistent with the alterity of the other person, as it amounts to one person occupying the point of view of the other, with their own point of view.

Even if we move beyond reasoning from our own experience with attitudes of consent and consider how others *generally* express attitudes of acceptance and willingness, we encounter again inferences that are inconsistent with the alterity of the other person. If the expression of a consensual attitude is taken

[48] Overgaard, 'Rethinking Other Minds' (n 4) 261.

to be a conventional, scripted, social phenomenon, then we treat consent as something that is 'plastic', able to be moulded into shape, in the sense that it 'manifests something as something'.[49] Consent becomes plastic when we treat 'consent' as something that 'is at hand', 'just stands there', and merely 'renounces ... its hitherto unpublished existence'.[50] Consent then becomes a social artefact that we can identify and comprehend. A person may perceive a series of cues from another person that form part of a conventional sexual script: a way of talking, dressing, dancing, a repertoire of intimate acts, and so on. The sexual script may be conventional and widespread, but the 'consent' is still moulded into shape by social force; it is something that stands 'outside' the mental state of the person to whom the consent is attributed.

When 'consent' becomes plastic, the empirical task 'of forming beliefs or judgments about others' mental states'[51] can therefore be performed in the same way that we identify any other social artefact. We can infer from an open-ended set of observations and social conventions. What counts as an inference to the best explanation of a person's behaviour depends on the inference that an ordinary member of the social group (and ordinary practitioner of the linguistic practice) would take as consent. The 'consent' has a form that is moulded by social practice. This enables the open-ended set of inferences: just as drops of water on windows usually mean that it is raining outside, body language *like that* usually means consent to sex.

Both the analogical inference and the inference from social practices are accommodated by the attitudinal consent standard and the descriptive approach to the expressive consent standard. If the inference from observable behaviour to an internal attitude is an open-ended inference (under attitudinal consent), then any inference (or linking assumption)—analogical or social—is available to the finder of fact. Equally, if the inference (or linking assumption) is informed by what externalised behaviour an ordinary person would take as indicating consent, then an inference based on an ordinary social practice would be available to the finder of fact.

That is, an assumption that allows the movement from *what is being observed* to *what can be inferred*. If we are concerned by linking assumptions that ought not to be available when inferring consent, then it is tempting to prescribe inference-blocking rules. As we have encountered in the previous essay (at 7.3), we could amass a list: (i) lack of protest or resistance does not mean

[49] Levinas, *Totality and Infinity* (n 33) 296.
[50] Levinas, *Totality and Infinity* (n 33) 296.
[51] Goldman (n 10) 402.

consent, (ii) silence does not mean consent, (iii) prior consent is not present consent, (iv) pressured consent is not consent, (v) consent is only verbalised consent, (vi) foreplay is not consent, and so on. In doing so, we would be prescribing which words or overt actions of a person indicate an internal attitude of willingness, acceptance, or acquiescence. As we know, this approach encounters problems (of context-insensitivity and culpability gaps).

Rather than prescribing *which* inferences can be drawn, the contention here is that we need to prescribe *how* the inferences are drawn. Specifically, to respect the alterity of the person, we need to make the move from *what is being observed* to *what can be inferred* epistemically burdensome. The epistemic standard that is being imported suggests that a justified belief in the presentation of a mental state of another person must be predicated on reasons to take the presentation to be a person attending to their own presentation. Burdened by this epistemic standard, the expressive consent standard requires not only 'words and conduct that manifest an attitude of willingness or acceptance' but also reasons to suggest that the consenting person is attending to their own presentation through such words and conduct.

In the same way that when a person states his or her own name, they are attending to their own presentation, when a person expresses their willingness to engage in a sexual act, they are attending to their own presentation. This is the relevant 'linking assumption' between *what is being observed* and *a justified belief*. When applied to empirical questions, the standard of consent requires reasons for believing that another person is using a set of communicative techniques or conventions to express an attitude of acceptance, willingness, or acquiescence. In this way, the epistemic standard places the other person—and not social phenomena—as the source of meaning.

The empirical task of 'going about' forming a justified belief will always encounter conventional practices, communicative techniques, implicature, and sexual scripts. However, it is because 'the other' is transcendent—because there remains a 'dimension of the other person that essentially escapes my comprehension' (our first intuition)—that we need to find reasons to believe that the other person is relying upon a certain set of conventional practices, communicative techniques, and so on. At the same time, it is because the other does present and express themselves to us that our beliefs in their mental state can sometimes be certain and reliable (our second intuition). Another person's mental states are always inaccessible to us, but only in the sense that they are presented to us by another person. We can, nonetheless, act on, and rely on, the consent of another person provided that our inferences about their attitude confront the epistemic problem of other minds.

8.5

We now have a new formulation of the expressive consent legal standard, one that is burdened by an epistemic requirement. Under this expressive (epistemic) standard, reliance on the 'words and conduct that indicate an attitude of willingness or acceptance' must be supported with reasons for taking those words or conduct as the other person's presentation of that attitude. In other words, A's belief in B's attitude must be grounded in B-specific reasons for taking B to be expressing that attitude. In terms of the language of the standards themselves, incorporating the epistemic standard into a legal standard merely requires a substitution of 'her'/'his'/'their' for 'an'. The contrast between legal standards is now between

attitudinal standard: where consent is an internal attitude of willingness, acceptance, or acquiescence;

expressive (descriptive) standard: where consent is the words or overt actions of a person that indicate *to an ordinary person* an internal attitude of willingness, acceptance, or acquiescence;

expressive (prescriptive) standard: where consent is *particular* words or overt actions of a person that indicate an internal attitude of willingness, acceptance, or acquiescence; and

expressive (epistemic) standard: where consent is the words or overt actions of a person that indicate *her/his/their* internal attitude of willingness, acceptance, or acquiescence.

Sitting behind the simple shift from 'an' to 'her'/ 'his'/'their' is the alterity of the other person—the expectation on a person who acts on, and relies upon, a belief in the consent of another person to provide reasons for why 'the words and conduct that indicate an attitude' are *her/his/their* words and conduct that manifest *her/his/their* attitude.

There remains, however, a lot of unfinished business. Recall from the previous essay that the principal concern with the attitudinal standard is that it accommodates any inference from behaviour to attitude. And yet, the alternative—the expressive standard—was either equally accommodating or was context-insensitive whilst only capturing culpable ignorance rather than culpable wrongdoing. Hence, the final question for this essay is whether the expressive (epistemic) consent standard both resists collapse into the attitudinal standard and captures only culpable and criminalisable conduct.

Let us start with the first horn of the dilemma and consider how the expressive (epistemic) consent standard avoids the collapse into the attitudinal standard. In the previous essay, the collapse of the distinction between attitudinal and expressive consent unfolded in two stages. First, the focal point of any finding of fact is the inference from externalised (public or objective) behaviour to the internal (private or subjective) attitude. Under either legal standard, a belief in consent is located in the inference from another person's behaviour to that other person's attitude. Note how the discussion in this essay has further affirmed the inferential basis of both self-knowledge and a justified belief in a mental state of another person. Second, if the standard of inference (ie how that inference can be drawn) is determined descriptively (how ordinary people would draw that inference), then the expressive consent standard accommodates the same inferences that are available to a defendant under the attitudinal standard. To put the same point in the terms of this essay, if the problem of other minds is only an empirical problem, then the legal standard of a belief in the consenting attitude of another person is only concerned with what, in the ordinary course of life, we (ordinary people) look for when we are assessing consensual mental states of others.

As we can anticipate, since the expressive (epistemic) standard represents a response to the epistemological problem of other minds, the expressive (epistemic) standard resists the collapse back into the attitudinal standard. This is an important shift, from an empirical-descriptive standard of inferences (how, in the ordinary course of life, ordinary people assess others' consenting attitudes) to an epistemological standard of inference (how a person can have a justified belief in the consenting attitude of another person). The expressive (epistemic) standard represents a heightened evidential burden on A to show how—whatever behaviour is relied upon—there were reasons to take that behaviour as B expressing her attitude, as B 'attending to her presentation'.

The second horn of the dilemma arises when the expressive consent standard prescribes rules of inference, rather than describing them. The initial problem with this prescriptive approach is that the rules of inference (from behaviour to attitude) are context-insensitive. Silence cannot mean consent (even when it can); enthusiastic and unassisted undressing is not enough for consent (even when it is); 'no' always means 'no' (regardless of the context, social practice, and implicature). These practices are not, according to the prescriptive approach, how people *ought to be* inferring a consenting attitude. The expressive (prescriptive) approach prohibits social practices at the expense of the choice to engage in certain consensual, albeit morally risky, sexual acts (such as nonverbal consent, false protest, kinky or domineering sex, and so on). In comparison, the expressive (epistemic) standard is more context-sensitive, insofar as the defendant has the opportunity to discharge the evidential burden and show how the person-specific context enables the inference about the complainant's expression of consent. In this way, the epistemic standard is compatible with sexual autonomy; it permits people to exercise their rights as self-owners to engage in morally risky sexual acts.

The more challenging problem arises when the defendant cannot discharge this burden. Namely, when the defendant (A) relies upon a set of words or overt actions of the complainant (B) to infer B consented to A's treatment of B, in circumstances where B's words and overt actions might be consistent with how 'ordinary' people in B's position communicate consent to people in A's position. This, you may recall, is 'plastic consent'—the meaning of consent that is shaped and moulded by social forces alone. Such circumstances would satisfy the expressive (descriptive) standard, may or may not clear the expressive (prescriptive) standard (depending on whether the words or overt actions fit the prescribed sexual script), but do not satisfy the requirements of the expressive (epistemic) standard.

Still under the second horn of the dilemma, it is now a real challenge to say that person A is responsible (for the purposes of the criminal law) for relying upon plastic consent, for acting as an 'ordinary' person whilst presuming that B is doing the same. Part of this challenge is to show how the expressive (epistemic) consent standard captures criminalisable conduct and aligns with principles of retribution, which is especially challenging in light of my earlier suggestion that the expressive (prescriptive) consent standard does not. As discussed in the previous essay (at 7.3), if the expressive consent standard is to be squared with the retributive morality of the criminal law, then it must clear two hurdles. Hence, to avoid the second horn of the expressive consent dilemma, the epistemic standard will need to clear these hurdles that the prescriptive standard tripped on.

Responding to this challenge requires some finesse. Clearing each hurdle requires three manoeuvres (and each manoeuvre draws upon ideas developed in earlier essays). By way of overview, these hurdles, manoeuvres, and callbacks are as follows:

> *The ignorance hurdle* requires that we attribute moral responsibility only to those who acted contrary to reasons that they knew applied to their situation.

> *The first manoeuvre (ignorance hurdle)* relies on the moral mismanagement inculpatory exception to displace the general exculpatory principle (developed in Essay 4 at 4.4).
>
> *The second manoeuvre (ignorance hurdle)* connects the moral mismanagement inculpatory exception with the moral mismanagement (encountered in Essay 2 at 2.4).
>
> *The third manoeuvre (ignorance hurdle)* delineates the form of 'culpability' that follows from the moral mismanagement inculpatory exception (from Essay 4 at 4.4).

The criminalisation hurdle limits the criminal law's retributive response to conduct that represents an unwillingness to be guided by an interest or value that the state is responsible for promoting.

> *The first manoeuvre (criminalisation hurdle)* reconnects the state's responsibility for vindicating the right to self-ownership (discussed in Essay 5 at 5.4) with the principle of consent-astuteness (developed in Essay 1 at 1.2).
>
> *The second manoeuvre (criminalisation hurdle)* further burdens the principle of consent-astuteness with the alterity of the other (introduced at 8.2 and developed at 8.4).
>
> *The third manoeuvre (criminalisation hurdle)* answers doubts about criminalisation by showing how the expressive (epistemic) consent standard can satisfy the principles of criminalisation (posited in Essay 3 at 3.5).

Let us start by clearing *the ignorance hurdle*. The general principle of moral responsibility excuses a person who is unaware of the reasons that they acted contrary to (here, we are concerned with A's unawareness that B does not consent to sex with A). As we have encountered in Essay 4 (at 4.4), one way to depart from the general principle is through the procedural failings exception, where:

> *inculpatory exception (procedural failings)*: a person is blameworthy for acting contrary to reasons that they were unaware applied to their moral situation if their unawareness is a result of a failure to perform their procedural epistemic obligations to understand their moral situation.

This is the philosophical equivalent of the 'failure to ascertain' legal standard. Recall (from Essay 7 at 7.3) that the failure to ascertain legal standard 'requires, in order for an exculpatory state of mind to exist, that a sexual agent "stop and ask", by way of words or gestures'.[52] The requirement to 'stop and ask' is a procedural requirement (which we encountered in Essay 4) to '*do* . . . certain things: to ask certain questions . . . to stop and think, to focus one's attention in a certain direction'.[53] The concern (which we encountered in Essays 4 at 4.4 and 7 at 7.3) is that the requirement itself—to act out a certain process—cannot attribute the blameworthy attitude or *mens rea* sufficient to impute culpability.

At the same time, the 'failure to ascertain' and the failure 'to focus one's attention in a certain direction' can be indicative of a blameworthy attitude (and can be a practical means of evidencing a blameworthy attitude). I suggested that procedural failings are symptoms of a disease, where the disease (and the source of moral responsibility) represents a failing to orientate oneself properly towards moral reasons. According to this alternative account of imputing moral responsibility, we can displace the general exculpatory principle where a person fails to properly orientate themselves towards their moral situation. According to this exception:

> *inculpatory exception (moral mismanagement)*: a person is blameworthy for acting contrary to reasons that they were unaware applied to their moral situation if their unawareness is a result of the mismanagement of their moral outlook.

We can begin to clear the first hurdle by relying on this exception to displace the general exculpatory principle, in a way that continues to 'proceed from the subjective perspective of the agents themselves'.[54]

However, clearing the first hurdle requires a second and third manoeuvre. The second manoeuvre connects the moral mismanagement inculpatory exception with the moral mismanagement that we encountered in Essay 2. Recall that for Nicola Gavey, 'everyday taken-for-granted normative forms of heterosexuality work as a cultural scaffolding for rape'.[55] Insofar as 'discourses of sex and gender . . . produce forms of heterosex that set up the preconditions for rape—women's passive, acquiescing (a)sexuality and men's forthright, urgent

[52] Anna High, 'Comparing Affirmative Consent Models: Confusion, Substance, and Symbolism' (2023) 45 Syd LR 467, 489.

[53] Gideon Rosen, 'Skepticism about Moral Responsibility' (2004) 18 Philos Perspect 295, 301.

[54] Douglas Husak, *Ignorance of Law: A Philosophical Inquiry* (OUP 2016) 154.

[55] Nicola Gavey, *Just Sex? The Cultural Scaffolding of Rape* (Routledge 2005) 2.

pursuit of sexual "release"', we can appreciate how '[t]hese script a relational dynamic that arguably authorizes sexual encounters that are not always clearly distinguishable from rape'.[56] The connection lies in how the cultural scaffolding of heterosex sets up the preconditions of a mismanaged moral outlook, with an obvious example being pornography. As Vadas explains, 'where pornography is manufactured-for-use, men's sexual relations with women are conceptually unrelated to their female partner's personhood'.[57] It then follows 'that men's sexual relations with women will, under these conditions, be conceptually unrelated to any and all person-related characteristics or abilities their female partners might have'.[58] The further point to add here is that acting contrary to the principle of alterity amounts to the mismanagement of a person's moral outlook, a sexual solipsism that denies the alterity of the person. A range of blameworthy attitudes might qualify as a mismanagement of a person's moral outlook: a self-centredness that disregards the point of view of another, wishful thinking that is preoccupied with one's own immediate interests, an arrogance that presumes that the other's interests are the same interests, and a reductionist attitude of treating a person as if they were a thing.

Given the connection between the moral mismanagement inculpatory exception and the cultural scaffolding of heterosex, the third manoeuvre (required to clear the first hurdle) delineates the 'culpability' that follows from the inculpatory exception. Beyond the culpability *for* being ignorant (of the moral reasons that apply), I have suggested before that the culpability from moral mismanagement also renders the wrongdoer culpable *through* their ignorance, in the sense that the responsibility for the original wrong is *derived from* the blameworthy behaviour that rendered the person ignorant of the applicable moral reasons[59] (or a person can be responsible for acting against reasons, and the accompanying blameworthy ignorance of moral reasons works *to sustain* their responsibility for their actions). In this way, the failure to satisfy the requirements of the expressive (epistemic) consent standard is a failure to be consent-astute. It is a failure that attracts culpability for the wrong: the wrong of acting without a belief in consent, since the belief that the wrongdoer held was not an epistemically justified one.

Herein lies an important turning point. Since contemporary legal standards determine the culpability of a defendant in terms of their honest belief in their

[56] Gavey (n 55) 3.
[57] Melinda Vadas, 'The Manufacture-for-use of Pornography and Women's Inequality' (2005) 13 J Political Philos 174, 190.
[58] Vadas (n 57) 190.
[59] Rosen (n 53) 300.

moral situation, the 'cultural scaffolding of sexual solipsism' is exculpatory—it accommodates the mismanaged moral outlook. In contrast, under the approach taken here, the mismanaged moral outlook is *inculpatory*; it is a way of sustaining responsibility for the wrong of acting without being consent-astute. Simply put: if the wrongdoing is acting without a justified belief in consent, and an honest belief in consent is asserted, then the inculpatory exception explains why an honest belief from a mismanaged moral outlook does not sever responsibility for the wrongdoing. As promised, in reply to Conaghan, this is how the 'cultural embeddedness of rape and its normative investment in a particular conception of sexual relations' is relevant to the formal elements of sexual offences.[60]

To clear the second hurdle (criminalisation), we require again three manoeuvres. The first manoeuvre is the connection with the state's responsibility for promoting 'the value of having a system of sexual relations in which people control . . . the treatment of their own bodies'[61] that vindicates the right to self-ownership, by giving legal effect to the principle of consent-astuteness (the requirement that A must have reasons to believe that B would accept A's treatment of B). By requiring consent-astuteness, the state carves out a sphere of control around the body, unspecified by a person's choices but recognising the exclusive right to make those choices. In this way, the state protects and promotes the 'non-use value' of every person.

The second manoeuvre (which we can take from this essay) is to further burden the principle of consent-astuteness. If another person's acceptance (agreement or willingness) is a point of view on the world that I cannot adopt, share, or have a point of view on, then to have reasons to believe that another person agrees to my treatment of them is to have reasons to believe that they are attending to their own presentation. In analytical terms, this means that to discharge the duty of consent-astuteness, and to have reasons to believe that B agrees to the treatment, is to also have B-specific reasons about how B communicates her acceptance of, or opposition to, the treatment. It follows from the first two manoeuvres that the state is responsible for enforcing a duty of consent-astuteness that extends to the requirement of B-specific reasons about how B expresses their attitudes of acceptance or opposition.

The third manoeuvre attempts to answer doubts about criminalisation. If criminalisation requires the punishable conduct to not only be morally

[60] Joanne Conaghan, 'The Essence of Rape' (2019) 39 OJLS 151, 163.
[61] Stephen Shute and John Gardner, 'The Wrongness of Rape' in John Gardner (ed), *Offences and Defences: Selected Essays in the Philosophy of Criminal Law* (OUP 2007) 19.

wrongful,[62] and harmful,[63] but also be the conduct that manifests an unwillingness to be guided by a value that the state is responsible for promoting,[64] then the question remains whether the expressive (epistemic) consent standard can satisfy these demanding conditions. It can, if we accept the first two manoeuvres (that the state is responsible for enforcing the extended principle of consent-astuteness). It is then possible to say that when a person (A) applies force to another person (B), and A's belief in B's consent has no B-specific content about how B communicates their acceptance of A's application of force, A is engaging in intentional conduct that is unguided by the non-use value of B (which is a value that the state is responsible for promoting). We see here (at the third manoeuvre) the momentum of the principle of alterity. It follows from the principle of alterity that what can qualify as a justification, or an excuse, must be grounded in not only words and overt actions but the words and overt actions of the specific person. The fundamental idea (developed in this essay) is that the principle of alterity also broadens the state's sphere of concern: that the right to sexual autonomy is a right to be taken as a specific, and not generic, person.

We can now solve our foreground and background puzzles. In the foreground of this essay, we were concerned with reconciling two intuitions about the problem of other minds: the alterity intuition and the knowledge intuition. We can have reliable knowledge about the mental states of other people (the knowledge intuition) because we can make reliable inferences from what we directly perceive about them, when, that is, we have reasons to take their presentation to be them attending to their own presentation. At the same time, there is a dimension of the other person that is beyond my knowledge of them (the alterity intuition), since our perceptions of the other person are presented to us from an independent and inalienable source—their point of view—that we can have no point of view on.

Note how the solution to the background puzzle mirrors this. If the expressive consent standard is to embody our concern for the alterity of the person, then it requires what sits behind 'the knowledge intuition'; it requires that a person has reasons to believe that another person is manifesting or presenting a specific attitude to them. Burdened by alterity, the expressive consent standard can resist the collapse into the attitudinal standard, since it moves the problem of other (consenting) minds from being an empirical problem (of the ordinary

[62] AP Simester and Andreas von Hirsch, *Crimes, Harms, and Wrongs: On the Principles of Criminalisation* (Hart Publishing 2011) 22.

[63] Simester and von Hirsch (n 62) 21.

[64] Jesse Wall, 'Public Wrongs and Private Wrongs' (2018) 31 CJLJ 177, 183–95.

practices of ordinary people) to an epistemic problem (of justified beliefs). As an epistemic standard, it avoids the pitfalls of prescribing social conventions or inference-negating rules. It instead requires that a person orientate their moral outlook towards the alterity of the other person, and it can evidence a maladjusted outlook with procedural failures. We can appreciate that when sex is presented as being with people without the person-related characteristics of people, an outlook that denies the alterity of the other person is both commonplace and problematic. The shift that is needed is to treat this moral mismanagement as inculpatory rather than exculpatory. This is what the expressive (epistemic) consent standard is able to achieve: capturing the culpability of mistaken beliefs in the consent of another that are the result of a mismanaged moral outlook, since it treats the mismanagement as inculpatory. Moreover, conduct that is unguided by the alterity of the other person, that relies upon generic persons and plastic consent, is ultimately intentional conduct that is unguided by the 'non-use value' of every person.

One final, and practical, question remains: whether the legal tests and standards advocated for over the past four essays can be implemented in practice. Specifically, implemented without departing from the principle of criminal procedure that requires the prosecution to carry the burden to prove the elements of an offence (and disprove any defences) beyond reasonable doubt. I conclude in the next discussion by answering this question, with a comparison between the law reform advocated here and the current law under particular criminal codes (the Sexual Offences Act 2003 (United Kingdom) and the Tentative Draft No 6 of the Model Penal Code (American Law Institute)).

Conclusion

'[T]he burden and standard of proof', Paul Robert explains, 'structure criminal proceedings so that the prosecution is obliged to make all the running in gathering, organizing, and presenting the evidence of crime'.[1] Because of the 'inequality of arms' between the defendant and the state,[2] the defendant has nothing to prove, and the prosecution has everything to prove. It then follows that, when it comes to prosecuting a sexual offence, 'the burden of proving nonconsent is on the government and therefore, in a loose sense, on the government's leading witness', the complainant.[3] This, in effect, 'shifts the inquiry from the behaviour of the accused to that of [the complainant]'.[4] This focus on the complainant is an unwelcome implication of the 'inequality of arms' that can be mitigated through the modest law reform that I will consider here.

In this conclusion, I will illustrate the law reform that has been advanced in these essays is consistent with 'the golden thread' of criminal proceedings: that 'the prosecution must prove every offense element (beyond reasonable doubt)' which 'means—procedurally speaking—it must also disprove—"negative"—justifications and excuses'.[5] Hence, the purpose of this discussion is to explain how and why:

1. *consent as a defence*: the provision of consent ought to be a justificatory defence, and a mistaken belief in the provision of consent ought to be an exculpatory defence (rather than the absence of consent being an inculpatory element of the offence);
2. *expressive consent*: consent itself ought to be defined with reference to the objective 'words and overt actions' that express a subjective attitude

[1] Paul Roberts, *Roberts & Zuckerman's Criminal Evidence* (3rd edn, OUP 2022) 66.

[2] Roberts (n 1) 58.

[3] David P Bryden and Sonja Lengnick, 'Rape in the Criminal Justice System' (1997) 87 J Crim Law Criminol 1194, 1316–17.

[4] Colleen Hall, 'Rape: The Politics of Definition' (1988) 105 SALJ 67, 74–75.

[5] Markus D Dubber, *An Introduction to the Model Penal Code* (2nd edn, OUP 2015) 143, citing American Law Institute, 'Model Penal Code: Official Draft and Explanatory Notes (Complete Text of Model Penal Code as Adopted at the 1962 Annual Meeting of the American Law Institute at Washington, D.C., May 24, 1962)' (1985) ss 1.12(1) and 1.12(2)(a).

of acceptance, willingness, or agreement (rather than defined in terms of the attitude of acceptance, willingness, or agreement itself); and

3. *complainant-specific reasons*: the reasons that can justify a mistaken belief that the complainant consented ought to be limited to complainant-specific reasons (rather than an open-ended category of reasons that can explain the mistake).

And to also explain how each reform (1–3) is consistent with the principle:

4. *the golden thread*: the prosecution ought to be required to discharge the formal burden of having to prove (beyond reasonable doubt) the elements of the offence, and disprove (beyond reasonable doubt) any justificatory or exculpatory defences.

Let us start with (1) *consent as a defence.* Early in this book, I argued for the primacy of 'consent-astuteness' (over consent in fact) as the antidote to the instrumental use of the body of another person. One reason given for adopting this 'second-person perspective' was that it helps us frame the 'non-use value' of the other person. By accepting that we need reasons to believe that another person agrees to our treatment of them, we respect that each person has a right to self-ownership (has exclusive use and control over their own body). In doing so, we respect a right that is valuable independently of how it is exercised, and we acknowledge the person has a value independently of the use we might make of them.

Midway through this book, the 'non-use value' of every person briefly returned when we considered which conventional practice—the 'no means no' convention or the 'yes means yes' convention—aligns with the right to self-ownership. The contention being that the criminal law ought to represent a normative practice (a set of rights and obligations) where there is an obligation not to apply force to a person's body unless and until that person suspends the obligation through their consent. It follows that the sexual use of, or application of force to, another person's body ought to be a *pro tanto* legal wrong, where the provision of consent can justify the wrong (and a mistaken belief in consent can excuse the wrong).

The *pro tanto* legal wrong thesis is, however, at odds with all criminal codes. In the United Kingdom, for instance, the absence of consent is an element of sexual offences. Section 1(1) of the Sexual Offences Act 2003 provides:

> (1) A person (A) commits an offence if—
> (a) he intentionally penetrates the vagina, anus or mouth of another person (B) with his penis,
> (b) *B does not consent to the penetration*, and
> (c) A does not reasonably believe that B consents.

The absence of consent is also an element of the offences of assault by penetration,[6] sexual assault,[7] and causing a person to engage in sexual activity without consent.[8]

Similarly, the American Law Institute's Tentative Draft No 6 of the Model Penal Code proposes a new offence, called 'Sexual Assault in the Absence of Consent'.[9] The offence provides:

> (1) An actor is guilty of Sexual Assault in the Absence of Consent when:
> (a) the actor engages with another person in, or causes another person to engage in, submit to, or perform, an act of sexual penetration or oral sex; and
> (b) *the other person does not consent to that act*; and
> (c) the actor is reckless with respect to the conduct, attendant circumstances, and results specified in paragraphs (a) and (b).

Here, again, the absence of consent is an element of the offence. Moreover, even when a particular state defines a sexual offence without reference to consent, the absence of consent is nonetheless treated as an element of the offence. For example, when the sexual offence is defined with reference to force or the threat of force,[10] and consent is available as a defence,[11] 'the [prosecution] has a burden of proof beyond reasonable doubt on the issue of consent as well as on the issue of force'.[12] The jury is then directed as if the absence of consent is an element of the offence of criminal sexual assault, as an Illinois direction explains:

> To sustain the charge of criminal sexual assault, the State must prove the following propositions:

[6] Sexual Offences Act 2003, s 2(1)(c).
[7] Sexual Offences Act 2003, s 3(1)(c).
[8] Sexual Offences Act 2003, s 4(1)(c).
[9] American Law Institute, 'Model Penal Code: Sexual Assault and Related Offenses, Tentative Draft No. 6' (April 2022) s 213.6.
[10] 720 ILCS 5/11-1.20.
[11] 720 ILCS 5/11-1.70(a).
[12] *People v Haywood* 118 Ill 2d 263 (1987) 274.

> First Proposition: That the defendant committed an act of sexual penetration upon []; and
> Second Proposition: That the act was committed by the use of force or threat of force; and
> Third Proposition: That [] did not consent to the act of sexual penetration.[13]

This is because, even if the provision of consent is legislated as a justification or excuse, the prosecution retains the formal/persuasive burden of disproving any justifications or excuses (after the defence has discharged a procedural/evidential burden to adduce the evidence to support the justification or excuse). As the Michigan Sexual Assault Benchbook explains:

> Consent may be raised as an affirmative defense to criminal sexual conduct offenses when a defendant produces enough evidence to place consent at issue, and the defense of consent is not precluded by law. *People v Thompson*, 117 Mich App 522, 528 (1982) . . . When a defendant produces sufficient evidence to give rise to the issue of an affirmative defense, the prosecutor must disprove the affirmative defense beyond a reasonable doubt.[14]

We return, therefore, to Michelle Madden Dempsey's doubt: that the *pro tanto* legal wrong thesis 'marks no significant practical distinction because . . . the burden of persuasion remains on the prosecution as to both offence elements and (the absence of) affirmative defences'.[15] Because of (4) *the golden thread*, even if we were to remove the absence of consent as an inculpatory element, and (1) allow the provision of consent to be raised as a justification or excuse, nothing changes in a criminal trial.

In isolation, Dempsey is right. However, when we consider the standard of practical reasoning that justifications and excuses are required to satisfy, we can appreciate the change that the *pro tanto* legal wrong thesis precipitates. Since justifications require that the defendant acted on 'explanatory' reasons (the reasons that the defendant did act on) and 'guiding' reasons (the reasons that the defendant ought to have acted on), and since excuses require the defendant be justified in acting on their explanatory reasons, the standard of

[13] Illinois Pattern Jury Instructions, Criminal, No 27.03, [11.56].

[14] Michigan Judicial Institute, *Sexual Assault Benchbook—Third Edition* (rev edn, Michigan Judicial Institute 2024) 4-1.

[15] Michelle Madden Dempsey, 'The Normative Force of Consent in Moral, Political, and Legal Perspective' in Tatjana Hörnle (ed), *Sexual Assault: Law Reform in a Comparative Perspective* (OUP 2023) 24.

practical reasoning is more demanding than if the absence of consent were an inculpatory element. One way to encapsulate this more demanding standard is to define consent itself as an external or objective phenomenon that expresses that attitude through overt words or actions ('expressive consent'). This is because only the objective elements of consent can furnish a defendant with the guiding and explanatory reasons that the practical reasoning of justifications and excuses requires of the defendant.

In terms of (2) *expressive consent*, most criminal codes still posit the attitudinal standard. In the United Kingdom under the Sexual Offences Act 2003, 'a person consents if he agrees by choice, and has the freedom and capacity to make that choice'.[16] This is consistent with the approach by the courts to treat consent as representing 'a wide range of states of mind in the context of intercourse between a man and a woman, ranging from actual desire on the one hand to reluctant acquiescence on the other'.[17]

The Tentative Draft No 6 of the Model Penal Code seeks to define 'consent' and does so by adopting the attitudinal standard. Consent, under the Tentative Draft, 'means a person's willingness to engage in a specific act of sexual penetration, oral sex, or sexual contact'.[18] Samantha Newman traces the drafting history of this consent definition.[19] Newman notes that the Institute's Tentative Draft No 1 featured an *affirmative* consent definition, where '[consent]' means 'a person's positive agreement, communicated by either words or actions, to engage in sexual intercourse or sexual contact'.[20] This definition was abandoned following 'heightened criticism that an actor could face criminalization if there was not "positive agreement communicated by either words or action"'.[21]

This is a concern we encountered in 'the expressive consent dilemma'. The finder of fact's dilemma is either accommodating the social and semantic rules as they are practised ('describing the sexual script') or requiring that certain social and semantic rules be followed ('prescribing the sexual script'). By describing the script, the finder of fact can make the same accommodations for mistaken beliefs in consent that we are permitted under the attitudinal standard (the collapse). By prescribing the script—which appears to be the Institute's concern—the finder of fact conflates culpability for wrongdoing

[16] Sexual Offences Act 2003, s 74.
[17] *R v Olugboja* [1982] QB 320 (CA) 321.
[18] American Law Institute, 'Model Penal Code, Tentative Draft No. 6' (n 9) s 213.0(2)(e)(i).
[19] Samantha Newman, 'Reexamining the Consent Definition Under Article 213: Sexual Assault and Related Offenses of the Model Penal Code and Its Troubling Influence on Affirmative Consent Definition States' (2023) 1(2) Ga Crim Law Rev 101.
[20] Newman (n 19) 118.
[21] Newman (n 19) 118ff.

with culpability for being ignorant of the applicable social and semantic rules (the culpability gap). The way out of the dilemma is ultimately found in requiring (3) *complainant-specific reasons* for a mistaken belief in consent (discussed below).

Newman expresses concern that the new attitudinal definition will likely influence 'legislative word choices, statute construction, and proposed amendments to current law', including states that have adopted the expressive consent standard.[22] These states, which depart from the Model Penal Code, include

> Vermont, where consent is defined as 'the affirmative, unambiguous, and voluntary agreement to engage in a sexual act, which can be revoked at any time';[23]
>
> New Jersey, where sexual assault is defined by an actor committing an act, without the victim's 'affirmative and freely-given permission';[24]
>
> Wisconsin, where consent is defined as 'words or overt actions by a person who is competent to give informed consent indicating a freely given agreement to have sexual intercourse or sexual contact';[25]
>
> District of Columbia, where consent 'means words or overt actions indicating a freely given agreement to the sexual act or contact in question';[26] and
>
> Minnesota, where consent means 'words or overt actions by a person indicating a freely given present agreement to perform a particular sexual act with the actor'.[27]

We will return to these expressive consent states in a moment. The question, for now, is whether (2) *expressive consent* is consistent with the (4) *the golden thread*. The shift in the standard of practical reasoning might appear to be a

[22] Newman (n 19) 129–30.
[23] 13 VSA, s 3251(3). See also *State v Snow* 193 Vt 390 (2013) 391.
[24] NJ Rev Stat, s 2C:14-2 (2023). See also *State in Interest of MTS* 129 NJ 422 (NJ Super Ct App Div, 1992) 443; *State in Interest of KB* 2013 WL 3340654 (NJ Super Ct App Div, 2013) 1.
[25] 940 Wis Stat Ann, ss 225(3)(a)–(4) (2018); *State v Perkins* No 95-1353-CR (Wis Ct App August 7, 1996) 1.
[26] DC Code, s 22-3001(4). The provision goes on to state that '[l]ack of verbal or physical resistance or submission by the victim, resulting from the use of force, threats, or coercion by the defendant shall not constitute consent'.
[27] Minn Stat, s 609.341(4). The provision goes on to state that '[c]onsent does not mean the existence of a prior or current social relationship between the actor and the complainant or that the complainant failed to resist a particular sexual act'.

shift of a burden from the prosecution to the defendant. For instance, Lois Pineau argues:

> Where communicative sex does not occur, this establishes a presumption that there was no consent. The importance of this presumption is that we are able . . . to shift the burden of proof from the plaintiff . . . to the defendant who must then give some reason why she [consented].[28]

Pineau then suggests that a cross-examiner could use the affirmative consent model

> to discover how much respect there had been for the dialectics of desire. Did he ask her what she liked? If she was using contraceptives? If he should? What tone of voice did he use? How did she answer? Did she make any demands? Did she ask for penetration? How was that desire conveyed? Did he ever let up the pressure long enough to see if she was really that interested? Did he ask her which position she preferred?[29]

Despite how pertinent these questions are (that the expressive consent standard succeeds in foregrounding), there is no shift in the burden of proof under the expressive consent standard. To understand why, we need to distinguish between (a) the legal standard: *what* an (offence) or defence requires and (b) the burden of proof: *who* has to (dis)prove the offence or defence. Under the proposed reform ((2) *expressive consent*), (a) the legal standard is a definition of consent (in terms of the 'words and overt actions that express an attitude of willingness, acceptance, or agreement'), whilst (b) the burden of proof remains on the prosecution to disprove the consent (as defined in that manner). As Deborah Tuerkheimer emphasises, '[d]espite some confusion, an affirmative consent definition does not shift the burden of proof to the defendant'.[30] She explains:

> [T]he burden of proving guilt beyond a reasonable doubt remains on the state. In order to convict, the prosecution must demonstrate that the defendant engaged in intercourse without the alleged victim's consent, which must be manifested in an affirmative manner.[31]

28 Lois Pineau, 'Date Rape: A Feminist Analysis' (1989) 8 L & Phil 217, 240–41.
29 Pineau (n 28) 240–41; Bernadette McSherry, 'No! (means no?)' (1993) 18 Alt LJ 27, 29.
30 Deborah Tuerkheimer, 'Affirmative Consent' (2016) 13 Ohio St J Crim L 441, 449, fn 34.
31 Tuerkheimer (n 30) 448–449.

Whilst the burden of proof remains unchanged, the change of the legal standard (from attitudinal to expressive consent) changes the shape of the factual inquiry into a mistaken belief. By way of an informal/evidential burden, the defendant needs to show (by way of evidence) that the belief that the complainant consented can raise reasonable doubt. But it now needs to be reasonable doubt as to whether the belief in consent was grounded in the 'words and overt actions' of the complainant themselves. This follows from (what I have termed) an epistemic burden: to have a justified belief in the mental state of another person is to provide the 'linking assumption' to establish or ground the B-specific reasons that B is expressing the mental state. The epistemic burden is two-fold: it requires not only evidence that the belief in consent was based on objective or observable 'words or overt actions' but also reasons in favour of 'the linking assumption' that those words and overt actions were her (his/their) expression of her (his/their) attitude of willingness or acceptance. The point is that this narrows the inquiry into whether an exculpatory mistaken belief arose in fact.

Further narrowing is articulated in the third reform: (3) *complainant-specific reasons*, where the reasons that can explain and justify a mistaken belief that the complainant consented ought to be limited to reasons that pertain only to the complainant and their expressive behaviour. In comparison, the criminal law often (if not invariably) accommodates an open-ended category of reasons that can explain and justify the mistake. For instance, in the United Kingdom, Section 1(2) of the Sexual Offences Act 2003 provides that '[w]hether a belief is reasonable is to be determined having regard to *all the circumstances*, including any steps A has taken to ascertain whether B consents'.

The United Kingdom Crown Prosecution Service guidance on rape and sexual offences explains that this Section 1(2) inquiry will likely include consideration of

> a suspect's attributes, such as disability or extreme youth, but not if (s)he has any particular fetishes. . . . The provision does not expressly change the concept of consent, nor does it go so far as to require the accused to have taken positive steps to avoid criminal liability, but it does shift the focus toward the accused's actions rather than concentrating solely on the complainant's.[32]

[32] Crown Prosecution Service, 'Prosecution Guidance: Rape and Sexual Offences—Chapter 6 Consent' (21 May 2021) <www.cps.gov.uk/legal-guidance/rape-and-sexual-offences-chapter-6-consent> accessed 1 December 2024.

The guidance then notes that '[i]t will be important for the police to ask the suspect in interview what steps (s)he took to satisfy him or herself that the complainant consented'.[33]

As discussed, the Tentative Draft No 6 of the Model Penal Code proposes an attitudinal definition of consent ('a person's willingness . . .'). The proposal then goes on to state that '[c]onsent may be express or it may be inferred from behavior—both action and inaction—*in the context of all the circumstances*'.[34] Whilst the Sexual Offences Act 2003 might 'shift the focus towards the accused's actions', both the Sexual Offences Act 2003 and the Tentative Draft No 6 provide for an open-ended set of circumstances from which a person may infer that another person consents to the treatment of them. The concern that I have expressed here is that when the state of mind of another person is an open-ended question of fact, the question of fact can accommodate any inference from behaviour to attitude (and expressive consent standards collapse back into attitudinal consent standards).

In this way, if the inferential basis is open-ended ('having regard to all the circumstances'), then any victory for expressive consent advocates will be an empty one. For instance, several of the US 'expressive consent' states have jury directions that allow consideration of 'all of the surrounding circumstances' in determining the issue of consent. The New Jersey Criminal Jury Instructions on 'consent' provide:

> In determining whether the consent of the victim was freely and voluntarily given, you are advised that consent may be openly expressed, implied, or apparent from the victim's willing participation in the activity in question. Further, you may consider *all that (he/she) said and did at the particular time and place, all of the surrounding circumstances* and whether a normal competent person would freely and seriously consent to the conduct with which the defendant is charged.[35]

Similarly, the Wisconsin Jury Instructions for third-degree sexual assault provide:

[33] Crown Prosecution Service (n 32).

[34] American Law Institute, 'Model Penal Code, Tentative Draft No. 6' (n 9) s 213.0(2)(e)(ii) (emphasis added).

[35] NJ JI CRIM 2C:2-10 (emphasis added).

> **Statutory Definition of the Crime**
> Third degree sexual assault, as defined in § 940.225(3)(a) of the Criminal Code of Wisconsin, is committed by one who has sexual intercourse with another person without consent.
>
> **Meaning of 'Did Not Consent'**
> 'Did not consent' means that (name of victim) did not freely agree to have sexual intercourse with the defendant. In deciding whether (name of victim) did not consent, you should consider *what [he] [she] said and did, along with all the other facts and circumstances.* This element does not require that (name of victim) offered physical resistance.[36]

This might explain why, in states that have adopted expressive or 'free agreement' reform standards, there is no significant increase in the conviction rate or prosecutors' charging practices.[37] This is because the open-ended inquiry into how a belief in consent was grounded allows the expressive consent standard to collapse into the attitudinal standard.

To avoid these empty victories (and avoid the collapse), the set of circumstances in which a person can justify an (albeit mistaken) belief in consent ought to be a closed set of circumstances, limited to how the complainant themselves employs words or overt conduct to express an attitude of acceptance, willingness, or agreement. Thus the requirement of (3) *complainant-specific reasons.*

We have already encountered a legal standard that approximates this requirement: the 'failure to ascertain' legal standard, which 'requires, in order for an exculpatory state of mind to exist, that a sexual agent "stop and ask", by way of words or gestures'.[38] We also encountered two main problems with this standard. One problem has been that the 'procedural failure to ascertain' is a symptom of a disease (and not the disease itself), where the disease itself (and the source of moral responsibility) represents a failing to orientate oneself properly towards moral reasons. However, when it comes to the practical task of 'shaping the inquiry into an exculpatory belief' for the finder of fact, we can look to the *symptoms* of the disease, and rely on *evidence of* the underlying 'failure to orientate' (provided that the 'failure to orientate' is sufficiently

36 Wis JI—Criminal 1218A (2018) (emphasis added).
37 Philip NS Rumney, 'The Review of Sex Offences and Rape Law Reform: Another False Dawn?' (2001) 64 MLR 890, 909.
38 Anna High, 'Comparing Affirmative Consent Models: Confusion, Substance, and Symbolism' (2023) 45 Syd LR 467, 489.

proximate to the 'failure to ascertain'). This is because the best available evidence of the 'failure to orientate' may be the 'failure to ascertain'.

The second problem has been that the 'failure to ascertain' legal standard was caught within the expressive consent dilemma: either the required efforts to ascertain consent are understood in terms of the extent to which an 'ordinary person' would 'stop and ask' (and the expressive standard collapses into the attitudinal standard), or the standard represents a required set of steps and becomes 'an overly prescriptive and inappropriate expansion of the *mens rea* of rape to require active ascertainment in all cases'.[39] To avoid the expressive consent dilemma, the 'failure to ascertain' standard needs to avoid being a prescribed checklist. Rather, the failure to ascertain needs to represent a failure to attend to 'the linking assumption' that connects a person's behaviour with the attitudinal consent they are expressing through their behaviour. Understood in this way, the gap between 'the failure to orientate oneself properly towards moral reasons' and the 'failure to take steps to attend to another's consent' begins to close. It closes when the moral reasons a person ought to be orientated towards *are* the complainant-specific reasons for a belief in the consent of the complainant. In this way, the 'failure to ascertain' is at least sufficiently proximate, or perhaps practically equivalent, to the 'failure to orientate'.

When it comes to law reform, the key point of contrast is that the 'failure to ascertain' standard represents a closed set of circumstances for a permissible inference (from the complainant's behaviour to the complainant's attitude). It is a departure from an open set of 'all the circumstances' for a permissible inference. This is not merely a 'shift in focus' (under the Sexual Offences Act) but, instead, a legal standard that reshapes the factual inquiry and the evidential burden. As Susan Caringella explains, it requires the defence to

> show that (a) the defendant took reasonable steps to ascertain voluntariness, agreement and (b) the voluntariness, agreement to the sex acts was not withdrawn by the alleged victim.[40]

In modifying Section 1(2) of the Sexual Offences Act 2003, the suggested reform requires:

[39] High (n 38) 489.
[40] Susan Caringella, *Addressing Rape Reform in Law and Practice* (Columbia UP 2008) 183.

> Whether a belief is [exculpatory] is to be determined *solely* by having regard to the steps (if any) A has taken to ascertain whether B consents [by expressing B's agreement through words and overt actions].

The proposed change here is a significant one, from (the open-ended) 'having regard to all the circumstances' directions to (the closed) 'having regard to the steps A has taken to ascertain whether B consents' standard. It is also a reform that sustains the distinction between attitudinal and expressive consent. In this way, any reasons that A can introduce in order to justify A's mistaken belief in B's consent are reasons that are (3) complainant-specific (and (2) grounded in the words and overt communicative acts of B). The complainant will remain the 'government's leading witness',[41] but the change in legal standard will also shift the inquiry and interrogation to the behaviour of the defendant (in ascertaining consent) and away from the general behaviour of the complainant.

The remaining question is whether this requirement of (3) *complainant-specific reasons* is consistent with (4) *the golden thread*. There is a formal answer to this question and a substantive one. The formal answer (that we encountered above) is that the persuasive burden has not shifted: the onus remains on the prosecution to disprove (beyond reasonable doubt) the excuse that the defendant had a belief that the complainant consented. The legal standard—for what qualifies as an exculpatory belief—has changed, and that change narrows how a defendant can discharge their evidential burden, but the persuasive burden remains on the prosecution.

The formal answer, however, is just another lawyers' gambit. The real question is whether we *ought to be* narrowing the factual inquiry that ultimately reshapes what the prosecution needs to disprove and reshapes how a defendant can discharge their evidential burden, given the principle that 'the prosecution has everything to prove, and the defendant has nothing to prove'. The overarching purpose of these essays has been to explain why we ought to. Whilst the defendant has nothing to prove, the defendant had something to attend to; namely, the non-use value of the person.

Let me then conclude by rehearsing the central argument, to illustrate how the central argument justifies the narrowing of the factual inquiry into the exculpatory belief in consent. If we accept that each person has a 'non-use value',

[41] Bryden and Lengnick (n 3) 1316–17.

then it follows that the principle of consent-astuteness requires that we have reasons to believe that the other person agrees to our treatment of them. The normative practice that aligns with the non-use value of each person and the principle of consent-astuteness is the positing of the right of self-ownership and the 'yes means yes' convention. This normative practice treats the application of force or the sexual use of the body as a *pro tanto* legal wrong, which calls for justification. Herein lies the tectonic shift towards requiring the defendant to perform a justificatory or exculpatory task. Following the tectonic shift, it is then a question of how the justificatory and exculpatory tasks can be performed (in a way that is consistent with the retributive morality of the criminal law, principles of criminalisation, and the golden thread of criminal procedure). As justificatory and exculpatory tasks, claims about consent need to be grounded in explanatory and guiding reasons. Moreover, as claims about the mental state of another person, the justificatory and exculpatory tasks also need to satisfy an epistemic standard (for beliefs in the mental states of others). The point is that the accumulative weight of these demands narrows how a defendant ought to be able to be excused for a wrong on the basis of a mistaken belief in consent, by limiting the factual inquiry to the steps the defendant had taken to attend to and ascertain whether the complainant consented through words or overt acts.

So, in the end, after starting with sweeping philosophical themes (instrumentalism, objectification, choice and coercion, and normative phenomena) and constructing a controversial claim (that sex is a *pro tanto* legal wrong that can only be justified or excused by redefining consent itself), we arrive at a small-scale law reform: that the considerations that go to identifying an exculpatory mistaken belief in consent ought to be grounded in words or overt acts that express consent and limited to the approach taken to ascertain that belief in consent. The modest scale of the reform reflects how the central argument has sought to *maintain the retributive morality of the criminal law*, a morality that captures culpability in terms of how the defendant acted contrary to moral reasons they knew applied to their moral situation; it has also sought to *be consistent with principles of criminalisation*, principles that limit state punishment to conduct that is antithetical to the values that the state is responsible for promoting; and it has sought to *not derogate from the golden thread of criminal procedure*, which requires that the prosecution prove (beyond reasonable doubt) every element of the offence and disprove any justifications or excuses. Whilst we can gesture as much as we like in philosophical arguments, criminal law reform ought to be done straightjacketed by these commitments. I like to think, therefore, that the proposed reforms of the criminal law are neither 'trivial'[42] nor 'extreme'.[43] I know, at least, that (taken together) they cannot be both trivial and extreme.

[42] Dempsey (n 15) 24.

[43] John Child and David Ormerod, *Smith, Hogan, and Ormerod's Essentials of Criminal Law* (2nd edn, OUP 2017) 279.

Bibliography

Ahmed E, Syed SA and Parveen N, 'Female Consensual Coital Injuries' (2006) 16 J Coll Physicians Surg Pak 333.

Alexander L, 'The Moral Magic of Consent (II)' (1996) 2 Leg Theory 165.

—— 'The Ontology of Consent' (2014) 55 Anal Philos 102.

American Law Institute, 'Model Penal Code: Official Draft and Explanatory Notes (Complete Text of Model Penal Code as Adopted at the 1962 Annual Meeting of the American Law Institute at Washington, D.C., May 24, 1962)' (1985).

—— *Restatement (Third) of Restitution and Unjust Enrichment* (American Law Institute 2011).

—— 'Model Penal Code: Sexual Assault and Related Offenses, Tentative Draft No. 2' (15 April 2016).

—— 'Model Penal Code: Sexual Assault and Related Offenses, Council Draft No. 6' (15 September 2017).

—— 'Model Penal Code: Sexual Assault and Related Offenses, Council Draft No. 7' (20 December 2017).

—— 'Model Penal Code: Sexual Assault and Related Offenses, Tentative Draft No. 6' (April 2022).

Anderson MJ, 'Campus Sexual Assault Adjudication and Resistance to Reform' (2016) 125 Yale LJ 1940.

Anthony L, 'Is There a "Feminist" Philosophy of Language?' in Louise Anthony (ed), *Only Natural: Gender, Knowledge, and Humankind* (OUP 2022).

Ball M, *Criminology and Queer Theory: Dangerous Bedfellows?* (Palgrave Macmillan 2016).

Beaulieu G, 'Can Explanatory Reasons Be Good Reasons for Action?' (2013) 44 Metaphilosophy 440.

Bergelson V, 'The Meaning of Consent' (2014) 12 Ohio St J Crim L 171.

Berlin I, *The Hedgehog and the Fox* (Weidenfeld & Nicolson 1953).

Berman MN, 'The Normative Functions of Coercion Claims' (2002) 8 Leg Theory 45.

Boghossian PA, 'Content and Self-knowledge' in Peter Ludlow and Norah Martin (eds), *Externalism and Self-knowledge* (CSLI Publications 1998).

Brett N, 'Sexual Offenses and Consent' (1998) 11 CJLJ 69.

Brudner A, *Punishment and Freedom: A Liberal Theory of Penal Justice* (OUP 2009).

Bryden DP, 'Redefining Rape' (2000) 3 Buff Crim L Rev 317.

—— and Lengnick S, 'Rape in the Criminal Justice System' (1997) 87 J Crim Law Criminol 1194.

Buist CL and Lenning E, *Queer Criminology* (Routledge 2016).

Campbell K, 'Offence and Defence' in Ian Dennis (ed), *Criminal Law and Justice: Essays from the W.G. Hart Workshop, 1986* (Sweet and Maxwell 1987).

Caringella S, *Addressing Rape Reform in Law and Practice* (Columbia UP 2008).

Carman T, *Merleau-Ponty* (Routledge 2008).

Cassam Q, 'What Asymmetry? Knowledge of Self, Knowledge of Others, and the Inferentialist Challenge' (2017) 194 Synthese 723.

Chang R, 'Do We Have Normative Powers?' (2020) 94 Proc Aristot Soc Suppl Vol 275.

Child J and Ormerod D, *Smith, Hogan, and Ormerod's Essentials of Criminal Law* (2nd edn, OUP 2017).

Cohen GA, *Self-Ownership, Freedom and Equality* (CUP 1995).

Colb SF, 'Conversation Before Penetration?', comment accompanying Michelle J Anderson, 'Rape Law Reform Based on Negotiation: Beyond the No and Yes Models' in Paul H Robinson, Stephen Garvey and Kimberly Kessler Ferzan (eds), *Criminal Law Conversations* (OUP 2011).

Conaghan J, 'The Essence of Rape' (2019) 39 OJLS 151.

Conly S, 'Seduction, Rape, and Coercion' (2004) 115 Ethics 96.

Cowan S, 'Freedom and Capacity to Make a Choice: A Feminist Analysis of Consent in the Criminal Law of Rape' in Vanessa Munro and Carl Franklin Stychin (eds), *Sexuality and the Law: Feminist Engagements* (Taylor & Francis 2007).

Crown Prosecution Service, 'Prosecution Guidance: Rape and Sexual Offences—Chapter 6 Consent' (21 May 2021) www.cps.gov.uk/legal-guidance/rape-and-sexual-offences-chapter-6-consentacces sed 1 December 2024.

Darwall SL, *The Second-Person Standpoint: Morality, Respect, and Accountability* (Harvard UP 2006).

—— 'What Are Moral Reasons?' (The Amherst Lecture in Philosophy, 2017) <https://www.amherstlecture.org/darwall2017/darwall2017_ALP.pdf>.

De Beauvoir S, *The Ethics of Ambiguity* (first published 1948, Bernard Frechtman tr, Citadel Press 1976).

—— *The Second Sex* (first published 1949, HM Parshley tr, Vintage Books 1989).

Deigh J, 'Reactive Attitudes Revisited' in Carla Bagnoli (ed), *Morality and the Emotions* (OUP 2011).

Dempsey MM, 'Victimless Conduct and the Volenti Maxim: How Consent Works' (2013) 7 Crim Law Philos 11.

—— 'Coercion, Consent, and Time' (2021) 131 Ethics 345.

—— 'The Normative Force of Consent in Moral, Political, and Legal Perspective' in Tatjana Hörnle (ed), *Sexual Assault: Law Reform in a Comparative Perspective* (OUP 2023).

—— and Herring J, 'Why Sexual Penetration Requires Justification' (2007) 27 OJLS 467.

Dougherty T, '*Yes Means Yes*: Consent as Communication' (2015) 43 Philos Public Aff 224.

Dressler J, 'Where We Have Been, and Where We Might Be Going: Some Cautionary Reflections on Rape Law Reform' (1998) 46(3) Clev St L Rev 409.

Dretske FI, *Seeing and Knowing* (Routledge & Kegan Paul 1969).

Dubber MD, *An Introduction to the Model Penal Code* (2nd edn, OUP 2015).

Duff RA, *Answering for Crime: Responsibility and Liability in the Criminal Law* (Hart Publishing 2007).

—— and Marshall SE, 'Public and Private Wrongs' in James Chalmers, Fiona Leverick and Lindsay Farmer (eds), *Essays in Criminal Law in Honour of Sir Gerald Gordon* (Edinburgh UP 2010).

Du Toit L, *A Philosophical Engagement with Rape: The Making and Unmaking of the Feminine Self* (Routledge 2009).

Dworkin A, *Intercourse* (Free Press 1987).

Dwyer A, Ball M and Crofts T (eds), *Queering Criminology* (Palgrave Macmillan 2016).

Edwards J and Simester A, 'What's Public About Crime?' (2017) 37 OJLS 105.

Feinberg J, *The Moral Limits of the Criminal Law Volume 1: Harm to Others* (OUP 1987).

Ferrell J and Sanders C (eds), *Cultural Criminology* (Northeastern UP 1995).

Ferzan KK, 'Consent, Culpability, and the Law of Rape' (2016) 13 Ohio St J Crim L 397.

—— 'Consent and Coercion' (2018) 50 Ariz St LJ 951.

—— and Westen P, 'How to Think (Like a Lawyer) about Rape' (2017) 11 Crim Law Philos 759.

FitzPatrick WJ, 'Moral Responsibility and Normative Ignorance: Answering a New Skeptical Challenge' (2008) 118 Ethics 589.

Fletcher GP, *Rethinking Criminal Law* (Little Brown 1978).

—— 'The Nature of Justification' in Stephen Shute, John Gardner and Jeremy Horder (eds), *Action and Value in Criminal Law* (Clarendon Press 1993).

—— *Basic Concepts in Criminal Law* (OUP 1998).

Gardner J, 'Justifications and Reasons' in AP Simester and ATH Smith (eds), *Harm and Culpability* (Clarendon Press 1996).

—— 'The Mysterious Case of the Reasonable Person' (2001) 51 UTLJ 273.

—— 'Fletcher on Offences and Defences' (2003) 39 Tulsa L Rev 817.

—— 'Justification under Authority' (2010) 23 CJLJ 71.

—— 'Relations of Responsibility' in Rowan Cruft, Matthew H Kramer and Mark R Reiff (eds), *Crime, Punishment, and Responsibility: The Jurisprudence of Antony Duff* (OUP 2011).

—— 'In Defence of Offences and Defences' (2012) 4 Jerusalem Rev Leg Stud 110.

—— 'The Many Faces of the Reasonable Person' (2015) 131 LQR 563.

—— 'Reasonable Reactions to the Wrongness of Rape' (2017) 29 Denning LJ 3.

—— and Shute S, 'The Wrongness of Rape' in Jeremy Horder (ed), *Oxford Essays in Jurisprudence: Fourth Series* (OUP 2000).

Gavey N, *Just Sex? The Cultural Scaffolding of Rape* (Routledge 2005).

Giovanini V, 'Alterity in Simone de Beauvoir and Emmanuel Levinas: From Ambiguity to Ambivalence' (2019) 34 Hypatia 39.

Goldman AI, 'Theory of Mind' in Eric Margolis, Richard Samuels and Stephen P Stich (eds), *The Oxford Handbook of Philosophy of Cognitive Science* (OUP 2012).
Greasley K, 'Sex, Reasons, *Pro Tanto* Wronging, and the Structure of Rape Liability' (2021) 15 Crim Law Philos 159.
Green L, 'Pornographies' (2000) 8 J Polit Philos 27.
Green SP, *Criminalizing Sex: A Unified Liberal Theory* (OUP 2020).
Grice HP, 'Logic and Conversation' in Donald Davidson and Gilbert Harman (eds), *The Logic of Grammar* (Dickenson 1975).
—— 'Meaning' (1957) 66 Philos Rev 377.
Gruber A, 'Consent Confusion' (2016) 38 Cardozo L Rev 415.
—— 'Rape Law Revisited' (2016) 13 Ohio St J Crim L 279.
Hall C, 'Rape: The Politics of Definition' (1988) 105 SALJ 67.
Harman E, 'Does Moral Ignorance Exculpate?' (2011) 24 Ratio 443.
Harris JW, *Property and Justice* (Clarendon Press 1996).
Henderson LN, 'What Makes Rape a Crime' (1987) 3 Women's LJ 193.
Herman B, 'Could It Be Worth Thinking About Kant on Sex and Marriage?' in Louise Antony and Charlotte Witt (eds), *A Mind of One's Own: Feminist Essays on Reason and Objectivity* (Westview Press 1993).
—— 'Could It Be Worth Thinking About Kant on Sex and Marriage?' in Louise Antony and Charlotte Witt (eds), *A Mind of One's Own: Feminist Essays on Reason and Objectivity* (2nd edn, Westview Press 2002).
Hickman SE and Muehlenhard CL, '"By the Semi-Mystical Appearance of a Condom": How Young Women and Men Communicate Sexual Consent in Heterosexual Situations' (1999) 36 J Sex Res 258.
High A, 'Comparing Affirmative Consent Models: Confusion, Substance, and Symbolism' (2023) 45 Syd LR 467.
Hoffman RJ and Ganti S, 'Vaginal Lacerations and Perforation Resulting from First Coitus' (2001) 17 Pediatr Emerg Care 113.
Hume D, *A Treatise of Human Nature* (LA Selby-Bigge ed, PH Nidditch rev, 2nd edn, OUP 1978).
Humphreys TP and Brousseau MM, 'The Sexual Consent Scale—Revised: Development, Reliability, and Preliminary Validity' (2010) 47 J Sex Res 420.
Hurd HM, 'Justifiably Punishing the Justified' (1992) 90 Mich L Rev 2203.
—— 'The Moral Magic of Consent' (1996) 2 Leg Theory 121.
—— 'Justification and Excuse, Wrongdoing and Culpability' (1999) 74 Notre Dame L Rev 1551.
—— 'Was the Frog Prince Sexually Molested?: A Review of Peter Westen's "The Logic of Consent"' (2005) 103 Mich L Rev 1329.
—— 'The Normative Force of Consent' in Peter Schaber and Andreas Müller (eds), *Routledge Handbook on the Ethics of Consent* (Routledge 2018).
Hurtig K, 'Consent and Normativity' in Miguel Garcia-Godinez, Rachael Mellin and Raimo Tuomela (eds), *Social Ontology, Normativity and Law* (De Gruyter 2020).
Husak D, *Overcriminalization: The Limits of the Criminal Law* (OUP 2008).
—— *Ignorance of Law: A Philosophical Inquiry* (OUP 2016).
—— and Thomas III GC, 'Date Rape, Social Convention, and Reasonable Mistakes' (1992) 11 Law & Phil 95.
Kant I, *Lectures on Ethics* (Louis Infield tr, Harper and Row 1963).
—— 'Groundwork of the Metaphysics of Morals' in Mary Gregor (ed), *Practical Philosophy* (Mary Gregor tr, CUP 1996).
—— 'Metaphysics of Morals' in Mary Gregor (ed), *Practical Philosophy* (Mary Gregor tr, CUP 1996).
—— *Lectures on Ethics* (Peter Heath and JB Schneewind eds, Peter Heath tr, CUP 1997).
—— 'Conjectural Beginning of Human History' in RB Louden (ed), *Anthropology, History, and Education* (RB Louden tr, CUP 2007).
Katz C, 'Levinas Between Agape and Eros' (2007) 11 Symposium 333.
Knight C and Wilson K, *Lesbian, Gay, Bisexual, and Trans People (LGBT) and the Criminal Justice System* (Palgrave Macmillan 2016).
Korsgaard CM, *Creating the Kingdom of Ends* (CUP 1996).

Laitinen A, 'Normative Powers, Agency, and Time' in Carla Bagnoli (ed), *Time in Action: The Temporal Structure of Rational Agency and Practical Thought* (Routledge 2022).
Lamond G, 'What is a Crime?' (2007) 27 OJLS 609.
Langton R, *Sexual Solipsism: Philosophical Essays on Pornography and Objectification* (OUP 2009).
Lawlor K, 'Knowing What One Wants' (2009) 79 Philos Phenomenol Res 47.
Levinas E, *Totality and Infinity: An Essay on Exteriority* (Alphonso Lingis tr, Duquesne UP 1969).
—— *Time and the Other* (Richard A Cohen tr, Duquesne UP 1987).
MacKinnon CA, *Toward a Feminist Theory of the State* (Harvard UP 1989).
Malcolm N, 'Knowledge of Other Minds' (1958) 55 J Philos 969.
Marshall SE and Duff RA, 'Criminalization and Sharing Wrongs' (1998) 11 CJLJ 7.
McDowell J, 'On the Reality of the Past' in John McDowell (ed), *Meaning, Knowledge and Reality* (Harvard UP 1998).
McSherry B, 'No! (means no?)' (1993) 18 Alt LJ 27.
Melnyk A, 'Inference to Best Explanation and Other Minds' (1994) 72 Australas J Philos 482.
Mendus S, 'Kant: "An Honest but Narrow-Minded Bourgeois"?' in Howard Lloyd Williams (ed), *Essays on Kant's Practical Philosophy* (University of Wales Press 1992).
Merleau-Ponty M, *Phenomenology of Perception* (Donald A Landes tr, Routledge 2012).
Michigan Judicial Institute, *Sexual Assault Benchbook—Third Edition* (rev edn, Michigan Judicial Institute 2024).
Mogul JL, Ritchie AJ and Whitlock K, *Queer (In)Justice: The Criminalization of LGBT People in the United States* (Beacon Press 2011).
Montmarquet J, 'Zimmerman on Culpable Ignorance' (1999) 109 Ethics 842.
Moran R, 'Responses to O'Brien and Shoemaker' (2003) 11 Eur J Philos 402.
Muehlenhard CL and Hollabaugh LC, 'Do Women Sometimes Say No When They Mean Yes? The Prevalence and Correlates of Women's Token Resistance to Sex' (1988) 54 J Pers Soc Psychol 872.
Naffine N, 'The Legal Structure of Self-Ownership: Or the Self-Possessed Man and the Woman Possessed' (1998) 25 J Law Soc 193.
—— 'Possession: Erotic Love in the Law of Rape' (1994) 57 MLR 10.
Nagel T, *The View from Nowhere* (OUP 1986).
Nedelsky J, 'Law, Boundaries and the Bounded Self' (1990) 30 Representations 162.
Newman S, 'Reexamining the Consent Definition Under Article 213: Sexual Assault and Related Offenses of the Model Penal Code and Its Troubling Influence on Affirmative Consent Definition States' (2023) 1(2) Ga Crim Law Rev 101.
Nozick R, *Anarchy, State, and Utopia* (Basic Books 1974).
Nussbaum MC, 'Objectification' (1995) 24 Philos Public Aff 249.
Overgaard S, 'Rethinking Other Minds: Wittgenstein and Levinas on Expression' (2005) 48 Inquiry 249.
—— 'Other People' in Dan Zahavi (ed), *The Oxford Handbook of Contemporary Phenomenology* (OUP 2012).
—— 'Other Minds Embodied' (2017) 50 Cont Philos Rev 65.
Owens D, 'The Possibility of Consent' (2011) 24 Ratio 402.
—— *Shaping the Normative Landscape* (OUP 2012).
Pallikkathayil J, 'The Possibility of Choice: Three Accounts of the Problem with Coercion' (2011) 11 Philos' Impr 1.
Papadaki L, 'Kantian Marriage and Beyond: Why It Is Worth Thinking about Kant on Marriage' (2010) 25 Hypatia 276.
—— 'Treating Others Merely as Means: A Reply to Kerstein' (2016) 28 Utilitas 73.
Parfit D, *Reasons and Persons* (Clarendon Press 1984).
Pascoe J, 'I Hunger for You: Kant and Kinky Sex' in Sharon M Kaye (ed), *What Philosophy Can Tell You About Your Lover* (Open Court 2012).
—— 'Beyond Consent: On Setting and Sharing Sexual Ends' (2023) 8(2) Philosophies 21.
Penner JE, *The Idea of Property in Law* (OUP 1997).
Perpich D, 'From the Caress to the Word: Transcendence and the Feminine in the Philosophy of Emmanuel Levinas' in Tina Chanter (ed), *Feminist Interpretations of Emmanuel Levinas* (Pennsylvania State UP 2001).

Pineau L, 'Date Rape: A Feminist Analysis' (1989) 8 L & Phil 217.
Plaxton M, 'Nussbaum on Sexual Instrumentalization' (2016) 10 Crim Law Philos 1.
Raz J, *The Authority of Law: Essays on Law and Morality* (Clarendon Press 1979).
—— *The Morality of Freedom* (OUP 1986).
—— 'Autonomy, Toleration, and the Harm Principle' in Ruth Gavison (ed), *Issues in Contemporary Legal Philosophy: Influence of HLA Hart* (Clarendon Press 1987).
—— *Practical Reason and Norms* (2nd edn, OUP 1999).
—— *From Normativity to Responsibility* (OUP 2011).
—— 'Is There a Reason to Keep a Promise?' in Gregory Klass, George Letsas and Prince Saprai (eds), *Philosophical Foundations of Contract Law* (OUP 2014).
—— 'Normative Powers (revised)' (2019) Oxf J Leg Stud Research Paper 36/2019 <https://ssrn.com/abstract=3379368> accessed 1 December 2024.
Reece H, 'Rape Myths: Is Elite Opinion Right and Popular Opinion Wrong?' (2013) 33 OJLS 445.
Roberts P, *Roberts & Zuckerman's Criminal Evidence* (3rd edn, OUP 2022).
Rosen G, 'Culpability and Ignorance' (2003) 103 Proc Aristot Soc 61.
—— 'Skepticism about Moral Responsibility' (2004) 18 Philos Perspect 295.
Rumney PNS, 'The Review of Sex Offences and Rape Law Reform: Another False Dawn?' (2001) 64 MLR 890.
Ryle G, *The Concept of Mind* (Hutchinson's University Library 1949).
Schulhofer SJ, 'Rape in the Twilight Zone: When Sex is Unwanted But Not Illegal' (2005) 38 Suffolk UL Rev 415.
—— 'Consent: What It Means and Why It's Time to Require It' (2016) 47 U Pac L Rev 665.
Scruton R, *Sexual Desire: A Moral Philosophy of the Erotic* (Free Press 1986).
Searle J, 'Grice on Meaning: 50 Years Later' (2007) 26(2) Teorema 9.
Shafer CM and Frye M, 'Rape and Respect' in Mary Vetterling-Braggin, Fredrick Elliston and Jane English (eds), *Feminism and Philosophy* (Littlefield, Adams and Co 1977).
Shapiro S, 'Law, Plans, and Practical Reason' (2002) 8 Leg Theory 387.
Shiffrin SV, 'Promising, Intimate Relationships, and Conventionalism' (2008) 117 Philos Rev 481.
Shute S, 'Second Law Commission Consultation Paper on Consent: (1) Something Old, Something New, Something Borrowed: Three Aspects of the Project' (1996) Crim L R 684.
—— and Gardner J, 'The Wrongness of Rape' in John Gardner (ed), *Offences and Defences: Selected Essays in the Philosophy of Criminal Law* (OUP 2007).
Simester AP, *Fundamentals of Criminal Law: Responsibility, Culpability, and Wrongdoing* (OUP 2021).
—— and von Hirsch A, *Crimes, Harms, and Wrongs: On the Principles of Criminalisation* (Hart Publishing 2011).
Stanton-Ife J, 'Horrific Crime' in RA Duff and others (eds), *The Boundaries of the Criminal Law* (OUP 2010).
Strawson P, 'Freedom and Resentment' in Gary Watson (ed), *Free Will* (2nd edn, OUP 2003).
Tadros V, *Criminal Responsibility* (OUP 2005).
Tuerkheimer D, 'Affirmative Consent' (2016) 13 Ohio St J Crim L 441.
Turteltaub J, *While You Were Sleeping* (Buena Vista Pictures 1995).
Vadas M, 'The Manufacture-for-use of Pornography and Women's Inequality' (2005) 13 J Political Philos 174.
Varden H, 'Kant on Sex. Reconsidered—A Kantian Account of Sexuality: Sexual Love, Sexual Identity, and Sexual Orientation' (2018) 4(1) Fem Philos Q 1.
—— *Sex, Love, and Gender: A Kantian Theory* (OUP 2020).
Wall J, 'Sexual Offences and General Reasons Not to Have Sex' (2015) 35 OJLS 777.
—— 'Public Wrongs and Private Wrongs' (2018) 31 CJLJ 177.
—— 'The Margins of Private Law' in Kate Falconer, Kit Barker and Andrew Fell (eds), *Life and Death in Private Law* (Bloomsbury Publishing 2024).
Watt B, 'The Story of Rape: Wrongdoing and the Emotional Imagination' (2014) 26 Denning LJ 46.
Way K, 'I Went on a Date with Aziz Ansari. It Turned into the Worst Night of My Life' (*BABE*, 13 January 2018) <https://babe.net/2018/01/13/aziz-ansari-28355> accessed 1 December 2024.
Wertheimer A, *Coercion* (Princeton UP 1987).

—— 'Consent to Sexual Relations' in Franklin Miller and Alan Wertheimer (eds), *The Ethics of Consent: Theory and Practice* (OUP 2009).
West R, *Caring for Justice* (NYU Press 1997).
—— 'Sex, Law and Consent' in Franklin Miller and Alan Wertheimer (eds), *The Ethics of Consent: Theory and Practice* (OUP 2009).
—— 'Consent, Legitimation, and Dysphoria' (2020) 83 MLR 1.
Westen P, 'Offences and Defences Again' (2008) 28 OJLS 563.
—— *The Logic of Consent: The Diversity and Deceptiveness of Consent as a Defense to Criminal Conduct* (Routledge 2016).
Wiederman MW, 'The Gendered Nature of Sexual Scripts' (2005) 13 Fam J 496.
Williams G, 'Offences and Defences' (1982) 2 Leg Stud 233.
—— 'The Logic of Exceptions' (1988) 42 CLJ 261.
Wilson D, 'Kant and the Marriage Right' (2004) 85 Pac Philos Q 103.
Witmer-Rich J, 'Unpacking Affirmative Consent: Not as Great as You Hope, Not as Bad as You Fear' (2016) 49 Tex Tech L Rev 57.
Wittgenstein L, *Last Writings on the Philosophy of Psychology: The Inner and the Outer, 1949–1951, Vol 2* (GH von Wright and Heikki Nyman eds, CG Luckhardt and Maximilian AE Aue trs, Blackwell 1992).
Zimmerman MJ, *An Essay on Moral Responsibility* (Rowman and Littlefield 1988).

Cases

People v Haywood 118 Ill 2d 263 (1987).
R v JA [2011] SCC 28, [2011] 2 SCR 440.
R v Millar [1998] QCA 276, [2000] 1 Qd R 437.
R v Olugboja [1982] QB 320 (CA).
State in Interest of KB 2013 WL 3340654 (NJ Super Ct App Div, 2013).
State in Interest of MTS 129 NJ 422 (NJ Super Ct App Div, 1992).
State v Perkins No 95-1353-CR (Wis Ct App August 7, 1996).
State v Snow 193 Vt 390 (2013).

Legislation

Crimes Act 1900 (NSW).
Crimes Act 1958 (Vic).
Crimes Act 1961 (NZ).
Criminal Code Act 1899 (Qld).
Criminal Code Act 1924 (Tas).
Criminal Code Act Compilation Act 1913 (WA).
Criminal Code RSC 1985, c C-46.
Criminal Law Consolidation Act 1935 (SA).
DC Code, s 22 (2018).
720 ILCS 5.
Illinois Pattern Jury Instructions, Criminal.
Minn Stat, s 609 (2017).
NJ JI CRIM.
NJ Rev Stat, s 2C (2023).
Offences Against the Person Act 1861 (UK).
Rev Code Wash (ARCW) (2017), s 9A.
Sexual Offences Act 2003 (UK).
13 VSA.
Wis JI—Criminal.
940 Wis Stat Ann (2018).

Index

For the benefit of digital users, indexed terms that span two pages (e.g., 52–53) may, on occasion, appear on only one of those pages.